University Success

Success

TRANSITION LEVEL

ORAL COMMUNICATION

Christina Cavage

Series Editor: Robyn Brinks Lockwood

Authentic Content Contributors: Ronnie Alan Hess II and Victoria Solomon

University Success Oral Communication, Transition Level

Copyright © 2017 by Pearson Education, Inc.

All rights reserved.

No part of this publication may be reproduced, stored in a retrieval system, or transmitted in any form or by any means, electronic, mechanical, photocopying, recording, or otherwise, without the prior permission of the publisher.

Pearson Education, 221 River Street, Hoboken, NJ 07030

Staff credits: The people who made up the *University Success Oral Communication, Transition Level* team, representing content creation, design, manufacturing, marketing, multimedia, project management, publishing, rights management, and testing, are Pietro Alongi, Rhea Banker, Stephanie Bullard, Tracey Cataldo, Sara Davila, Mindy DePalma, Dave Dickey, Warren Fischbach, Nancy Flaggman, Gosia Jaros-White, Niki Lee, Amy McCormick, Jennifer Raspiller, Paula Van Ells, and Joseph Vella.

Project supervision: Debbie Sistino

Contributing editors: Eleanor Barnes, Andrea Bryant, Nancy Matsunaga, and Leigh Stolle

Cover image: Memorial Hall of Harvard University, © Roman Babakin/Shutterstock

Text and cover design: Yin Ling Wong

Video research: Constance Rylance

Video production: Kristine Stolakis

Text composition: MPS Limited

Library of Congress Cataloging-in-Publication Data

A catalog record for the print edition is available from the Library of Congress.

ISBN-10: 0-13-440027-5

ISBN-13: 978-0-13-440027-3

Printed in the United States of America

1 16

Contents

Welcome to *University Success* iv

Key Features of *University Success* viii

Scope and Sequence xiv

Acknowledgments xviii

PART 1: FUNDAMENTAL ORAL COMMUNICATION SKILLS

SOCIOLOGY: Active Participation 2

ECONOMICS: Idea Development 16

BIOLOGY: Extended Discourse 30

HUMANITIES: Speaking Styles 46

ENVIRONMENTAL ENGINEERING: Visuals 60

PART 2: CRITICAL THINKING SKILLS

SOCIOLOGY: Facts and Opinions 80

ECONOMICS: Implications and Inferences 96

BIOLOGY: Understanding and Presenting Processes 110

HUMANITIES: Analogies 126

ENVIRONMENTAL ENGINEERING: Summarizing and Synthesizing 140

PART 3: EXTENDED LECTURES

SOCIOLOGY: Five Revolutions 158

ECONOMICS: Supply and Demand 164

BIOLOGY: Are Viruses Alive? 170

HUMANITIES: Love and Education 176

ENVIRONMENTAL ENGINEERING: Air Filtration Systems in the Home .. 182

Credits 189

Index 190

Welcome to *University Success*

INTRODUCTION

University Success is a new academic skills series designed to equip transitioning English learners with the reading, writing, and oral communication skills necessary to succeed in courses in an English-speaking university setting. The blended instructional model provides students with an inspiring collection of extensive authentic content, expertly developed in cooperation with five subject matter experts, all "thought leaders" in their fields. By utilizing both online and in-class instructional materials, *University Success* models the type of "real life" learning expected of students studying for a degree. Unlike a developmental textbook, *University Success* recognizes the unique linguistic needs of English language learners. The course carefully scaffolds skill development to help students successfully work with challenging and engaging authentic content provided by top professors in their academic fields.

SERIES ORGANIZATION: *THREE STRANDS*

This three-strand series, **Reading**, **Writing**, and **Oral Communication**, includes five distinct content areas: the Human Experience, Money and Commerce, the Science of Nature, Arts and Letters, and Structural Science, all popular fields of study among English language learners. The three strands are fully aligned across content areas and skills, allowing teachers to utilize material from different strands to support learning. Teachers can delve deeply into skill development in a single skill area, or provide additional support materials from other skill areas for richer development across the four skills.

THE *UNIVERSITY SUCCESS* APPROACH: *AN AUTHENTIC EXPERIENCE*

This blended program combines the utility of an interactive student book, online learner lab, and print course to create a flexible approach that adjusts to the needs of teachers and learners. The skill-based and step-by-step instruction helps students master essential skills and become confident and successful in their ability to perform in academic-degree-bearing courses taught in English. Students at this level need to engage with content that provides the same challenges faced by native speakers in a university setting. Many English language learners are not prepared for the quantity of reading and writing required in college-level courses, nor are they properly prepared to listen to full-length lectures that have not been scaffolded for them. These learners, away from the safety of an ESL classroom, must keep up with the rigors of a class led by a professor who may be unaware of the challenges a second-language learner faces. *University Success* steps up to the podium to represent academic content realistically with the appropriate skill development and scaffolding essential for English language learners to be successful.

The program features the following:

- **Rigorous academic preparation** that allows students to build on their strengths and prior knowledge, develop language and study skills, and increase their knowledge of academic content related to the STEAM areas of study
- **Systematic skill development,** from strategies to critical thinking to application and assessment, that explicitly teaches students to notice, understand, and employ English language features in the comprehension and synthesis of new information
- **A fluency driven approach** designed to help learners with fluency, accuracy, and automaticity allowing them to process linguistically complex texts of significant length
- **Flexible three-part developmental English approach** that includes intensive skill development and extensive practice
- **Extensive work with authentic texts** and videotaped **lectures** created by dynamic Stanford University professors providing a challenging experience that replicates the authentic experience of studying in a mainstream university classroom
- **Flexible format** and sophisticated design for students who are looking for authentic academic content, comprehensive practice, and a true college experience
- **Global Scale of English for Academic Learners** alignment with content tied to outcomes designed to challenge students who have achieved a B2+ level of proficiency or higher
- **Content and fluency vocabulary approach** that develops learner ability to read words as multiword units and to process text more quickly and with greater ease
- **Strategies for academic success,** delivered via online videos, including how to talk to professors during office hours and time management techniques, that help increase students' confidence and ability to cope with the challenges of academic study and college culture
- **Continuous formative assessment** and extensive formative assessment built into the series, offering multiple points of feedback, in class or online, assessing the ability of students to transfer and apply skills with rigorous academic challenges

TEACHER SUPPORT

Each of the three strands is supported with:

- **Comprehensive downloadable teaching notes** in MyEnglishLab that detail key points for all of the specialized academic content in addition to tips and suggestions for teaching skills and strategies
- **An easy-to-use online learning management system** offering a flexible gradebook and tools for monitoring student progress
- **Audioscripts, videoscripts, answer keys, and word lists** to help in lesson planning and follow-up

BOOK ORGANIZATION: *THREE PARTS*

University Success is designed with a part structure that allows for maximum flexibility for teachers. The series is "horizontally" aligned allowing teachers to teach across a specific content area and "vertically" aligned allowing a teacher to gradually build skills. Each part is a self-contained module, offering teachers the ability to customize a nonlinear program that will best address the needs of students. The skills, like the content areas, are aligned, giving teachers and students the opportunity to explore the differences in application based on the type of study experience the students need.

In Part 1 and Part 2 students work with comprehensive skills that include:

- Working with and developing complex ideas reflecting areas of academic interest
- Using, creating, and interpreting visuals from data, experiments, and research
- Distinguishing facts and opinions and hedging when presenting, reviewing, or writing academic research
- Recognizing and using inference and implications in academic fields
- Identifying, outlining, and describing complex processes in research, lab work, and experiments

Part 3 provides a truly authentic experience for students with an extended essay (Reading strand), lecture (Oral Communication strand), and interview about the writing process (Writing strand) provided by the thought leader. Part 3 functions as a final formative assessment of a student's ability to apply skills with mainstream academic content. Part 3 content includes:

- Subject matter to which students can find personal connections
- Topics with interdisciplinary appeal
- Material that draws students into the most current debates in academia
- Topics that strengthen the cultural and historical literacy of students

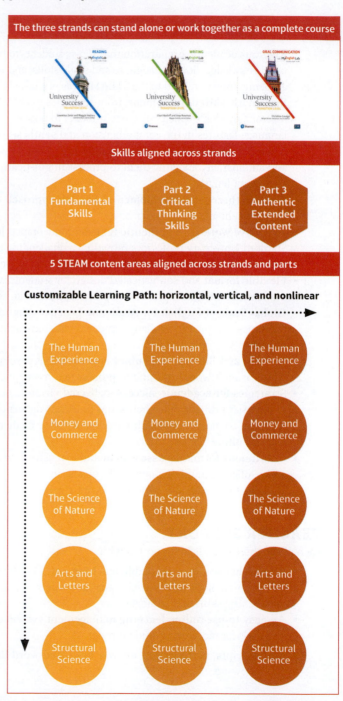

SUBJECT MATTER EXPERTS

Marcelo Clerici-Arias teaches undergraduate courses at Stanford University's Department of Economics, from principles of micro- and macroeconomics to upper-level courses in computational economics, behavioral economics, and economic policy. He has researched innovative pedagogies used in economics and other social and natural sciences. His main research areas are game theory, computational economics, and teaching and learning. Professor Clerici-Arias is a popular speaker and presenter, has participated in NSF-sponsored projects, and has co-edited an economics textbook.

Jonathan D. Greenberg is a lecturer in law at Stanford Law School; teaching fellow for the school's advanced degree program in International Economic Law, Business and Policy; and scholar-in-residence at the school's Gould Center for Conflict Resolution. He has published scholarly articles and chapters in a broad range of interdisciplinary journals and books.

Robert Pogue Harrison is a professor of French and Italian literature at Stanford University and author of six books, the most recent of which is *Juvenescence: A Cultural History of Our Age* (2014). He writes regularly for the *New York Review of Books* and hosts the radio podcast *Entitled Opinions*. He is a member of the American Academy of Arts and Sciences, and in 2014 he was knighted Chevalier of the French Republic.

Lynn Hildemann is a professor of civil and environmental engineering at Stanford University and currently is serving as department chair. She is an author on over 80 peer-reviewed publications. Her research areas include the sources and dispersion of airborne particulate matter in indoor environments and assessment of human exposure to air pollutants. She has served on advisory committees for the Bay Area Air Quality Management District and the California Air Resources Board and as an associate editor for *Environmental Science & Technology*.

Robert Siegel is a professor in the Department of Microbiology and Immunology at Stanford University. He holds secondary appointments in the Program in Human Biology, the Center for African Studies, and the Woods Institute for the Environment. He is the recipient of numerous teaching awards including Stanford's highest teaching accolade, the Walter Gores Award. Dr. Siegel's courses cover a wide range of topics including virology, infectious disease, and global health, as well as molecular biology, Darwin and evolution and island biogeography, and photography. He is an avid hiker, photographer, and dromomaniac.

SERIES EDITORS

Robyn Brinks Lockwood teaches courses in spoken and written English at Stanford University in the English for Foreign Students graduate program and is the program education coordinator of the American Language and Culture undergraduate summer program. She is an active member of the international TESOL organization, serves as chairperson of the Publishing Professional Council, and is a past chair of the Materials Writers Interest Section. She is a frequent presenter at TESOL regional and international conferences. She has edited and written numerous textbooks, online courses, and ancillary components for ESL courses and TOEFL preparation.

Maggie Sokolik holds a BA in anthropology from Reed College and an MA in romance linguistics and a PhD in applied linguistics from UCLA. She is the author of over 20 ESL and composition textbooks. She has taught at MIT, Harvard, Texas A&M, and currently UC Berkeley, where she is director of College Writing Programs. She has developed and taught several popular MOOC courses in English language writing and literature. She is the founding editor of *TESL-EJ*, a peer-reviewed journal for ESL/EFL professionals, one of the first online journals. She travels frequently to speak about grammar, writing, and instructor education. She lives in the San Francisco Bay area, where she and her husband play bluegrass music.

Lawrence J. Zwier is an associate director of the English Language Center, Michigan State University. He holds a bachelor's degree in English literature from Aquinas College, Grand Rapids, MI, and an MA in TESL from the University of Minnesota. He has taught ESL/EFL at universities in Saudi Arabia, Malaysia, Japan, Singapore, and the United States. He is the author of numerous ELT textbooks, mostly about reading and vocabulary, and also writes nonfiction books about history and geography for middle school and high school students. He is married with two children and lives in Okemos, Michigan.

Key Features of *University Success Oral Communication*

UNIQUE PART STRUCTURE

University Success employs a unique three-part structure, providing maximum flexibility and multiple opportunities to customize the flow of content.

Each part is a self-contained module allowing teachers to focus on the highest value skills and content. Parts are aligned around science, technology, engineering, arts, and mathematic (STEAM) content relevant to mainstream academic areas of study.

Part 1 and Part 2 focus on the fundamental and critical thinking skills most relevant for students preparing for university degrees. **Part 3** introduces student to extended practice with the skills. Students work directly with the authentic content created and delivered by top professors in their academic fields.

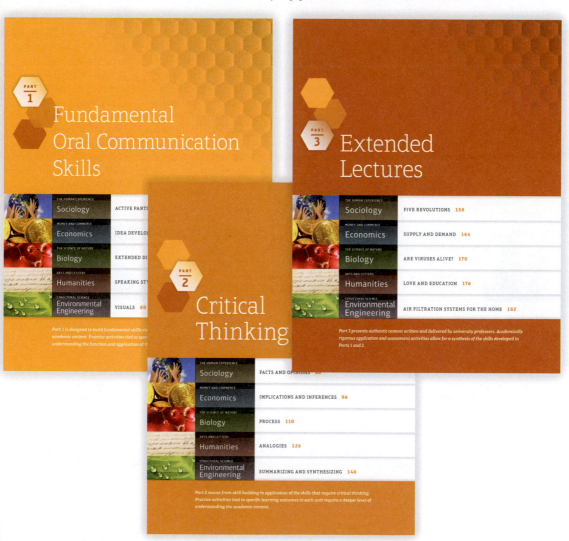

PART 1 AND PART 2

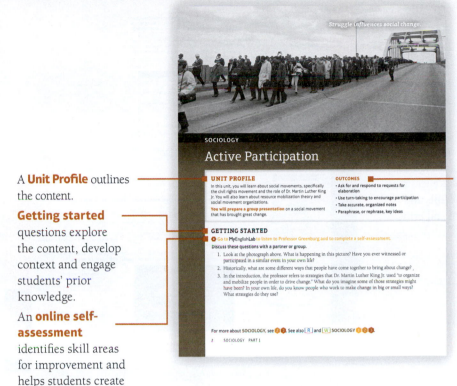

A **Unit Profile** outlines the content.

Getting started questions explore the content, develop context and engage students' prior knowledge.

An **online self-assessment** identifies skill areas for improvement and helps students create personal learning objectives.

Outcomes aligned with the Global Scale of English (GSE) are clearly stated to ensure student awareness of skills.

Professors provide a **preview** and a **summary** of the content.

Why It's Useful highlights the purpose for developing skills and supports transfer of skills to mainstream class content.

A **detailed presentation** contextualizes the skills value in academic study.

Noticing activities allow students to see skills demonstrated in the contexts of academic lectures, discussions, and question and answer sessions.

Each skill is divided into discreet **supporting skill** areas.

Multiple **excercises** encourage application of the skills and build fundamental and critical thinking skills.

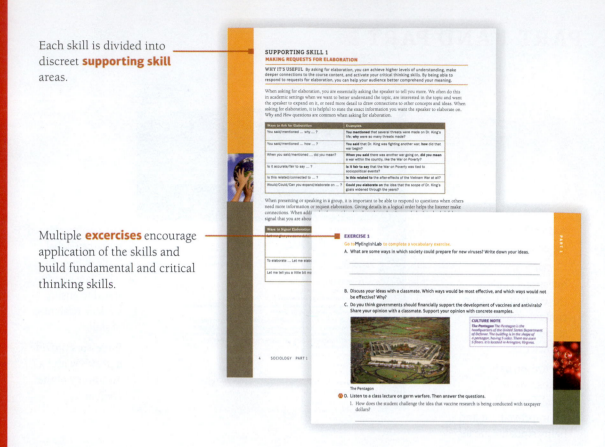

SUPPORTING SKILL 1
MAKING REQUESTS FOR ELABORATION

WHY IT'S USEFUL By asking for elaboration, you can achieve higher levels of understanding, make deeper connections to the course content, and activate your critical thinking skills. By being able to respond to requests for elaboration, you can help your audience better comprehend your meaning.

When asking for elaboration, you are essentially asking the speaker to tell you more. We often do this in academic settings when we want to better understand the topic, are interested in the topic and want the speaker to expand on it, or need more detail to draw connections to other concepts and ideas. When asking for elaboration, it is helpful to state the exact information you want the speaker to elaborate on. Why and How questions are common when asking for elaboration.

Ways to Ask for Elaboration	Examples
You said/mentioned … why … ?	**You mentioned** that several threats were made on Dr. King's life; **why** were so many threats made?
You said/mentioned … how … ?	**You said** that Dr. King was fighting another war; **how** did that war begin?
When you said/mentioned … did you mean ?	**When you said** there was another war going on, **did you mean** a war within the country, like the War on Poverty?
Is it accurate/fair to say … ?	**Is it fair to say** that the War on Poverty was tied to sociopolitical events?
Is this related/connected to … ?	**Is this related** to the after-effects of the Vietnam War at all?
Would/Could/Can you expand/elaborate on … ?	**Could you elaborate** on the idea that the scope of Dr. King's goals widened through the years?

When presenting or speaking in a group, it is important to be able to respond to questions when others need more information or request elaboration. Giving details in a logical order helps the listener make connections. When addi... signal that you are abou...

Ways to Signal Elaboration
Let me give you some detail...
To elaborate ... Let me elab...
Let me tell you a little bit mo...

4   SOCIOLOGY   PART 1

EXERCISE 1
Go to MyEnglishLab to complete a vocabulary exercise.

A. What are some ways in which society could prepare for new viruses? Write down your ideas.

_____

_____

B. Discuss your ideas with a classmate. Which ways would be most effective, and which ways would not be effective? Why?

C. Do you think governments should financially support the development of vaccines and antivirals? Share your opinion with a classmate. Support your opinion with concrete examples.

CULTURE NOTE
The Pentagon The Pentagon is the headquarters of the United States Department of Defense. The building is in the shape of a pentagon, having 5 sides. There are even 5 floors. It is located in Arlington, Virginia.

The Pentagon

D. Listen to a class lecture on germ warfare. Then answer the questions.
1. How does the student challenge the idea that vaccine research is being conducted with taxpayer dollars?

PART 1

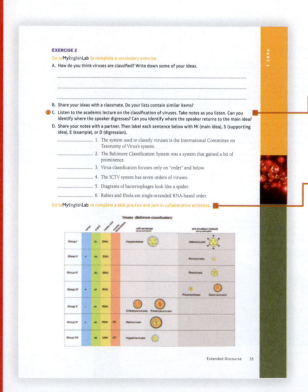

EXERCISE 2
Go to MyEnglishLab to complete a vocabulary exercise.

A. How do you think viruses are classified? Write down some of your ideas.

_____

_____

B. Share your ideas with a classmate. Do your lists contain similar items?

C. Listen to the academic lecture on the classification of viruses. Take notes as you listen. Can you identify where the speaker digresses? Can you identify where the speaker returns to the main idea?

D. Share your notes with a partner. Then label each sentence below with MI (main idea), S (supporting idea), E (example), or D (digression).

_____ 1. The system used to classify viruses is the International Committee on Taxonomy of Virus's system.

_____ 2. The Baltimore Classification System was a system that gained a bit of prominence.

_____ 3. Virus classification focuses only on "order" and below.

_____ 4. The ICTV system has seven orders of viruses.

_____ 5. Diagrams of bacteriophages look like a spider.

_____ 6. Rabies and Ebola are single-stranded RNA-based order.

Go to MyEnglishLab to complete a skill practice and join in collaborative activities.

Viruses (Baltimore classification)

Extended Discourse   35

A variety of listening types including lectures and academic discussions represent "real life" university experiences.

Online activities encourage students to personalize content with collaborative research activities.

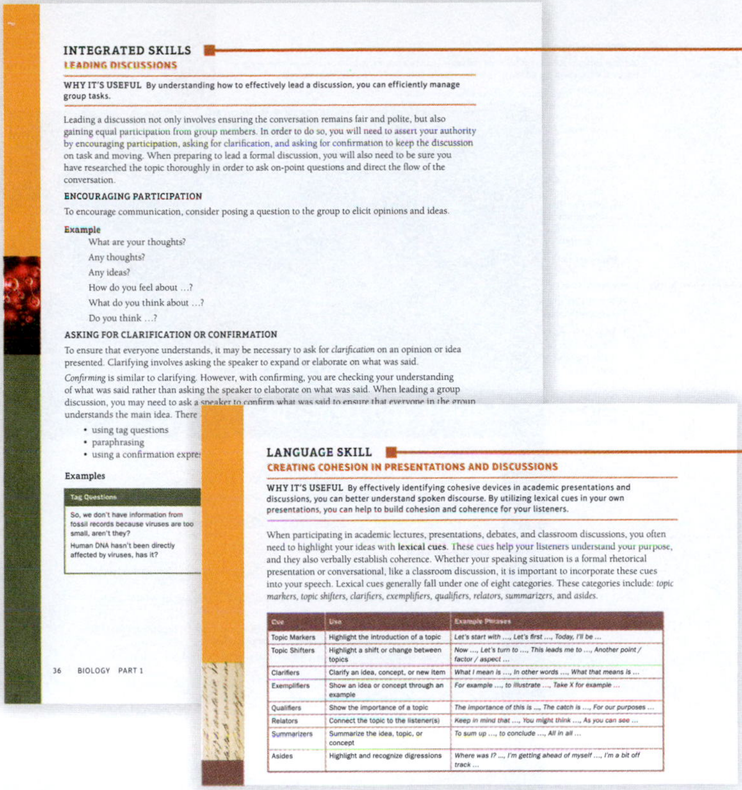

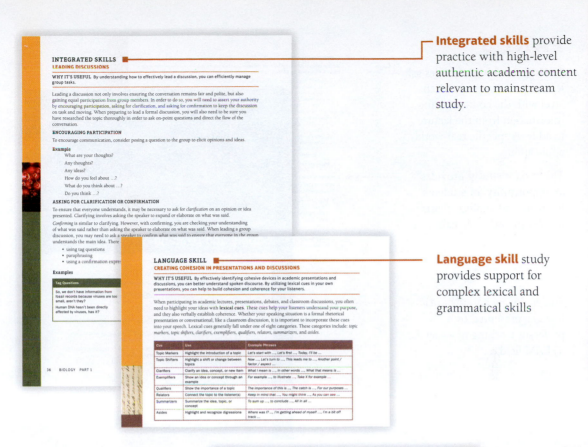

INTEGRATED SKILLS
LEADING DISCUSSIONS

WHY IT'S USEFUL By understanding how to effectively lead a discussion, you can efficiently manage group tasks.

Leading a discussion not only involves ensuring the conversation remains fair and polite, but also gaining equal participation from group members. In order to do so, you will need to assert your authority by encouraging participation, asking for clarification, and asking for confirmation to keep the discussion on task and moving. When preparing to lead a formal discussion, you will also need to be sure you have researched the topic thoroughly in order to ask on-point questions and direct the flow of the conversation.

ENCOURAGING PARTICIPATION

To encourage communication, consider posing a question to the group to elicit opinions and ideas.

Example
What are your thoughts?
Any thoughts?
Any ideas?
How do you feel about …?
What do you think about …?
Do you think …?

ASKING FOR CLARIFICATION OR CONFIRMATION

To ensure that everyone understands, it may be necessary to ask for *clarification* on an opinion or idea presented. Clarifying involves asking the speaker to expand or elaborate on what was said.

Confirming is similar to clarifying. However, with confirming, you are checking your understanding of what was said rather than asking the speaker to elaborate on what was said. When leading a group discussion, you may need to ask a speaker to confirm what was said to ensure that everyone in the group understands the main idea. There

- using tag questions
- paraphrasing
- using a confirmation expre

Examples

Tag Questions
So, we don't have information from fossil records because viruses are too small, aren't they?
Human DNA hasn't been directly affected by viruses, has it?

36 BIOLOGY PART 1

LANGUAGE SKILL
CREATING COHESION IN PRESENTATIONS AND DISCUSSIONS

WHY IT'S USEFUL By effectively identifying cohesive devices in academic presentations and discussions, you can better understand spoken discourse. By utilizing lexical cues in your own presentations, you can help to build cohesion and coherence for your listeners.

When participating in academic lectures, presentations, debates, and classroom discussions, you often need to highlight your ideas with **lexical cues**. These cues help your listeners understand your purpose, and they also verbally establish coherence. Whether your speaking situation is a formal rhetorical presentation or conversational, like a classroom discussion, it is important to incorporate these cues into your speech. Lexical cues generally fall under one of eight categories. These categories include: *topic markers, topic shifters, clarifiers, exemplifiers, qualifiers, relators, summarizers,* and *asides.*

Cue	Use	Example Phrases
Topic Markers	Highlight the introduction of a topic	*Let's start with …, Let's first …, Today, I'll be …*
Topic Shifters	Highlight a shift or change between topics	*Now …, Let's turn to …, This leads me to …, Another point / factor / aspect …*
Clarifiers	Clarify an idea, concept, or new item	*What I mean is …, In other words …, What that means is …*
Exemplifiers	Show an idea or concept through an example	*For example …, to illustrate …, Take X for example …*
Qualifiers	Show the importance of a topic	*The importance of this is …, The catch is …, For our purposes …*
Relators	Connect the topic to the listener(s)	*Keep in mind that …, You might think …, As you can see …*
Summarizers	Summarize the idea, topic, or concept	*To sum up …, to conclude …, All in all …*
Asides	Highlight and recognize digressions	*Where was I? …, I'm getting ahead of myself …, I'm a bit off track …*

Integrated skills provide practice with high-level authentic academic content relevant to mainstream study.

Language skill study provides support for complex lexical and grammatical skills

A **lecture** aligned with the academic content allows students to apply skills practiced in the unit. Critical thinking and thinking visually activities challenge students to dig deeper.

A **final project** allows students to integrate content and utilize all aspects of their oral communication skills. Projects include presentations, debates and panel discussions.

Parts 1 and 2 end with an extended **application of skills** that function as a formative assessment.

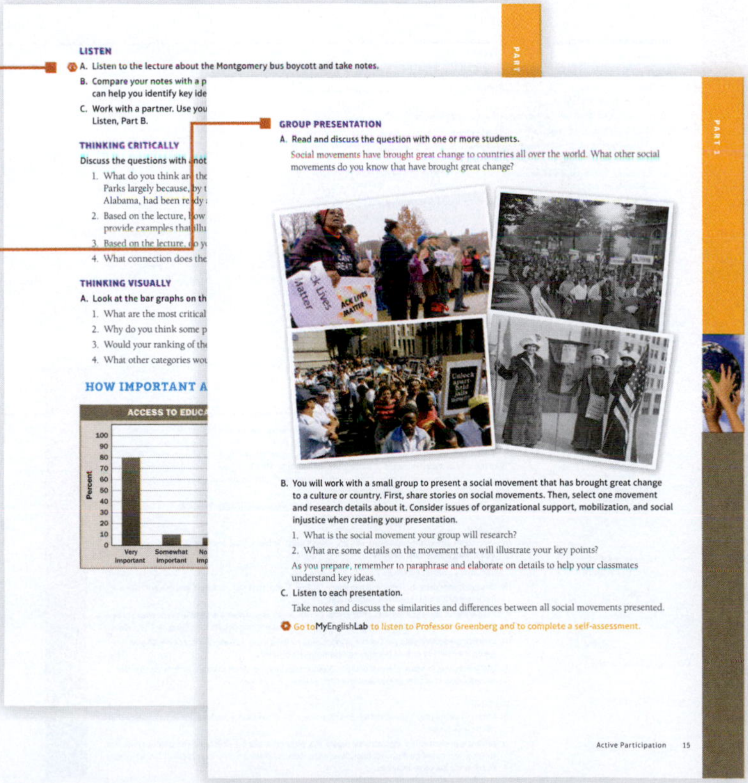

LISTEN
A. Listen to the lecture about the Montgomery bus boycott and take notes.
B. Compare your notes with a p… can help you identify key ide…
C. Work with a partner. Use you… Listen, Part B.

THINKING CRITICALLY
Discuss the questions with anot…
1. What do you think ar… the … Parks largely because, by t… Alabama, had been re…dy…
2. Based on the lecture, how … provide examples that illu…
3. Based on the lecture, do y…
4. What connection does the…

THINKING VISUALLY
A. Look at the bar graphs on th…
1. What are the most critical…
2. Why do you think some p…
3. Would your ranking of th…
4. What other categories wo…

HOW IMPORTANT A…

GROUP PRESENTATION
A. Read and discuss the question with one or more students.
Social movements have brought great change to countries all over the world. What other social movements do you know that have brought great change?

B. You will work with a small group to present a social movement that has brought great change to a culture or country. First, share stories on social movements. Then, select one movement and research details about it. Consider issues of organizational support, mobilization, and social injustice when creating your presentation.
1. What is the social movement your group will research?
2. What are some details on the movement that will illustrate your key points?
As you prepare, remember to paraphrase and elaborate on details to help your classmates understand key ideas.
C. Listen to each presentation.
Take notes and discuss the similarities and differences between all social movements presented.
Go to MyEnglishLab to listen to Professor Greenberg and to complete a self-assessment.

Active Participation 15

PART 3

Critical thinking activities ask learners to engage at a deep level with the content, using information from the lecture to address specific real-world applications.

Thinking visually provides an opportunity for students to create and analyze charts, graphs and other visuals.

Students view an **authentic lecture** presented by a professor working in a specific STEAM field.

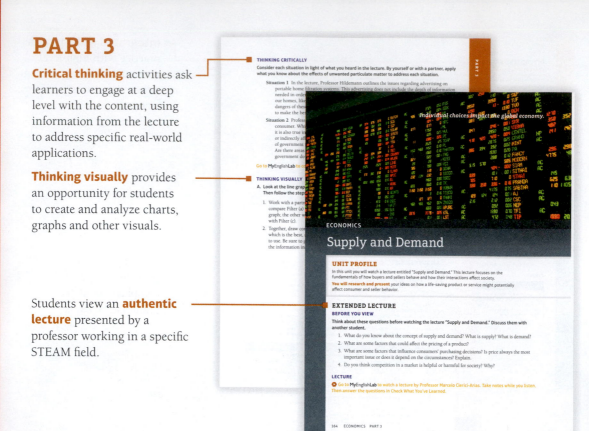

Language skills reviews language skills developed in Part 1 and Part 2, using the source content from the professor to provide final examples.

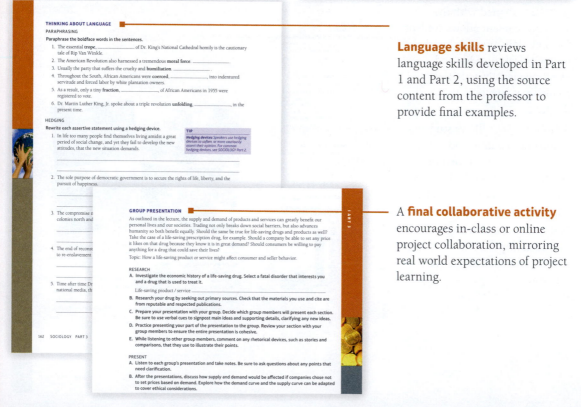

A **final collaborative activity** encourages in-class or online project collaboration, mirroring real world expectations of project learning.

TEACHER SUPPORT

Each of the three strands is supported with comprehensive **downloadable teaching notes** in MyEnglishLab that detail key points for all of the specialized, academic content in addition to tips and suggestions for how to teach skills and strategies.

Assessments on selected topics provide extra opportunities for students to demonstrate learning. Flexible design allows assessments to be used as unit reviews, mid-terms, or finals. Test bank presents multiple test versions for easy test proctoring.

An easy to use online learning management system offering a **Flexible Gradebook** and tools for monitoring student progress, such as audioscripts, videoscripts, answer keys, and word lists to help in lesson planning and follow up.

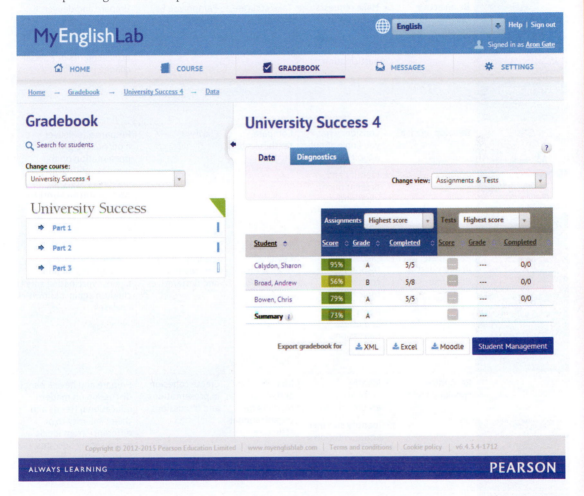

Scope and Sequence

PART 1

Fundamental Oral Communication Skills is designed to build fundamental skills step by step through exploration of rigorous, academic content.

	FUNDAMENTAL SKILLS	SUPPORTING SKILLS	INTEGRATED SKILLS	LANGUAGE SKILLS	APPLY YOUR SKILLS
SOCIOLOGY **Active Participation**	Be an active participant	• Make requests for elaboration • Use turn-taking to encourage participation	Take accurate, organized notes	Paraphrase key ideas	Prepare and deliver an informational group presentation on origins, evolution, and achievements of a social change movement
ECONOMICS **Idea Development**	Develop an idea	• Consider what you know about a topic • Identify and present main ideas and supporting details	Compare textbooks to lectures	Clarify	Prepare and deliver a persuasive group presentation on the business plan of an imaginary start-up company in an effort to gain start-up capital
BIOLOGY **Extended Discourse**	Participate in extended discourse	• Discuss and respond to controversial topics • Recognize and utilize digressions	Lead discussions	Identify and use interrogatives and declaratives	Prepare and have a class debate for and against vaccinating small children against known diseases
HUMANITIES **Speaking Styles**	Recognize speaking styles	• Identify emphatic argumentation • Identify succinct argumentation	Identify and utilize markers for organizational structure	Create cohesion in presentations and discussions	Prepare and have a panel discussion on modern educational trends and their similarity to or difference from ideals espoused by Socrates, Plato, Goethe, and Nietzsche
ENVIRONMENTAL ENGINEERING **Visuals**	Use visuals	• Connect visuals to a lecture • Read and interpret complex visuals	Synthesize text into a visual	Create and communicate visuals	Prepare and deliver an informational individual presentation on a "green" building and the systems and features that make it a model for green construction

PART 2
Critical Thinking Skills moves from skill building to application of the skills that require critical thinking.

	CRITICAL THINKING SKILLS	SUPPORTING SKILLS	INTEGRATED SKILLS	LANGUAGE SKILLS	APPLY YOUR SKILLS
SOCIOLOGY **Facts and Opinions**	Distinguish facts from opinions	• Identify facts through verbal and non-verbal signposts • Identify opinions through verbal and non-verbal signposts	Distinguish between facts and opinions in texts	Interpret and utilize hedging devices	Prepare and deliver a persuasive group presentation for an important change that needs to be made to a school or community
ECONOMICS **Implications and Inferences**	Understand implications and inferences	• Identify implied meaning • Determine a speaker's intent and degree of certainty	Synthesize information from multiple sources	Understand implied conditions	Prepare and have a class debate in favor of supply side-economics and demand–side economics
BIOLOGY **Process**	Understand and present processes	• Identify structure and purpose of a process presentation • Analyze flow of a process presentation	Explain a complex process	Use generalizations and specific information	Prepare and deliver an informational individual presentation on the origins, symptoms, and treatment of an infectious disease
HUMANITIES **Analogies**	Make analogies	• Use metaphors and similes • Make assumptions	Assess the quality of a conclusion	Use colloquial language	Prepare and deliver an informational group presentation on the continuing influence in society of a classic work of literature
ENVIRONMENTAL ENGINEERING **Summarizing and Synthesizing**	Summarize and synthesize research	• Select suitable research to support your ideas • Present well-integrated research	Understand and present a research report	Source academic references	Prepare and deliver an informational group presentation on the role that government regulations have played in health problems

PART 3

Extended Lectures presents authentic content written and delivered by university professors. Academically rigorous application and assessment activities allow for a synthesis of the skills developed in Part 1 and Part 2.

	LECTURE	RESEARCH/ASSIGNMENT
SOCIOLOGY	Five Revolutions	Research, prepare, and deliver an individual presentation on a grassroots social movement that has had an impact on society.
ECONOMICS	Supply and Demand	Research, prepare, and deliver a group presentation on the history of a lifesaving drug or service, and how its price might influence consumer and seller behavior.
BIOLOGY	Are Viruses Alive?	Research, prepare, and have a panel discussion on the potential benefits and repercussions of requiring genetic testing for fatal diseases.
HUMANITIES	Love and Education	Research, prepare, and deliver an individual presentation on volunteer organizations and private foundations that promote a "love for the world."
ENVIRONMENTAL ENGINEERING	Air Filtration Systems for the Home	Research, prepare, and have a class debate for and against the necessity of further federal regulation to protect consumers from false claims about health products.

A Note from Robyn Brinks Lockwood

Series Editor for *University Success Oral Communication*

Like many EAP students, my students have already been accepted into the university and are attending courses at the graduate level within their disciplines. They have studied English for years, but the realities of studying in an English-speaking university has come as a shock. Lectures are 50, 60, or 75 minutes long; far longer than the shorter excerpts included with their other ESL textbooks. Lecturers use slang, hesitations, or humor, and they don't adapt their vocabulary or style simply because there is a second-language speaker in the classroom. Students need material with which to transition to the next level: longer and authentic lectures with spoken language phrasing and activities that more closely mimic what they will encounter in an academic setting.

To this end, *University Success* has included materials that will provide this bridge and make students' transition from an EAP setting into a native-speaker setting easier. The Transition Level is ideal because it offers content that students need in which to succeed at the university level. It allows practice with real lectures given by Stanford University professors and lecturers—the type of materials they are likely to encounter as they begin academic courses. The text offers instruction in listening and speaking skills, but it also offers ample opportunity for students to actually apply the skills beyond scripted lectures and speaking activities. Students will feel a true sense of accomplishment after working with these materials. More importantly, they will succeed beyond the ESL classroom.

PART 1 – FUNDAMENTAL SKILLS

In the first five units of *University Success Oral Communication*, each of the five main subject areas (Economics, Sociology, Biology, Humanities, Environmental Engineering) is covered. Despite their chosen major, most students are required to take general education requirements in these different fields. Students might be familiar with some of the skills provided, but they likely have not had enough practice applying these skills to authentic content. The Stanford professors, who are the thought leaders for all the books in the series, introduce themselves and their fields via short vignettes that help students prepare for the materials. This section also includes shorter listening passages on which students can practice one skill at a time before tackling a full-length lecture in Part 3.

PART 2 – CRITICAL THINKING SKILLS

In these units, each main subject area is explored in greater depth. Longer listening passages demand more application and analysis. Critical-thinking is more directly elicited so that transition-level students engage in such processes as identifying generalizations in a lecture as well as: using generalizations to support their own points; identifying and using appropriate tone and register; and managing inferences and implications.

PART 3 – EXTENDED LECTURES

Part 3 units include university lectures given by Stanford thought leaders. Each lecture in this part is 20–25 minutes long, authentic in content, vocabulary, and details. The lectures are filled with the same humor, "imperfect" English, and digressions typical of the lectures the professors give in their classrooms. These lectures are not as high-interest as students are typically trained with, so they are challenging. The benefit, of course, is that this is exactly what they will have to do when they are in mainstream classes. In Part 3, *University Success* does something no other high-level EAP text does. It offers content from professors at a world-renowned university and gives them the chance to practice with materials that will help them cross that bridge into true academic studies.

Acknowledgments

It takes a village to produce an innovative, cutting-edge text like University Success. Many thanks to the highly professional staff at Pearson: Niki Cunnion, Sara Davila, Mindy DePalma, Gosia Jaros-White, Amy McCormick and all those working behind the scenes to create a wonderful tool for teachers and students. My deepest gratitude to Debbie Sistino for her guidance, leadership, and keen eyes and ears. Keen eyes and ears make for great editors, and I was fortunate enough to have two of the best: Nancy Matsunaga and Eleanor Barnes. Nancy and Eleanor both worked tirelessly to help me clarify complex topics, and make them approachable for our students. A special thanks to our Series Editor, Robyn Brinks Lockwood for brainstorming with me, answering my questions, and supporting me all along the way.

Great materials are often a result of great classroom experiences. I am especially grateful for the students at SCAD (Savannah College of Art and Design) who have challenged me to create materials that are dynamic, real-world and effective. To my colleagues near and far, I am indebted to you for our continuous discussions on how to best construct materials that meet student needs. A final thanks to my friends and family who have given me time, motivation, and laughter when I needed it the most. — *Christina Cavage*

Reviewers

We would like to thank the following reviewers for their many helpful comments and suggestions:

Jamila Barton, North Seattle Community College, Seattle, WA; **Joan Chamberlin**, Iowa State University, Ames IA; **Lyam Christopher**, Palm Beach State College, Boynton Beach, FL; **Robin Corcos**, University of California , Santa Barbara, Goleta, CA; **Tanya Davis**, University of California, San Deigo, CA; **Brendan DeCoster**, University of Oregon, Eugene, OR; **Thomas Dougherty**, University of St. Mary of the Lake, Mundelein, IL; **Bina Dugan**, Bergen County Community College, Hackensack, NJ; **Priscilla Faucette**, University of Hawaii at Manoa, Honolulu, HI; **Lisa Fischer**, St. Louis University, St. Louis, MO; **Kathleen Flynn**, Glendale Community College, Glendale, CA; **Mary Gawienowski**, William Rainey Harper College, Palatine, IL; **Sally Gearhart**, Santa Rosa Junior College, Santa Rosa, CA; **Carl Guerriere**, Capital Community College, Hartford, CT; **Vera Guillen**, Eastfield College, Mequite, TX; **Angela Hakim**, St. Louis University, St. Louis, MO; **Pamela Hartmann**, Evans Community Adult School, Los Angeles Unified School District, Los Angeles, CA; **Shelly Hedstrom**, Palm Beach State University, Lake Worth, FL; **Sherie Henderson**, University of Oregon, Eugene, OR; **Lisse Hildebrandt**, English Language Program, Virginia Commonwealth University, Richmond, VA; **Barbara Inerfeld**, Rutgers University, Piscataway, NJ; **Zaimah Khan**, Northern Virginia Community College, Loudon Campus, Sterling, VA; **Tricia Kinman**, St. Louis University, St. Louis, MO; **Kathleen Klaiber**, Genesee Community College, Batavia, NY; **Kevin Lamkins**, Capital Community College, Hartford, CT; **Mayetta Lee**, Palm Beach State College, Lake Worth, FL; **Kirsten Lillegard**, English Language Institute, Divine Word College, Epworth, IA; **Craig Machado**, Norwalk Community College, Norwalk, CT; **Cheryl Madrid**, Spring International Language Center, Denver, CO; **Ann Meechai**, St. Louis University, St. Louis, MO; **Melissa Mendelson**, Department of Linguistics, University of Utah, Salt Lake City, UT; **Tamara Milbourn**, University of Colorado, Boulder, CO; **Debbie Ockey**, Fresno City College, Fresno, CA; **Diana Pascoe-Chavez**, St. Louis University, St. Louis, MO; **Kathleen Reynolds**, William Rainey Harper College, Palatine, IL; **Linda Roth**, Vanderbilt University ELC, Greensboro, NC; **Minati Roychoudhuri**, Capital Community College, Hartford, CT; **Bruce Rubin**, California State University, Fullerton, CA; **Margo Sampson**, Syracuse University, Syracuse, NY; **Sarah Saxer**, Howard Community College, Ellicott City, MD; **Anne-Marie Schlender**, Austin Community College, Austin, TX **Susan Shields**, Santa Barbara Community College, Santa Barbara, CA; **Barbara Smith-Palinkas**, Hillsborough Community College, Dale Mabry Campus, Tampa, FL; **Sara Stapleton**, North Seattle Community College, Seattle, WA; **Lisa Stelle**, Northern Virginia Community College Loudon, Sterling, VA; **Jamie Tanzman**, Northern Kentucky University, Highland Heights, KY; **Jeffrey Welliver**, Soka University of America, Aliso Viejo, CA; **Mark Wolfersberger**, Brigham Young University Hawaii, Laie, HI; **May Youn**, California State University, Fullerton, CA.

Fundamental Oral Communication Skills

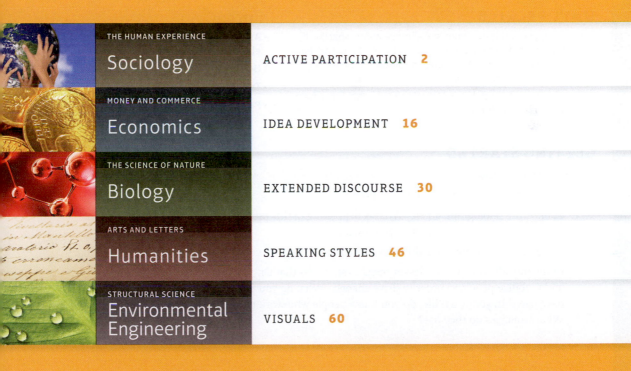

THE HUMAN EXPERIENCE
Sociology
ACTIVE PARTICIPATION   2

MONEY AND COMMERCE
Economics
IDEA DEVELOPMENT   16

THE SCIENCE OF NATURE
Biology
EXTENDED DISCOURSE   30

ARTS AND LETTERS
Humanities
SPEAKING STYLES   46

STRUCTURAL SCIENCE
Environmental Engineering
VISUALS   60

Part 1 is designed to build fundamental skills step by step through exploration of rigorous, academic content. Practice activities tied to specific learning outcomes in each unit focus on understanding the function and application of the skills.

Struggle influences social change.

EDMUND PETTUS BRIDGE

SOCIOLOGY

Active Participation

UNIT PROFILE

In this unit, you will learn about social movements, specifically the civil rights movement and the role of Dr. Martin Luther King Jr. You will also learn about resource mobilization theory and social movement organizations.

You will prepare a group presentation on a social movement that has brought great change.

OUTCOMES

- Ask for and respond to requests for elaboration
- Use turn-taking to encourage participation
- Take accurate, organized notes
- Paraphrase, or rephrase, key ideas

GETTING STARTED

▶ Go to MyEnglishLab to listen to Professor Greenberg and to complete a self-assessment.

Discuss these questions with a partner or group.

1. Look at the photograph above. What is happening in this picture? Have you ever witnessed or participated in a similar event in your own life?

2. Historically, what are some different ways that people have come together to bring about change?

3. In the introduction, the professor refers to strategies that Dr. Martin Luther King Jr. used "to organize and mobilize people in order to drive change." What do you imagine some of those strategies might have been? In your own life, do you know people who work to make change in big or small ways? What strategies do they use?

For more about **SOCIOLOGY,** see ② ③ . See also ⓡ and Ⓦ **SOCIOLOGY** ① ② ③ .

FUNDAMENTAL SKILL
BEING AN ACTIVE PARTICIPANT

WHY IT'S USEFUL By being an active participant, you can deepen your comprehension of a subject and identify key information, increasing your learning.

During college lectures, class discussions, and group work, you will be asked to participate in different ways. Participating is not simply listening but being an active member of the class. Understanding what it means to be an **active participant** is central to your success. Active participation involves being prepared, interacting and engaging in course dialogue, working in groups, and being involved in hands-on learning. These activities deepen your understanding and improve your overall classroom experience.

One strategy that will aid you in becoming an active participant is **asking for and responding to requests for elaboration**. Elaboration involves expanding the topic—going from the simple to the complex. It often involves gaining more insights into, or details about, the topic. There may be times when you do not fully understand the lecturer or a classmate, or when you simply would like to explore a particular area in greater depth. To better understand, or to get more detail, it's important to ask questions so that the speaker can give a deeper explanation. The same is true as a speaker. Your listeners may have questions about a point or idea you are making. Therefore, you will need to be prepared to respond to their questions in greater detail.

A second critical strategy is being able to know when to engage in a group or class discussion, as well as how to do so. This is referred to as **turn-taking**. Part of turn-taking also includes getting others' ideas, or **encouraging participation**. High-quality academic conversations involve the exchange of ideas, with a lot of turn-taking.

Go to **MyEnglishLab** to complete a vocabulary exercise.

NOTICING ACTIVITY

🎧 A. Listen to the beginning of an academic seminar. As you listen, consider where you might ask a question for more detail or deeper understanding.

🎧 B. Now listen to a conversation between two students who have just heard the academic seminar. What were they glad to hear more about? Why?

Go to **MyEnglishLab** to complete a skill practice and join in collaborative activities.

SUPPORTING SKILL 1
MAKING REQUESTS FOR ELABORATION

WHY IT'S USEFUL By asking for elaboration, you can achieve higher levels of understanding, make deeper connections to the course content, and activate your critical thinking skills. By being able to respond to requests for elaboration, you can help your audience better comprehend your meaning.

When asking for elaboration, you are essentially asking the speaker to tell you more. We often do this in academic settings when we want to better understand the topic, are interested in the topic and want the speaker to expand on it, or need more detail to draw connections to other concepts and ideas. When asking for elaboration, it is helpful to state the exact information you want the speaker to elaborate on. *Why* and *How* questions are common when asking for elaboration.

Ways to Ask for Elaboration	Examples
You said/mentioned … why … ?	**You mentioned** that several threats were made on Dr. King's life; **why** were so many threats made?
You said/mentioned … how … ?	**You said** that Dr. King was fighting another war; **how** did that war begin?
When you said/mentioned … did you mean?	**When you said** there was another war going on, **did you mean** a war within the country, like the War on Poverty?
Is it accurate/fair to say … ?	**Is it fair to say** that the War on Poverty was tied to sociopolitical events?
Is this related/connected to … ?	**Is this related to** the after-effects of the Vietnam War at all?
Would/Could/Can you expand/elaborate on … ?	**Could you elaborate on** the idea that the scope of Dr. King's goals widened through the years?

When presenting or speaking in a group, it is important to be able to respond to questions when others need more information or request elaboration. Giving details in a logical order helps the listener make connections. When adding details, consider *who, what, where, when, how,* and *why.* It is also helpful to signal that you are about to elaborate.

Ways to Signal Elaboration	Examples
Let me give you some details. First … Second …	**Let me give you some details. First,** the sociopolitical climate was one in which the country was divided by race. **Second,** the political climate was also divided, as many Americans were against the war, while others deemed it necessary.
To elaborate … Let me elaborate.	**Let me elaborate.** This took place in a very segregated town. Community members had literally drawn lines in the street.
Let me tell you a little bit more. What's more …	**What's more is** Dr. King recruited the poor from the city and rural areas and led them in a campaign for fair wages.

EXERCISE 1

Go to MyEnglishLab to complete a vocabulary exercise.

A. What do you know about Dr. Martin Luther King Jr.? Write down some things you know.

....

....

....

....

....

....

....

....

....

....

....

....

....

B. Work with a classmate. Share what you know. As you listen to your partner, ask for elaboration.

C. Listen to the lecture about Dr. King's early years. As you listen, think about which topics you would like the lecturer to elaborate on. Write down three questions.

1. ....

2. ....

3. ....

D. In a small group, share your requests for elaboration. Choose two or three questions to ask your instructor.

Go to MyEnglishLab to complete a skill practice and join in collaborative activities.

SUPPORTING SKILL 2
TURN-TAKING AND ENCOURAGING PARTICIPATION

WHY IT'S USEFUL By identifying techniques used in spoken discourse for turn-taking and for encouraging participation, you can better understand, and follow the unspoken regulations of organized academic discussions. By using these techniques when you speak, you can invite your listeners to actively engage in the topic with you.

Verbal interaction is a regular part of one's academic life. Understanding the unspoken rules for **turn-taking**, or when to enter or exit the conversation, is an important part of being an active participant.

ENTERING A CONVERSATION

You can enter the conversation when someone has finished his or her thought or idea. Some clues that the speaker has finished a thought are:

- a drop in intonation

  The college had few adult students, so it specifically opened up study to qualified younger students.

- a slower pace or lengthening of the last syllable

  His undergraduate degree was awarded by Morehouse College, a historically black college in At-lan-ta.

- a turn-taking signal, or cue

  … you know.
  What do you think?
  That's my idea.
  Well …
  Ah …

Hearing one of these turn-taking techniques signals listeners that they may speak. When entering a conversation, speakers may begin:

Expressions Used for Entering a Conversation	Utterances Commonly Used before a Phrase
Can I add to that by saying …	Well,
I'd like to say …	Yes,
I'd like to add to that …	So,
I'd like to give my two cents …	But,
My idea is …	Um,
One idea is …	No/Nah,

Examples

Well, I'd like to give my two cents. The political turmoil at the time definitely impacted the threats.

So, my idea is that many citizens chose not to engage, and that also created problems.

Um, I'm not sure about that. I think they were fighting their own battles.

EXITING A CONVERSATION

Turn-taking also involves giving up the floor, or allowing someone else to share his or her ideas. It is important to pay close attention to your listeners to determine if someone would like to ask a question, add to your ideas, or offer a new idea. Pay attention to:

- expressions
- body language (nodding in agreement or disagreement can indicate a listener has something to share)
- noises such as *uh-huh*, *hmmm*

ENCOURAGING PARTICIPATION

Lecturers often encourage listeners to participate and contribute ideas. This makes the class more dynamic and presents an opportunity for deeper learning. Lecturers may address you by name to ask you for your thoughts.

Example

How about you, Tiaxin?
What do you think, Ali?
Ming, can you add anything?
We haven't heard from you, Rosa.

Or, they may use an expression to encourage full participation.

Example

What does everyone think?
Any ideas or thoughts on that?
Does anyone want to add something here?

Go to MyEnglishLab to complete a vocabulary exercise.

EXERCISE 2

A. **Read the discussion excerpt between a student and tutor and add expressions to encourage participation. Then role-play the conversation with a partner. Be sure to signal turn-taking with a drop in pitch and lengthened final syllables.**

Tutor:	Let's review social movements. ....
Student:	Well, I think the professor defined social groups as large groups that don't have power, and they are trying to promote some sort of change in society.
Tutor:	Yeah, and let's not forget that they are organized, unlike collective behaviors. As far as King and the civil rights movement, ...
Student:	I think Dr. King's civil rights movement was definitely a social movement because it was organized, attempted to relieve tensions in society, and the group had legitimate expectations for change.
Tutor:	Yes. So let's talk about social change. King led the movement to bring about change through his ability to lead the group. He knew how to reach people and mobilize them. ....
Student:	Yes, I can add to that. He also was able to frame the group's message and advocate for them.
Tutor:	I think you got it! You might be ready for the test.

B. Listen to the academic discussion. Choose all the signals of turn-taking and encouraging participation that you hear.

Turn-taking signals when finished speaking:

☐ lengthened syllables

☐ drop in pitch

☐ you know

☐ That's my idea.

Turn-taking signals when beginning to speak:

☐ I'll add to that by saying …

☐ I'd like to say …

☐ My idea is …

☐ Well,

☐ Nah,

☐ Um

☐ Yeah

Encouraging participation:

☐ How about you …?

☐ … what do you think?

☐ Any ideas?

☐ We haven't heard from you.

☐ Does anyone want to add something here?

C. Listen again and take notes on what you hear. With a partner, share what you remember from the excerpt. Practice using signals for turn-taking and encouraging participation.

....

....

....

....

....

....

Go to MyEnglishLab to complete a skill practice and join in collaborative activities.

INTEGRATED SKILLS
TAKING ACCURATE, ORGANIZED NOTES

WHY IT'S USEFUL By developing a systematic note-taking method, you can easily identify key points of a lecture, better understand the connections between related ideas, and have the needed tools to improve your overall performance on assignments and tests.

One of the greatest cognitive demands you have as a college student is taking notes during a lecture. Academic listening involves much more than just listening passively. You need to:

- select important ideas;
- interpret the information;
- determine what to write down and;
- record it in an organized manner.

The more accurate and organized your notes are, the more likely you are to be successful in your comprehension of the subject. Part of being an organized note-taker is finding and utilizing a technique or method that works for you. You may find that one technique works better in one class, while a different method works in a different course. Common note-taking methods are:

- outlining
- the Cornell Method
- charting or mapping

OUTLINING

Outlining involves listening and writing key ideas based on space indentation. This makes it easy to identify the key ideas, supporting details, and examples. Information that is most general starts at the margin, while more specific details and examples are indented.

> I. Civil Rights social movement
>> A. Began in 1955 with Montgomery bus boycott
>> B. Rosa Parks arrested for not surrendering her seat
>>> 1. First lady of civil rights

THE CORNELL METHOD

The Cornell Method has two main parts: the first part you do in class, while listening, and the second part you do immediately after class. In class, you jot down notes on the right side of a paper. After class, you use the left side to pull out key ideas. This allows you to easily condense and identify key ideas within a lecture.

Social Movement Organization Leader: MLK	MLK as a SMO leader
Characteristics:	Leaders have all kinds of characteristics.
1. organize people	Organize people, frame a movement's
2. create/state message	message, exploit opportunities, gather
3. exploit opportunities	people.
	These characteristics are important for
	leaders. They represent the collective
	group.

CHARTING OR MAPPING

Charting or mapping contains all key information and visually illustrates the relationships between ideas.

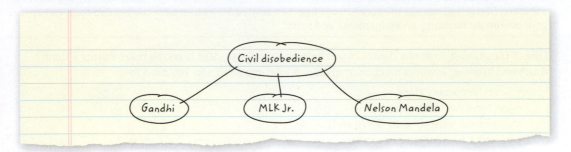

EXERCISE 3

A. **With a partner, review the three note-taking methods. What are the advantages and disadvantages of each method?**

B. **Now listen to a lecture on Dr. Martin Luther King's early adult life. Take notes using one of the methods.**

C. **Using your notes, answer the questions about the lecture.**

1. Can you number the events of Dr. King's life in chronological order?

.... Dr. King's house bombed

.... Married Coretta Scott

.... Graduated from Morehouse College

.... Earned PhD at Boston College

.... Wrote "Letter from Birmingham Jail"

.... Awarded Nobel Peace Prize

.... Led march on Washington, DC to bring attention to civil rights

.... Took leadership role after Montgomery bus boycott

.... Gave famous "I Have a Dream" speech

.... Assassinated in 1968

2. What were some results of Dr. King's efforts?

3. Why was Dr. King no longer the primary voice of the civil rights movement in 1964?

4. What are some other issues Dr. King spoke out against?

D. **With your partner, discuss which note-taking method you chose and why. Was it effective? Why or why not?**

Go to MyEnglishLab to complete a skill practice.

For more about NOTE-TAKING, see ⌐R⌐ SOCIOLOGY ①.

LANGUAGE SKILL
PARAPHRASING KEY IDEAS

WHY IT'S USEFUL By identifying paraphrasing, you can determine the meaning of complex terms. You can also utilize paraphrasing techniques when speaking or presenting to clarify technical language for your listeners.

In academic lectures and discussions, discipline-specific language is often used. Lecturers often restate the meaning of these terms in a way that is easier for listeners to understand. This is referred to as **paraphrasing**, or rephrasing. For example, a lecturer might state:

"Dr. King's <u>ascribed status</u>, *or social position given by birth,* played a role in his desire to advocate."

The lecturer used the term *ascribed status,* followed by its definition. This is one common way lecturers paraphrase.

Language for Paraphrasing	Examples
By that I mean …	Dr. King had great discipline. **By that I mean** he was motivated to produce particular realities.
It's …	Remember when we discussed normalization? **It's** a social process by which some practices are marked as "normal," while others are marked as "abnormal."
In other words,	The ruling class ideology prevailed. **In other words**, those in charge promoted the idea that African Americans were different.
In a word,	King worked to lift the underclass—**in a word**, the poorest and most underprivileged.
Or	Dr. King's ascribed status, **or** social position given by birth, played a tremendous role in his desire to advocate.
That is to say,	Class conflicts, **that is to say**, the differences between the varying social classes, were also a concern of King's.
Use of appositive (definition)	The sanctions **(punishments)** put upon King did not slow his efforts.

EXERCISE 4

A. **Look at the word list from this unit. Choose the words and phrases you know. If you don't remember the meaning, ask a classmate.**

☐ boycott   ☐ promised land   ☐ segregate

☐ propel   ☐ shoulder the responsibility ☐ scrutinize

☐ grassroots   ☐ charisma   ☐ passive resistance

B. **Read the sentences, which include words and phrases from Part A. Add paraphrases of the terms where indicated.**

1. Dr. King served as the primary spokesman for the bus boycott, ...

2. While the civil rights campaign began in the South, Dr. King propelled the movement,

   .... , to a national level.

3. The work of civil rights leaders was frequently scrutinized, ... , by others.

4. Although Dr. King was the face of the Civil Rights movement, it was truly a grassroots effort.

   ....

5. One critical leadership characteristic noted by sociologists is charisma. ....

C. **Work with a partner. Make sentences using the words and phrases in Part A that are not used in Part B. Practice paraphrasing.**

Go to **MyEnglishLab** to complete a skill practice.

APPLY YOUR SKILLS

WHY IT'S USEFUL   By applying the skills you have learned in this unit, you will be able to more actively participate and engage in a college-level sociology lecture.

ASSIGNMENT

Prepare a group presentation on a social movement. Your group will present key elements of the movement, such as organizational support and mobilization, to explain how the movement started and gained momentum, as well as what changes it achieved.

BEFORE YOU LISTEN

A. Before you listen, discuss the questions with one or more students.

1. How do most grassroots efforts begin? How about the civil rights movement?

2. What is a boycott, and what do people boycott?

3. Why do you think Dr. King led a variety of boycotts?

B. You will listen to a lecture about the Montgomery bus boycott. As you listen to the lecture, think about these questions.

1. Why is Rosa Parks so well known for the Montgomery bus boycott?

2. What effect did her arrest have on the civil rights movement?

3. How was Dr. King involved?

4. What impact did the bus boycott have on the city of Montgomery?

C. Review the Unit Skills Summary. As you listen to the lecture and prepare for your group presentation, apply the skills you learned in this unit.

UNIT SKILLS SUMMARY

BE AN ACTIVE PARTICIPANT USING THESE SKILLS:

Utilize strategies for elaboration and turn-taking.
- Ask for and respond to questions to get and give more details.
- Use your voice and signposts to signal the end or beginning of your ideas.
- Identify when others want to take a turn.

Take accurate, organized notes.
- Utilize a method to help you systematically organize key ideas.
- Select, interpret, determine, and write down key ideas.

Paraphrase.
- Listen for restatements of key terms to determine meaning.
- Restate discipline-specific vocabulary to clarify technical language.

LISTEN

A. Listen to the lecture about the Montgomery bus boycott and take notes.

B. Compare your notes with a partner. Do you both have the same key ideas? What skills from this unit can help you identify key ideas?

C. Work with a partner. Use your notes on the listening to answer the questions from Before You Listen, Part B.

THINKING CRITICALLY

Discuss the questions with another student.

1. What do you think are the primary implications of the speaker's statement, "We remember Rosa Parks largely because, by the time of her arrest, the African American community of Montgomery, Alabama, had been ready and waiting for a 'test case' to oppose bus segregation laws"?

2. Based on the lecture, how would you describe the speaker's point of view? In your discussion, provide examples that illustrate your understanding.

3. Based on the lecture, do you think individuals can greatly influence social change? How?

4. What connection does the speaker suggest exists between everyday citizens and social change?

THINKING VISUALLY

A. Look at the bar graphs on this page and on the next page. Discuss the questions with a partner.

1. What are the most critical civil rights for the respondents?

2. Why do you think some people answered "Not at all important" to some categories?

3. Would your ranking of these issues be similar or different? How?

4. What other categories would you add to these?

HOW IMPORTANT ARE THESE CIVIL RIGHTS ISSUES TO YOU?

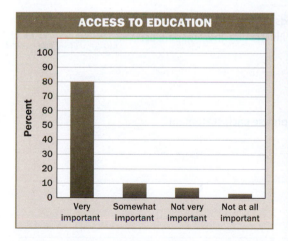

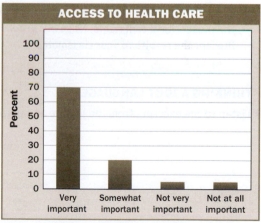

Continued

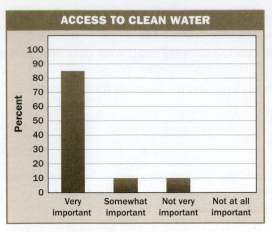

ACCESS TO CLEAN WATER

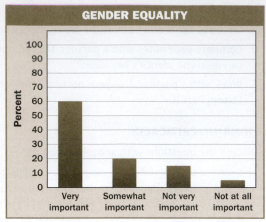

GENDER EQUALITY

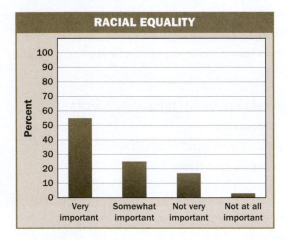

RACIAL EQUALITY

B. Conduct a survey in class or online of 10 friends regarding their beliefs on the most critical civil rights. Make bar graphs illustrating their responses. Present the results to your classmates.

For help interpreting and creating graphs, refer to ENGINEERING Parts 1 and 2.

Go to MyEnglishLab to listen again and answer critical thinking questions.

THINKING ABOUT LANGUAGE

Listen to the excerpts from the lecture and paraphrase each statement.

1. ....

2. ....

3. ....

4. ....

GROUP PRESENTATION

A. Read and discuss the question with one or more students.

Social movements have brought great change to countries all over the world. What other social movements do you know that have brought great change?

B. You will work with a small group to present a social movement that has brought great change to a culture or country. First, share stories on social movements. Then, select one movement and research details about it. Consider issues of organizational support, mobilization, and social injustice when creating your presentation.

1. What is the social movement your group will research?

2. What are some details on the movement that will illustrate your key points?

As you prepare, remember to paraphrase and elaborate on details to help your classmates understand key ideas.

C. Listen to each presentation.

Take notes and discuss the similarities and differences between all social movements presented.

▶ Go to MyEnglishLab to listen to Professor Greenberg and to complete a self-assessment.

Individual choices impact the global economy.

ECONOMICS

Idea Development

UNIT PROFILE

In this unit, you will learn how economists model the behavior of consumers and firms using the economic theories of supply and demand. You will also learn how competitive markets reach equilibrium.

You will prepare a presentation on a potential start-up. Each group will pitch its group product or service to the class in order to gain capital.

OUTCOMES

- Consider what you already know about a topic
- Identify and present main ideas and supporting details
- Compare textbooks to lectures
- Clarify your ideas

GETTING STARTED

▶ Go to MyEnglishLab to listen to Professor Clerici-Arias and to complete a self-assessment.

Discuss these questions with a partner or group.

1. What does the saying "money makes the world go around" mean to you? Is gaining and maintaining wealth one of your top priorities?

2. How is the price of a product or service determined? How important is price to you when you shop?

3. In the introduction, Professor Clerici-Arias says that "small, brand new companies can challenge and even surpass, larger, more established businesses." How do you think small companies might do this? Can you think of some examples of companies like this?

For more about **ECONOMICS** see 2 3. See also R and W **ECONOMICS** 1 2 3.

FUNDAMENTAL SKILL
DEVELOPING AN IDEA

WHY IT'S USEFUL By understanding idea development, you can be a more active participant in class lectures and academic discussions. By utilizing idea development, you can prepare cohesive, interesting presentations.

During your college career, you will attend a number of class lectures and presentations. Some lectures may last up to two hours. Understanding the main ideas in a lecture and making connections between those ideas is an important part of college success.

Your professor has developed the idea for his lecture by considering the topic and the key points related to the topic. Noticing how a presenter develops an idea will help you better understand both the topic and how ideas are related to one another.

There are several strategies that can help you determine someone else's idea development. First, before you listen to a lecture, **consider what you already know about the topic**. There are many ways to get your thoughts flowing. One activity is brainstorming. Imagine you are sitting in an economics class and the topic is product development. The first thing you need to do is ask yourself what you already know about the topic. What words or phrases related to product development come to mind? Brainstorming is the first step in helping you consider everything you already know about the topic.

Lecturers often give verbal cues when speaking that signal a speaker's **main ideas and supporting details**. These cues, or *signal words*, can help you better understand the speaker's organization.

As a college student, you will also be required to prepare oral presentations. Organizing your ideas in a clear, cohesive manner is an important part of giving a presentation. You can use the same strategies to prepare your own presentation that you use to prepare yourself to hear a professor's lecture. Start by considering what you know about the topic you will present. Brainstorm and jot down any ideas that come to mind. Consider which ones are main ideas and which ones are supporting details and organize them accordingly. As you give your presentation, remember to use signal words to help your listeners understand the connections between your ideas.

Go to MyEnglishLab to complete a vocabulary exercise.

NOTICING ACTIVITY

A. Listen to the beginning of a lecture. As you listen, try to identify the main ideas and supporting details. Discuss your ideas with a classmate.

B. Listen to two students discussing the lecture. Did they focus on the same ideas and details as you did?

> **CULTURE NOTE**
> *Silicon Valley* Silicon Valley is near San Francisco in northern California. It is home to hundreds of start-up companies, many in the field of technology. Google®, Apple®, and Facebook all call Silicon Valley home. When North Americans hear a reference to Silicon Valley, they immediately associate it with small start-up companies that have grown big.

Go to MyEnglishLab to complete a skill practice and join in collaborative activities.

SUPPORTING SKILL 1
CONSIDERING WHAT YOU KNOW ABOUT A TOPIC

WHY IT'S USEFUL By considering what you already know about a topic, you can make connections to new information you hear in a lecture or discussion. These connections improve your comprehension.

There are many ways you can consider what you know about a topic:

- Create a mind map of related concepts and words.
- Scan the related textbook chapter.
- Talk to a classmate about the topic.
- Look up key vocabulary.
- Conduct an Internet search on the title, topic, or speaker.

When you are sitting in a lecture class, the professor may say something that sparks an idea or concept in your mind. For example, if a professor lectures on how Facebook founders saw a gap in the market for college-aged people to share and connect with others, you may immediately think of concepts like *social media*, *profile*, *friend requests*, and more. This is **activating your prior knowledge** and making connections between related concepts and words. This can also be done using a visual map, or "mind map."

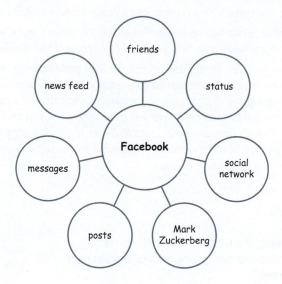

Another strategy is to utilize other course resources, like your textbooks. Many college lectures correlate to the reading material—in textbooks, articles, or other materials suggested by the professor. Skim and scan that material before the lecture. By doing so, you can connect new ideas to what you already know. You will also familiarize yourself with vocabulary words you are likely to hear as well as important ideas and relevant details. When the professor talks about these things during the lecture, you will recognize what he or she is talking about, making the lecture more understandable.

When you skim, pay attention to headings, bulleted lists, words and phrases in italics or boldface type, and the chapter introduction and conclusion. These will give you a good sense of the main ideas of the topic. When you scan, pay attention to details, such as dates, percentages, and examples. These will help you identify some of the supporting information on the topic.

For more about skimming and scanning, refer to [R] **SOCIOLOGY** 1.

EXERCISE 1

Go to MyEnglishLab to complete a vocabulary exercise.

A. What do you know about start-up companies? Write down any concepts, words, or phrases you associate with a start-up.

B. Share your list with another student. Together create a mind map with your ideas.

C. Listen to the conversation about start-ups. Complete the mind map as you listen.

CULTURE NOTE

Facebook Facebook is a world-reknowned start-up company. It is the first social networking company of its kind. It was started by a young college student who wanted to be virtually connected to his friends and family. Since the launch of Facebook, many other social networking companies have emerged, including Instagram and LinkedIn® professional networking services.

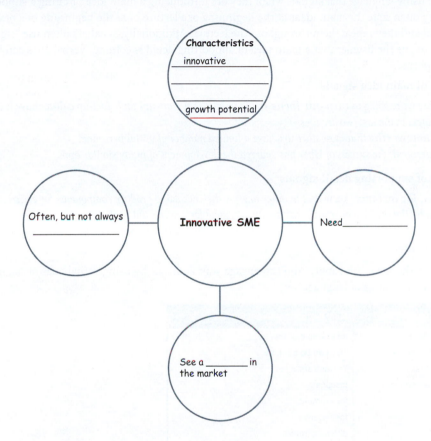

D. Compare your completed mind map with a partner. What information did you already know about start-ups? What information was new?

Go to MyEnglishLab to complete a skill practice and join in collaborative activities.

SUPPORTING SKILL 2

IDENTIFYING AND PRESENTING MAIN IDEAS AND SUPPORTING DETAILS

WHY IT'S USEFUL By identifying the main ideas and supporting details of a lecture or discussion, you can comprehend the meaning of a lecture and, in turn, participate in discussions. Understanding how to express main ideas and supporting details will also help you convey your ideas clearly and to develop your own presentations.

Speakers want the audience to follow what is being presented. Professors and professional speakers are mindful of using language that signals when they are introducing a main idea or citing a supporting detail. They often state the main ideas at the beginning of a lecture or at the beginning of a new portion of a lecture, and they repeat them throughout the lecture. Additionally, speakers often use "signposting," or signals, to cue the listener that a main idea or supporting detail is coming. Verbal cues can be either a word or a phrase.

Examples of main idea signals

- *Today we're going to **turn our focus to** the impact that start-ups and start-up culture have had on business in the last two decades.*
- *It's **noteworthy** that most start-ups have a limited number of initial personnel.*
- ***In general**, the success of Uber has spurred the development of many similar apps.*

Examples of supporting detail signals

- *Tesla, **for instance**, knew that in order to grow they needed to produce components for electric cars as well.*
- ***Much like** the idea of growth, scalability is critical for a successful SME.*
- *For an SME to gain capital, it must be ambitious. **Things like** integration of economic and social value demonstrate ambition.*

As a speaker, the same rules apply. You can engage your audience by using verbal cues or "signposting" your ideas with chunks of language.

More Main Idea Signals	More Supporting Detail Signals
Our topic today is…	An example of this is…
Let's discuss/look at…	This can be seen by…
My key point is…	To illustrate…
The main/key idea is…	Imagine…
Remember…	for example
above all	for instance
in general	different from
in reality	much like
most importantly	similarly
noteworthy	specifically
the objective	such as
obviously	first …, second …
overall	things like …
significant	in 2015
	statistically, … one in ten

EXERCISE 2

Go to MyEnglishLab to complete a vocabulary exercise.

A. Complete this lecture excerpt using verbal cues.

Let's get started. Yesterday we looked at how consumers create demand. Today .... how businesses generate demand for a product or service. The first way in which a company creates demand is by developing their brand—making it desirable and recognizable, ... Apple®. Even if you don't have an iPhone© or iPad©, you recognize their brand. .... being recognizable, a product has to evoke strong feelings of satisfaction. Companies do this, ..., by posting reviews and consumer ratings.

B. Listen to three lecture introductions. Choose all of the main ideas you hear in each.

1. a. the supply of goods
   b. factors in shifting demand
   c. consumer taste and preference
   d. consumer income
   e. world events that affect demand

2. a. influences on demand
   b. international trade
   c. consumer preferences
   d. luxury clothing
   e. nonessential commodity

3. a. consumer needs in the 19th century
   b. consumer taste and consumer preference
   c. ways of changing consumer tastes
   d. advertising in business
   e. consumer demand drives everything

C. Listen to each introduction again. Circle the verbal cues you hear.

1. let's discuss, let's examine, of all, for example, different from, obviously

2. the main idea, above all, to illustrate, for instance, for example

3. look at, in reality, remember, the key point, much like

Go to MyEnglishLab to complete a skill practice and join in collaborative activities.

INTEGRATED SKILLS
COMPARING TEXTBOOKS TO LECTURES

WHY IT'S USEFUL By noticing how textbooks and lectures present information differently, you can be a more informed and engaged learner. You can use textbooks to activate prior knowledge, support what you have heard, predict main ideas, or figure out what you may not have understood. You can use lecture notes to make connections to text content and to interpret the critical ideas of a course.

Both lectures and textbooks contain information you need to succeed in a college or university setting. They present critical information in different formats: lectures present information orally, while textbooks present information in written form. Which is easier to understand—lectures or textbooks? Some students feel it is much easier to understand written material. Textbooks are often better organized and easier to follow than lectures. Bold-faced words and headings often give clues to key information. Moreover, if you don't understand textbook material the first time you read it, you can easily read it again until you do. You can always refer to written information.

On the other hand, lecturers are not always as organized as a textbook. You have to listen carefully for verbal cues to indicate main ideas. Lecturers sometimes stray, or digress, from their main ideas, making it harder to follow the information. Furthermore, spoken information from lectures and discussions vanishes after it is delivered; unless it is recorded, you cannot refer to it again.

Feature	Textbook	Lecture
Organization	Patterned and predictable organizational structure (chapters, sections, headings)	Some lecturers tell stories or get off topic.
Important Ideas	Bold or italic type and underlining to show emphasis; bulleted lists	Lecturers often repeat. They "signal" important ideas using words and phrases and may increase volume.
Visual Cues	Photographs, charts, tables, graphs	Visuals are similar but often are presented on PowerPoint slides or on a board.
Extra Information	Table of contents, glossary, index	There are a variety of ways to include extra information: stories, anecdotes, asides, digressions.
Perspective	Objective and formal	Generally less formal than a book and contains more bias and opinions than a textbook.
Repetition	Via bulleted lists and end-of-chapter summaries	Speakers use verbal repetition and signal words and phrases, such as "what I mean is" or "to summarize."
Grammar	Long sentences with detail; grammatically correct	Grammar is less formal, sometimes ungrammatical (doesn't always follow rules). Sentences are usually shorter.

Textbooks and lectures serve different purposes, and both have strengths and weaknesses. While textbooks tend to be more direct and objective, they often contain dated material and do not allow for any type of interaction. Lectures, on the other hand, are interactive. You can ask the lecturer questions, have information clarified, and be exposed to real-life, real-time examples. Lecturers often provide students with the most up-to-date and current information in the field.

EXERCISE 3

A. Read the passage and look at the visual aid below.

A **market** refers to all of the buyers and sellers of a given commodity. Markets can range from the very specific, such as the emerald market of central Thailand, to the especially large, such as the worldwide petroleum market. Markets are not restricted to goods; they can also include services—cab drivers in Los Angeles, window washers of Vancouver, and so on. A **competitive market** is one that has a large number of buyers and sellers, making each individual buyer or seller incapable of directly influencing market price. Thus, new producers are subject to predetermined prices as set by supply and demand. Using the supply-and-demand model, economists analyze competitive markets and potential price leveraging.

The price of goods in a competitive market tends toward the **equilibrium price**, which is the price where supply matches demand (see fig 2.3). The buyers and sellers in a competitive market are known as **price takers**; they are stuck with the equilibrium price and can do little to influence it.

In a **perfectly competitive market**, *all* goods or services involved are the same, and market price is *not* influenced by an individual buyer or seller. Perfectly competitive markets may not describe many markets in the real world, but they are a useful hypothetical situation that allows economists to explain certain trends and behaviors.

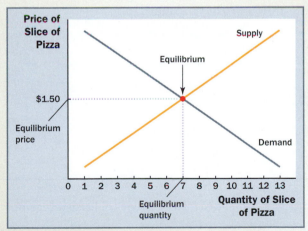

(Figure 2.3)

B. **Answer the questions with another student.**

1. How can one identify key ideas?
2. Discuss the organization. Is it easy to follow? Why or why not?
3. How are key terms defined?
4. Are examples given for key terms?
5. How does the visual help you understand the concept?

C. **Now listen to a lecture excerpt on the same topic. Answer the questions with your partner.**

1. How can one identify key ideas?
2. How does the organization differ from the text excerpt?
3. How does the speaker define key terms?
4. Are examples given?
5. What is something that the speaker does that the textbook excerpt does not do?

D. **With your partner, complete the chart comparing the textbook passage to the lecture.**

Feature	Textbook	Lecture
Organization		
Important Ideas		
Visual Cues		
Extra Information		
Perspective		
Repetition		
Grammar		

E. **Discuss with your partner if you prefer to read a textbook or listen to lecture. Which is easier for you and why?**

Go to MyEnglishLab to complete a skill practice.

LANGUAGE SKILL
CLARIFYING

WHY IT'S USEFUL By learning how to clarify, you can make sure you understand spoken information correctly. When speaking, you can also clarify for your listeners to ensure that they comprehend the information and remain engaged.

To clarify means to make something easier, or more clear, to understand. Both speakers and listeners use clarifying language to "check in" with the person they're communicating with.

Speakers ...	Listeners ...
may ask listeners during a lecture, discussion, or speech if they understood the content:	**can ask for clarification by saying:**
Do you see what I mean?	I'm not following you …
Does that make sense?	I'm not sure I understand …
Is that clear?	I'm not sure I'm clear about what you mean by that.
Does everyone understand?	I'm sorry, but I didn't catch what you said. Could you say it again?
Are there any questions?	I didn't follow what you said about …
may signal that they are clarifying by confirming the content:	**can ask for confirmation:**
That's not exactly what I meant. What I meant was …	Correct me if I'm wrong, but are you saying …
Let me put it another way.	When you say …, do you mean …
What I'm trying to say is …	Would I be correct if I said …
Perhaps I can make it clearer by …	Did you say …
What I mean is …	Let me see if I understood. You said …

A third person may confirm the speaker's message to help the listener understand
What Jose meant was …
Lee said …
I believe Mikhail's point was …
I think Franz said …. Is that right, Franz?
We all agree that …, right?

EXERCISE 4

A. Listen again to the student discussion of the professor's lecture. Answer the questions.

1. What three things did the woman not understand?

   ....

   ....

   ....

2. What words and phrases did the woman use to ask for clarification or confirmation?

....

....

....

....

....

3. What words did the woman use to signal she was clarifying or asking for clarification or confirmation?

....

....

....

....

....

B. **Read these passages silently. Working with another student, take turns as listener and speaker. Speakers: explain each passage and use clarification language to check understanding. Listeners: confirm your understanding using clarification language.**

1. The digital age has created more opportunities for SMEs. One trait of SMEs is innovation—the ability to do something very different than it has typically done in the past. Uber and Tesla are just two examples of how technology has positively affected their innovation.

2. Scalability is another critical trait for SMEs. Positioning a start-up to be scalable often leads to success. Without having a replicable business model, preparation for growth potential, and distribution potential, an SME will most likely fail.

3. Venture capital groups often work with the most innovative potential start-ups to ensure their business model has the characteristics needed for success in building equity.

4. Demand for a good is determined by a number of factors. These factors are not limited to price, consumer desire, price of related goods, or market trends.

5. Individual demand is directly related to an individual's income as well as preferences set by the individual. The individual can represent either self or family.

6. Increasing production for technological goods is a direct effect of the supply shift. This increase also lowers the price point and moves the equilibrium.

C. **Work with a small group. Each group member should tell the group about a successful start-up. Listen to each group member and ask clarification questions for anything that is unclear.**

Example

Student A: I love Edible Arrangements®. They are one of my favorite companies. You can have fresh fruit delivered to someone. The company started about ten years ago, and they are everywhere now.

Student B: When you say they deliver fresh fruit, do you mean just like having fresh flowers delivered?

Go to **MyEnglishLab** to complete a skill practice.

APPLY YOUR SKILLS

WHY IT'S USEFUL By applying the skills you have learned in this unit, you can actively participate and engage in a college-level economics lecture by making connections between the ideas you hear and by confirming or clarifying your understanding. You can also prepare and participate in a presentation with your classmates.

ASSIGNMENT

Prepare a presentation on a potential start-up. You and your group members will use the theories of supply and demand to pitch the product or service to the class in order to gain capital.

BEFORE YOU LISTEN

A. Discuss these questions with one or more students.

1. What products or services are in high demand?

2. Are suppliers able to meet the demands of the market? Why or why not?

3. Can you think of some products or services that compete against one another? How do these products compare as far as price?

4. What are some other factors that influence the price of a product or service?

B. You will listen to a lecture on the theories of supply and demand. Before you listen, brainstorm on this topic with one or more classmates. Think of as many words, phrases, and concepts that you can connect to supply and demand. Complete the mind map with your ideas.

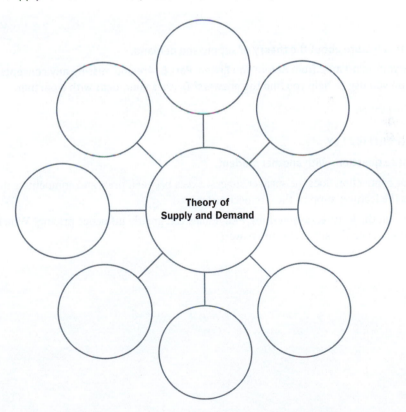

Theory of
Supply and Demand

C. Review the Unit Skills Summary. As you listen to the lecture and prepare for your group presentation, apply the skills you learned in this unit.

UNIT SKILLS SUMMARY

Activate your prior knowledge.
- Brainstorm related concepts and ideas.
- Scan course materials such as textbooks or handouts.
- Look up key vocabulary.
- Talk to a classmate about the topic.
- Conduct an Internet search on the title, topic, or speaker.

Identify and present main ideas and supporting details.

As a listener:

- notice the signal words speakers use for main ideas.
- notice the signal words speakers use for supporting details.

As a speaker:

- brainstorm main ideas and details using graphic organizers.
- use language signposts to highlight main ideas and details in your presentation.

Clarify.
- As a listener, ask questions to clarify or confirm your understanding.
- As a speaker, use clarification questions to be sure your listeners are following.

LISTEN

A. Listen to a lecture about the theory of supply and demand.

B. Review your mind map from Before You Listen, Part B. Are you missing any concepts? What listening skills can you use to help you find the answers? Discuss your ideas with a partner.

Go to MyEnglishLab to listen again and answer critical thinking questions.

THINKING CRITICALLY

Discuss these questions with another student.

1. What connection does the speaker suggest exists between price and competitive markets? How does the lecturer support that connection?

2. Based on the lecture, do you think individuals can greatly influence pricing? Which of the lecturer's remarks support your answer?

THINKING VISUALLY

A. Based on this graph of demand meeting supply, what other goods and services are likely to be represented by this equilibrium? Why do you think this is true?

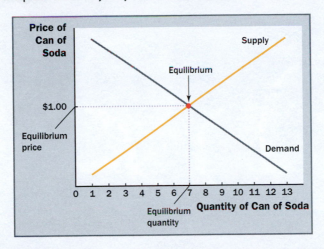

B. Conduct an online search on a product or service that interests you. Investigate the supply and demand of that product or service. Make a graph to show the demand and supply of that product or service. Is it at equilibrium? Present it to the class.

THINKING ABOUT LANGUAGE

🔊 Listen to these excerpts from the lecture. After each excerpt, ask for clarification or confirm your understanding with another student.

GROUP PRESENTATION

A. Read and discuss these questions with one or more students. Take notes on your discussion.

Professor Clerici-Arias described the theories of supply and demand and reviewed how these theories impact market trends and prices. How do start-ups like Facebook, Uber, and Tesla use these theories to gain capital? How might they have effectively pitched their ideas to receive financial support using these theories?

B. Work with a small group and create your own start-up company. Your company will pitch a product or service to the class. First, research market trends and determine potential demand to establish a gap in the market. Apply the theories of supply and demand to gain the capital you need.

1. What is the main idea behind your start-up?

2. What are three key ideas you could use to support the funding of your start-up?

3. What supporting information adds details to your start-up?

C. Prepare your group presentation.

Remember to use signposts to present your main idea and supporting details effectively. Use clarifying language to help your classmates understand your business plan.

D. Listen to each start-up presentation.

Listen carefully to all groups. Ask clarifying questions to learn more about their product or service. After the presentations are completed, take a vote on which start-up is most likely to succeed. Award that group the capital they need.

▶ Go to MyEnglishLab to listen to Professor Clerici-Arias and to complete a self-assessment.

Exploring the secret lives of viruses.

Extended Discourse

UNIT PROFILE

In this unit you will learn what a virus is and how it is transmitted, diagnosed, and treated. You will also learn about the dangers of 21st century viruses.

You will prepare a class debate on the use of immunizations in small children.

OUTCOMES

- Participate in extended discourse
- Respond to and discuss controversial topics
- Recognize and use digressions
- Lead discussions
- Utilize interrogatives and declaratives to gain, confirm, and assert support

GETTING STARTED

▶ Go to MyEnglishLab to listen to Professor Siegel and to complete a self-assessment.

Discuss these questions with a partner or group.

1. What are some common childhood viruses? What are some effective ways to treat those viruses? Thinking of your native country, what preventative measures are taken to avoid some of these viruses? What policies do you think should be in place?

2. In today's world, viruses know no boundaries. What are some viruses that are currently plaguing the world? What could be done to contain these viruses?

3. In the introduction, Professor Siegel refers to the classification of cellular organisms. What are the four classifications the professor mentions? Are you familiar with each of these?

For more about **BIOLOGY**, see ② ③. See also R and W **BIOLOGY** ① ② ③.

FUNDAMENTAL SKILL
PARTICIPATING IN EXTENDED DISCOURSE

Being an active member of an academic discussion involves participating, engaging your peers, and helping to keep the conversation going. This is often known as **extended discourse**. Extended discourse refers to in-depth, interactive communication on a particular topic. Professors and lecturers often use group discussion as a regular learning activity. In these situations, students are expected to initiate, maintain, and guide extended discourse as a way to gain deeper understanding into course content. Extended discourse allows you to fully interact with new information through questioning, clarifying, discussing, and reflecting.

Lively interaction is commonplace when **discussing and responding to controversial topics**. In these types of discussions, you need to understand how to effectively **challenge others' ideas**. Challenging ideas involves critiquing and evaluating the validity of an argument. To effectively critique an argument, you first must recognize specific, concrete language. This type of language helps you identify others' arguments and respond appropriately.

Listening actively is an important part of discussing and responding to controversial topics. Communication can often break down when group members become more interested in speaking than in listening. When listening actively to everyone's point of view, it is important to recognize any **digression or aside** that might interfere with the main topic. Digressions are ideas that have moved away from the main topic. They are usually not relevant to the discussion. Like digressions, asides are also short strays from the main idea. Asides usually take the form of a story.

Go to MyEnglishLab to complete a vocabulary exercise.

NOTICING ACTIVITY

A. Listen to an academic discussion in a natural sciences course. As you listen, pay attention to how each participant keeps the conversation going or extends the discourse.

B. Now listen to two students talking about the discussion. What do the students observe about the discussion?

Go to MyEnglishLab to complete a skill practice and join in collaborative activities.

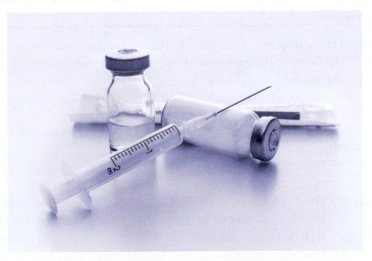

SUPPORTING SKILL 1
DISCUSSING AND RESPONDING TO CONTROVERSIAL TOPICS

WHY IT'S USEFUL By participating in a discussion on a controversial topic, you can develop skills in constructing an argument, clarifying your ideas, evaluating others' ideas, and critiquing.

Discussing controversial topics is a common practice in an academic environment. Professors often ask students to take a stance on a contentious or debatable issue. This serves many purposes. First, it allows you as a student to apply abstract ideas to a real situation. In doing so, you need to think critically about a topic. Thinking critically involves analyzing a topic deeply and formulating your stance or argument. Once you have established your position, you need to develop a justification for your ideas with specific, concrete language. Presenting those ideas involves giving an opinion and responding to the opinions of others. Look at the phrases below. Can you add to the list?

Giving an Opinion	Responding to or Challenging an Opinion
In my opinion …	I see your point, but …
I see it as …	That's true, but don't you think that …
I think it's reasonable to say that …	I'm not sure I agree. Reason being …
It would seem to me that …	Would/Wouldn't you say …?
I tend to favor …	Correct me if I'm wrong, but …

Second, you need to be an active listener. Often, when topics are highly controversial, there is a lot of talk and little listening. This causes communication to break down. Being an active listener means giving a speaker your full attention, taking notes, asking for clarification, and evaluating a speaker's main ideas.

When responding to a speaker's ideas, be sure to use effective clarification strategies. Be sure to restate what you think the speaker means and add a clarifying question.

Clarifying Questions
When you said …, did you mean …?
I'm not sure I followed your idea about …. Can you explain what you meant?
What did you mean by …?
Could you explain what you meant by …?

Evaluating another position requires you to identify the main points, the context, any potential bias, and fallacies in reasoning. Consider these questions when responding to or challenging other ideas:

- Do the main points support the overall position?
- Do the main points fit into the context of the discussion? That is, are they applicable to the current discussion?
- Is the speaker objective? Are the ideas supported with evidence rather than personal experience or anecdotes?
- Is the position grounded in sound reasoning?

Example

Professor: **I tend to favor** a focus on developing a viable vaccine as quickly as possible while you advocate an early focus on creating antivirals. **Why is that?**

Dr. Hastings: **Well, to clarify that a bit** … I certainly understand and appreciate the value of immunizations.

By asking yourself these questions, you can either prepare a well-thought out counterargument, modify your original idea, or accept some or all of the position presented. Considering another side, or opposing argument, can better help you refine your position.

EXERCISE 1

Go to MyEnglishLab to complete a vocabulary exercise.

A. What are some ways in which society could prepare for new viruses? Write down your ideas.

....

....

....

B. Discuss your ideas with a classmate. Which ways would be most effective, and which ways would not be effective? Why?

C. Do you think governments should financially support the development of vaccines and antivirals? Share your opinion with a classmate. Support your opinion with concrete examples.

The Pentagon

CULTURE NOTE

The Pentagon The Pentagon is the headquarters of the United States Department of Defense. The building is in the shape of a pentagon, having 5 sides. There are even 5 floors. It is located in Arlington, Virginia.

D. Listen to a class lecture on germ warfare. Then answer the questions.

1. How does the student challenge the idea that vaccine research is being conducted with taxpayer dollars?

....

2. How does the professor support Galloway's work?

....

3. Is the professor objective? How do you know?

....

4. Do you think the funding of this research is grounded in sound reasoning? Why or why not?

....

E. Compare your answers with a partner. Do you have similar or differing opinions on the use of government funds to cover germ warfare?

Go to MyEnglishLab to complete a skill practice and join in collaborative activities.

SUPPORTING SKILL 2
RECOGNIZING AND UTILIZING DIGRESSIONS

WHY IT'S USEFUL By identifying digressions, you can distinguish between necessary information and extra information. Using digressions in your own speech can help make your speech more interesting and more relatable to the audience.

Speakers often digress, or talk about something that is not directly related to the topic. We refer to these off-topic comments as *digressions*. Digressions are not only common in daily conversation, but also an academic classroom. Lecturers often purposely use digressions. There are many reasons a lecturer may digress; some reasons are the lecturer

- has a story that relates indirectly to the topic.
- wants to exemplify an idea or point.
- wants the audience to relax and take a short break.
- wants to connect the content of the lecture to the audience's experience.

When a lecturer digresses, he or she often signals a digression with signposting language, and subsequently signals a return to the topic.

Signposts for a Digression	Signals for a Return to Topic
As an aside …	As I was saying …
By the way …	Anyway,
If I may digress …	Enough of that, let's go back to …
This reminds me of …	Let me return to …
Oh, that reminds me …	So, where was I …?
This makes me think of …	To continue …
Let me just mention …	To get back to the topic at hand …
To change the subject for a minute …	To return to …
To go on a tangent for a moment …	Well, back to business.
To wander for a minute …	
You may be interested to know …	

Examples

Viruses are warfare. They kill. **By the way**, did anyone see the news last night? About what's happening with the Ebola virus? **Anyway …**

Influenza is deadly. It kills thousands of people a year in the USA alone. The virus can lasts for weeks, and weakens your body. **This reminds me of** the year 2004. I had the flu. I was in bed for a week. It was just awful … **Anyway, enough of that …**

EXERCISE 2

Go to MyEnglishLab to complete a vocabulary exercise.

A. How do you think viruses are classified? Write down some of your ideas.

....

....

....

B. Share your ideas with a classmate. Do your lists contain similar items?

C. Listen to the academic lecture on the classification of viruses. Take notes as you listen. Can you identify where the speaker digresses? Can you identify where the speaker returns to the main idea?

D. Share your notes with a partner. Then label each sentence below with MI (main idea), S (supporting idea), E (example), or D (digression).

.... 1. The system used to classify viruses is the International Committee on Taxonomy of Virus's system.

.... 2. The Baltimore Classification System was a system that gained a bit of prominence.

.... 3. Virus classification focuses only on "order" and below.

.... 4. The ICTV system has seven orders of viruses.

.... 5. Diagrams of bacteriophages look like a spider.

.... 6. Rabies and Ebola are single-stranded RNA-based order.

Go to MyEnglishLab to complete a skill practice and join in collaborative activities.

Viruses (Baltimore classification)

	sense	strand	nucleic acid	reverse transcriptase	with envelope (some examples)		w/o envelope (naked) (some examples)	
Group I		ds	DNA		Herpesviruses		Adenoviruses	
Group II	+	ss	DNA				Parvoviruses	
Group III		ds	RNA				Reoviruses	
Group IV	+	ss	RNA				Picornaviruses	Coronaviruses
Group V	–	ss	RNA		Orthomyxoviruses	Paramyxoviruses		
Group VI	+	ss	RNA	RT	Retroviruses			
Group VII		ds	DNA	RT	Hepadnaviruses			

INTEGRATED SKILLS
LEADING DISCUSSIONS

WHY IT'S USEFUL By understanding how to effectively lead a discussion, you can efficiently manage group tasks.

Leading a discussion not only involves ensuring the conversation remains fair and polite, but also gaining equal participation from group members. In order to do so, you will need to assert your authority by encouraging participation, asking for clarification, and asking for confirmation to keep the discussion on task and moving. When preparing to lead a formal discussion, you will also need to be sure you have researched the topic thoroughly in order to ask on-point questions and direct the flow of the conversation.

ENCOURAGING PARTICIPATION

To encourage communication, consider posing a question to the group to elicit opinions and ideas.

Example

> What are your thoughts?
>
> Any thoughts?
>
> Any ideas?
>
> How do you feel about …?
>
> What do you think about …?
>
> Do you think …?

ASKING FOR CLARIFICATION OR CONFIRMATION

To ensure that everyone understands, it may be necessary to ask for *clarification* on an opinion or idea presented. Clarifying involves asking the speaker to expand or elaborate on what was said.

Confirming is similar to clarifying. However, with confirming, you are checking your understanding of what was said rather than asking the speaker to elaborate on what was said. When leading a group discussion, you may need to ask a speaker to confirm what was said to ensure that everyone in the group understands the main idea. There are three main ways to confirm:

- using tag questions
- paraphrasing
- using a confirmation expression

> **TIP**
> ....
> For specific ways of asking elaboration, see SOCIOLOGY Part 1.

Examples

Tag Questions	Paraphrasing	Confirmation Expressions
So, we don't have information from fossil records because viruses are too small, aren't they? Human DNA hasn't been directly affected by viruses, has it?	What Bill means is that … I believe Emma's point is … I think Jamie feels …	If I understand you correctly, … Let me see if I understand you … In other words, you are saying … In a nutshell … What you're saying is …

RESEARCHING INFORMATION

When preparing for a formal discussion, like a panel discussion, not only the discussion moderator, but also each participant, needs to research information ahead of time to be adequately prepared to present his or her viewpoint. Research involves looking at the literature, building background knowledge, and drawing conclusions based on the literature. Selecting detailed examples to support those conclusions drawn are an integral part of your argument.

EXERCISE 3

A. Read an excerpt from a recent publication on viral evolution. As you read, underline where key terms are defined. How would these definitions help you as a panelist?

When examining any scientific evolution, it is critical to look at the information gained from fossil records. However, in the case of viral evolution, there is little gained from fossils due to the fact that viral organisms are minuscule. It is known that human DNA, the carrier of our genetic information, has been directly affected by viruses throughout the course of our evolution. It is through this evolution that scientists today are  able to speculate about how viruses evolved. There are three main hypotheses. First, a great number of scientists argue that viruses are remnants of early pre-cellular forms of life. The use the word *pre-cellular* means that there's still much left to learn about the origins of life between inorganic material and even the simplest of present-day prokaryote cells, those cells that are unicellular, such as bacteria. Other microbiologists assert that somewhere along the line, pieces of cells became detached and began reproducing parasitically. Finally, there's the chance that viruses began as parasitic cells that, through evolution, moved toward more efficient structures until they dwindled down to what we have today. As with the previous two theories, the cell is the foundation. There are numerous existing cells that are parasites or predators, feeding off of other cells. Over time, organisms can gradually develop through evolution structures and traits that aid in their reproduction. If a cellular parasite ended up requiring fewer resources by hijacking those of a host cell, then it could reproduce more efficiently. Over generations you could see an organism that started as a cell become a virus.

B. **Listen to the panel discussion. Write the phrase you hear that matches each strategy below.**

1. Signpost to encourage communication ....

2. Tag question for confirmation ....

3. Paraphrasing for confirmation ....

4. An expression for confirmation ....

5. Clarifying statement ....

C. **Read the next part of the excerpt from the publication and complete the tasks.**

> Evolutionary fitness needs to be considered when reviewing each of these theories. Evolutionary fitness refers to the concept of how well a species is able to reproduce in its environment. In the case of viruses, how rapidly are they able to branch out and diversify? Imagine two animals that share a common ancestor—it would have taken hundreds or thousands of years at the *least* for them to evolve into distinct species. Because viruses consist of very little actual genetic material, a small mutation can have a big impact on the virus. With so many viruses from each cell producing so rapidly in so many different cells in so many different hosts, you're more likely to encounter mutations. Take influenza, for example: each year there is a circulating strain that may not have been present the year before.

1. Paraphrase the sentence.

   Evolutionary fitness refers to the concept of how well a species is able to reproduce in its environment.

   ....

2. Use an expression to confirm understanding of the sentence.

   Imagine two animals that share a common ancestor—it would have taken hundreds or thousands of years at the *least* for them to evolve into distinct species.

   ....

3. Confirm understanding of the sentence with a tag question.

   Because viruses consist of very little actual genetic material a small mutation can have a big impact on the virus.

   ....

D. **Imagine you are having a panel discussion on viral fitness. Work in groups of three with one moderator and two panelists. Discuss the information in Part B and Part C using signposts for encouraging participation, clarifying meaning and confirming understanding.**

Go to MyEnglishLab to complete a skill practice.

LANGUAGE SKILL
IDENTIFY AND USE INTERROGATIVES AND DECLARATIVES

WHY IT'S USEFUL By recognizing how interrogatives and declaratives are used to confirm support and assert authority, you can better gain the support of your audience.

When working in a group, you often need to gain the support of your group members. One effective way to do this is by setting up a proposition and asking for support. A proposition is similar to a suggestion. However, it uses assertive language that often elicits a positive response from listeners. Propositions are formed by presenting a scenario, and then adding a negative interrogative or strong declarative.

INTERROGATIVES
Once you present a scenario or a situation, add a negative interrogative. A negative interrogative is a question formed with a modal + negative or *do* + negative.

Example
Situation: There is a flu pandemic and medical research has been developing vaccines rather than antivirals.

- **Wouldn't** *it be tragic for millions?*
- **Couldn't** *we have prevented this situation?*
- **Don't** *you think we should have done something different?*

It is hard to answer "no" to these questions. By using these interrogatives, you are likely going to gain support from your audience.

DECLARATIVES
Declaratives, like interrogatives, are used to assertively show the validity of your position or argument because they state a fact or an argument. By adding an action statement, you can strongly assert your authority. The action statement often tells listeners what should be done. To form an action statement, use *it is* + adjective + *clause*.

Examples
Situation: Imagine biological weapons have been used and have taken vast numbers of human lives as a result.

- **It is necessary** *to prevent that situation from happening through medical research.*
- **It is essential** *to prevent something like this from happening before it happens.*
- **It is prudent** *to prepare ourselves for a situation like this.*
- **It is imperative** *to prevent something like this from happening before it happens.*
- **It is critical** *to take steps now to avert such a situation.*

Declaratives can also include a noun clause.

Examples
- *It is critical* **that we** *be* **prepared for a mass viral outbreak.**
- *It is recommended* **that children under five** *be* **vaccinated.**
- *The government suggests* **that a traveler** *read* **the current viral outbreaks of his or her destination.**

When a noun clause is preceded by a verb or an adjective of urgency or suggestion, the verb in the noun clause is in the subjunctive form. This chart shows some examples of verbs and adjectives of urgency or suggestion. Can you think of others?

Verbs of Urgency / Suggestion	Adjectives of Urgency / Suggestion
advise	advisable
ask	critical
demand	crucial
insist	imperative
recommend	mandatory
request	recommended
suggest	vital

CHALLENGING OTHERS' IDEAS

In order to gain support, it is often necessary to challenge others' ideas. To effectively challenge, you must question or refute the argument made. In an academic environment, this is often a two-step process. First, it is important to acknowledge your understanding of his or her main point.

Examples

> While I understand your position on vaccines, …
>
> I agree with your idea on vaccines …
>
> I concur with your ideas on vaccines …

Next, give a specific flaw in the argument. This can be done by using an interrogative, stating a fact, or showing a weakness in the argument presented.

Examples

> While I understand your position on vaccines, don't you think more research needs to be conducted?
>
> I agree with your idea on vaccines; however, according to the CDC, 12 million children go unvaccinated a year.
>
> I concur with your ideas on vaccines in theory; however, I don't see the hard evidence to support them.

EXERCISE 4

A. Write an interrogative or declarative sentence for each imaginary situation.

1. Imagine a limit on the research dollars for antivirals and vaccines. (Add an interrogative.)

   ....

2. Imagine if taxpayers don't support this research for antivirals and vaccines. (Add a declarative.)

   ....

3. Imagine a mass outbreak of a virus that is slowly killing the young and the elderly. (Add an interrogative.)

   ....

4. Imagine a mass outbreak of a virus that is slowly killing the young and the elderly. (Add a declarative.)

....

5. Imagine prioritizing medical research to focus only on the prevention of viruses. (Add an interrogative.)

....

6. Imagine prioritizing medical research to focus only on the prevention of viruses. (Add a declarative.)

....

B. Read this final excerpt from the publication.

> Pharmaceutical companies are looking to government programs to fund research toward developing new drugs and vaccines that would fight against the flu. The government is contracting pharmaceutical companies and paying close to two million dollars for the development. Because of time and personnel restrictions, the government feels the viability of development lies with private industry rather than with governmental offices.

C. Work with a partner. Imagine you are preparing a presentation on this excerpt. Present an argument supporting or opposing the ideas given in the excerpt. Your partner will listen to your argument and respond with a counterargument.

Go to MyEnglishLab to complete a skill practice.

APPLY YOUR SKILLS

WHY IT'S USEFUL By applying the skills you have learned in this unit, you can better extend discourse, respond to and discuss controversial topics, and recognize and utilize digressions. You can also lead a discussion in which you encourage participation and utilize interrogatives and declaratives to gain support and assert authority.

ASSIGNMENT

Prepare a debate on whether or not small children should be vaccinated to immunize them from potentially harmful viruses. Use what you have learned about viruses as well as your research into the advantages and disadvantages of vaccines to develop your position.

BEFORE YOU LISTEN

A. Discuss the questions with one or more students.

1. In addition to what you have learned in this unit, what are some current deadly viruses?

2. Why do you think new viruses surface?

3. Are you familiar with a time in history where thousands or millions of people died due to viral outbreak? What was the disease, and what happened?

B. You will listen to a panel discussion about viruses in the 21st century. As you listen, think about these questions.

1. What are two of the deadliest 21st century viruses?

2. What are some characteristics of deadly viruses?

3. Is the world prepared for an epidemic? Why or why not?

4. What are some factors which make it easy to spread a virus?

C. Review the Unit Skills Summary. As you listen to the lecture and begin preparing your debate, apply the skills you learned in this unit.

UNIT SKILLS SUMMARY

Participate in extended discourse.
- Respond to and discuss controversial topics.
  - Give your opinion.
  - Respond to or challenge others' opinions.
  - Ask for clarification.

Recognize and use digressions.
- Identify common signposts for digressions.
- Recognize signals for a returns to topic.

Lead discussions.
- Encourage communication in a group.
- Confirm others' ideas through the use of tag questions, paraphrasing and expressions of confirmation.

Identify and utilize interrogatives and declaratives to gain, confirm, and assert support.
- Utilize questions and declarative statements to challenge ideas.

LISTEN

A. Listen to the panel discussion on 21st century viruses. Take notes as you listen.

B. Reread the questions from Before You Listen, Part B. Is there anything you cannot answer? What skills can you use to help find the answers?

Go to MyEnglishLab to listen again and answer critical thinking questions.

CULTURE NOTE
The Spanish Influenza The Spanish Influenza epidemic occurred in 1918. It was one the deadliest disasters in human history, infecting approximately five hundred million people across the globe. Many believe that it originated in Spain, or that it infected the greatest number of citizens of Spain. However, that was not the case. It was given the name the "Spanish Flu" during World War I. Due to the war, many countries did not report on the number of citizens infected, but Spain was a neutral country and did report the number of people who fell ill.

THINKING CRITICALLY

Discuss the questions with another student.

1. How are the three viruses similar? How do they differ?

2. Based on the lecture, what connection can be made between education and the containment of viruses?

THINKING VISUALLY

A. Using information from the lecture, complete the Venn diagram below with characteristics of Ebola, influenza, and HIV.

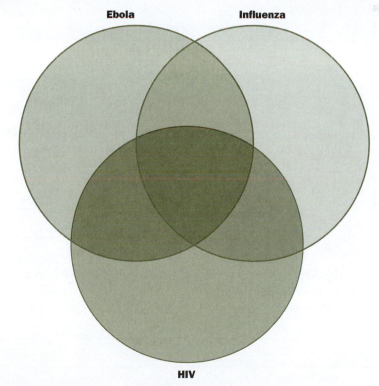

Ebola   Influenza

HIV

B. Compare your Venn diagram with a classmate.

Read the quotes. Write a proposition for each with either an interrogative or a declarative. Then, work with a partner. Take turns stating and responding to each proposition.

Quote One

The flu mutates extremely fast, and certain cramped quarters situations like prisons, barracks, and mass migrations of refugees can be a perfect breeding ground for deadly new strains. We have no shortage of such conditions today, despite our modern advances. Finally, we have the risk posed by a disease like bird flu—right now, this form of influenza is only transmissible via direct contact. The fatality rate is incredibly high.

Proposition:

....

....

....

Quote Two

The disease owes much of its high fatality rate to blood loss. Since Ebola is transmitted via bodily fluids, medical personnel are especially vulnerable; this understandably hinders any attempts at containment.

Proposition:

....

....

....

Quote Three

A number of factors worked together to make the flu so deadly—modern society had, for the first time, placed millions of people in close proximity to one another in major metropolitan centers.

Proposition:

....

....

....

Quote Four

Modern antiviral drugs have made having HIV much less deadly. With early treatment, many people with HIV can live well into old age in spite of the disease. While many are still at risk, awareness and treatment gets better every day.

Proposition:

....

....

....

CLASS DEBATE

A. Read and discuss the questions with a small group.

Many parents in the Western world are caught up in a debate over immunizations for infants and young children. This controversy surrounding vaccines is not new. A large number of parents feel vaccinations are causing more harm than good. What do you think? What are the advantages of infant vaccinations? What are the disadvantages?

B. You will participate in a class debate. Divide your class into two teams—for immunizations and against immunizations. With your team members, research the arguments both for and against the use of vaccines. Follow these steps:

1. Work with your team to determine the best arguments.

2. Assign each member one argument to support your team's position.

3. Each member prepares a brief for their team's position.

4. Elect a team leader to help lead the debate.

C. Debate the issue. Follow the steps.

1. Establish the rules of your debate.

2. Each team takes a turn presenting its claims using interrogatives and declaratives.

3. As the opposing team speaks, take notes.

4. Once the opposition has presented its arguments, ask questions to confirm or clarify your understanding.

5. After the debate, take a class vote to determine which team made the strongest claim.

▶ Go to **MyEnglishLab** to listen to Professor Siegel and to complete a self-assessment.

Education teaches you to love the world.

HUMANITIES

Speaking Styles

UNIT PROFILE

In this unit you will learn how great thinkers have influenced modern education and how education transforms and transcends generations. Specifically, you will learn about intellectual theorists Plato, Goethe, and Nietzsche.

You will participate in a panel discussion about the educational methods and goals in past societies and how they have influenced modern education.

OUTCOMES

• Recognize speaking styles
• Identify emphatic argumentation
• Utilize succinct argumentation
• Identify and utilize markers for organizational structure
• Utilize words and phrases to create cohesion in discussions and presentations

GETTING STARTED

▶ Go to MyEnglishLab to listen to Professor Harrison and to complete a self-assessment.

Discuss these questions with one or more students.

1. What changes have taken place in elementary, secondary, and post-secondary education between the time of your parents' schooling and your schooling?

2. What are some factors that have influenced educational change? Were their origins political, financial, or cultural?

3. In the introduction, Professor Harrison states that you might be surprised how similar today's curriculum is to ancient curriculums. In what ways do you think education has stayed the same?

For more about **HUMANITIES,** see 2 3. See also R and W **HUMANITIES** 1 2 3.

FUNDAMENTAL SKILL
RECOGNIZING SPEAKING STYLES

WHY IT'S USEFUL By identifying a speaker's style, you can better predict the argument, identify key ideas, and evaluate main points.

Every speaker has a unique style of speaking and presenting. Some speakers are direct and formal; others may be less explicit and informal. Speaking styles vary depending on the situation. When presenting in front of a class, you may require a more formal style. When sharing ideas in a group, you may choose a more casual style. Your speaking style will also vary, based on the type of discourse. If you are speaking to inform, such as explaining a process, you will likely be very succinct. When you are speaking to persuade, you may appeal to the listeners' emotions.

Expressing your point of view often involves argumentation. Argumentation is making a claim about a debatable issue and providing reasons to support that claim. There are several ways to present an argument. One such way is hypothetical argumentation. Hypothetical argumentation refers to presenting an argument by using an unreal situation or condition. These arguments are not based on evidence but on an imagined situation used as an example. For example, if speaking about education in ancient Greece, you could make an argument by placing the listener in that time period. While this helps the listener better understand your argument, the evidence is not real. Hypothetical arguments are quite common in academic discussions and debates.

When making an argument, consider what your speaking style will be. In one style, emphatic argumentation, you express your point assertively and with passion. The language may be formal, neutral, or informal. Another common style is succinct argumentation. With succinct argumentation you present your point briefly and with precision.

NOTICING ACTIVITY

Go to **MyEnglishLab** to complete a vocabulary exercise.

🔊 **A.** Listen to the lecture about the philosopher Plato. As you listen, notice what the professor's speaking style is.

The Greek philosopher Plato

Socrates, Plato's most influential teacher

🔊 **B.** Now listen to two students discussing the lecture. How do the students connect the lecture to their own campus experience?

Go to **MyEnglishLab** to complete a skill practice and join in collaborative activities.

SUPPORTING SKILL 1
IDENTIFYING EMPHATIC ARGUMENTATION

WHY IT'S USEFUL By identifying techniques of emphatic argumentation, you can understand how the speaker appeals to the emotions of his or her audience. By using these techniques, you will be able to better assert your own point of view on controversial topics.

Emphatic argumentation is making an argument assertively and with passion. This style of making a claim appeals to emotions and is common when discussing or debating topics that are highly controversial, personal, or theoretically based. There are several techniques used in an emphatic argument. The first is the language that is used. Emphatic claims use language that emphasizes, or strengthens, the speaker's point. This is usually done with intensifiers, like adverbs. These adverbs are often collocated with a verb.

Adverb / Intensifier	Meaning	Common Collocation
categorically	in every way, without hesitation	categorically believe / think
deeply	very strongly	deeply regret
enthusiastically	with great excitement	enthusiastically support
freely	without hesitation	freely admit
fully	completely	fully appreciate
honestly	truly, very strongly	honestly believe / think
positively	without a doubt	positively indicate
readily	without hesitation	readily accept
sincerely	with sincerity	sincerely believe / think
strongly	with a strong belief	strongly recommend
totally	completely	totally be
undoubtedly	without any doubt	undoubtedly be
utterly	completely	utterly oppose

Second, a speaker will use his or her voice to *stress the key word or words* of the claim. Like most stressed words, the speaker will lengthen the syllable and use a higher pitch. With emphatic claims, the syllable may sound even longer than normal. This is a common way to inject fervor into speech.

Last, the speaker will often *repeat key words*. This not only serves as a powerful cohesive device when speaking, but underscores the critical message and encourages acceptance of the claim.

An emphatic argument can be made formally or informally. Formal arguments generally have a clearly stated claim, rarely use the first person *I*, and include academic vocabulary. Conversely, informal arguments tend to begin with *I* and include less formal vocabulary. While emphatic argumentation can be made formally or informally, it is rarely neutral. Listeners can clearly determine the speaker's belief and position.

Examples
🔊 **Use of intensifier**

> The works of Plato take the form of dialogues—conversations between different people—and these dialogues **categorically** present an idealized version of Socrates as a wise and clever teacher.

🔊 **Use of intensifier and voice**

> Plato has positively had an enormous influence on education in the Western world, and many schools base their mission statements on the same terms Plato used to describe an ideal education.

⬡ **Repetition**

The students of Socrates have knowledge, but they do not yet have the judgment or experience that allows them to deal with complexity. Complexity.

EXERCISE 1

Go to MyEnglishLab to complete a vocabulary exercise.

A. What are some teaching methods that you are familiar with? Write them down.

....

....

....

B. With a classmate, generate a list of effective teaching methods. Discuss how these methods differ from those of the past. What influences how we teach and learn?

⬡ C. Listen to a student presentation on Johann Wolfgang von Goethe. As you listen, write down the phrases the student uses to make an emphatic argument.

Ways to Make an Emphatic Argument	Examples from Listening
Use of intensifiers	
Use of voice	
Use of repetition	

CULTURE NOTE

Goethe *Johann Wolfgang Von Goethe was born in 1749 in Germany. He was a writer and philosopher. His works have crossed cultures and eras and continue to influence writers, philosophers, and educators today. His most well-known work is* Faust. Faust *is a two-part drama that Goethe began when he was in his twenties and did not complete until shortly before his death in 1832.*

D. Compare your answers with a partner. Do you think the student make a strong emphatic argument in his presentation? Why or why not?

Go to MyEnglishLab to complete a skill practice and join in collaborative activities.

SUPPORTING SKILL 2
IDENTIFYING SUCCINCT ARGUMENTATION

WHY IT'S USEFUL By identifying succinct argumentation, you can easily distinguish the topic and key features of the argument. By utilizing succinct argumentation, you can better present a clear, straightforward claim that is based on facts.

Succinct argumentation refers to making an argument directly, clearly, and factually. This style of argument is common when discussing or debating topics that have distinct opposing views. Research is presented; however, counterarguments, based on research, may also exist. Like emphatic argumentation, there are several techniques used in a succinct argument.

Succinct argumentation is direct and literal. There is usually a clear one-sentence statement of the claim. Unlike emphatic argumentation, there is little word repetition or use of intensifiers. Ambiguous words (words that can be understood differently by different people) and rhetorical phrases (phrases used only for rhetorical effect) are avoided. Some common rhetorical phrases include: *it is a fact, it is known, it is true, it is clear, it is likely,* and *it appears*.

Succinct argumentation is *clear*. As a speaker, you will need to develop your argument much like you develop an essay. Begin with an overall thesis—your argument. Then, develop your argument with supporting ideas that directly link back to the thesis. Use specific details and examples, based on facts. Be sure to end with a summary that concludes your argument and support.

Last, because succinct argumentation uses evidence and direct language to present a claim, the language is *neutral*. Using neutral language allows the listeners to focus on the content and logic behind the argument rather than on the way in which the argument was presented.

EXERCISE 2

Go to MyEnglishLab to complete a vocabulary exercise.

A. In what ways does great literature influence future generations? Write down your ideas.

....

....

....

B. Share your ideas with a classmate. Do your lists contain similar items?

C. Listen to a presentation about Goethe's influence on Friedrich Nietzsche and take notes. Can you identify the speaker's argument and supporting ideas?

> **CULTURE NOTE**
> **Nietzsche** Friedrich Nietzsche (1844–1900) was a German philosopher, poet, and scholar. He greatly influenced Western philosophy through his writings, which used metaphors and irony to critique human morality.

D. Share your notes with a partner. Answer these questions.

1. What is the speaker's one-sentence argument?

2. What support does the speaker offer?

3. How does the speaker conclude?

4. Do you think the speaker presented a succinct argument? Why or why not?

Go to MyEnglishLab to complete a skill practice and join in collaborative activities.

INTEGRATED SKILLS
IDENTIFYING AND UTILIZING MARKERS FOR ORGANIZATIONAL STRUCTURE

WHY IT'S USEFUL By identifying its organizational markers within a text, you can better understand structure of a text, comprehending and distinguishing between various types of arguments.

RECOGNIZING ATTITUDE IN A TEXT

Recognizing a speaker's claim and inferring attitude and mood are often straightforward tasks when someone is speaking. Voice, facial expressions, and gestures often give clues to mood and attitude. In textual material, however, there is no voice, expression, or gesture. Being able to determine the mood and attitude of the writer, though, is critical to discovering the organizational structure as well as to identifying the writer's main argument. There are several steps you can follow while reading to fully comprehend the text.

1. **Read with the writer's purpose in mind.** There are five main purposes in academic reading: to educate, to examine, to entertain, to persuade, and to reflect.

Purpose	Description
Educate and explain	Author "teaches" in writing. Explains new concepts, findings.
Examine	Author looks thoroughly at a topic and uses evidence to investigate aspects of a topic.
Entertain	Author writes for pleasure of audience.
Persuade	Author is attempting to convince readers; uses concrete evidence and hypothetical situations to support the claim.
Reflect	Author expresses own ideas about a topic, problem, or situation.

2. **Determine attitude or mood by assessing word choice, examples used, and sentence structure.**

    You can determine the writer's attitude by asking these questions while reading:

    What kind of words does the writer use?
    - Are the words emotional or neutral?
    - Is the vocabulary academic or familiar and common?

    Is the writer giving specific examples, or making general statements?
    - Are the writer's examples supported by evidence?
    - Are the writer's examples personal, unreal, or hypothetical?

    What types of sentences exist?
    - Are there complex sentences with a third-person point of view?
    - Are there more simple sentences with a first-person point of view?

    Is the overall tone subjective or objective?

3. **Look for a writer's claim.**

    A writer's claim establishes the writer's position on a topic and often illustrates the organization of the argument. If a writer is examining a topic, there may not be a claim but instead an overall theme of the reading.

4. **Look for transitional words and phrases.**

    Transitional words and phrases help determine the order of the argument and provide the reader with a logical connection between ideas.

5. **Distinguish between concrete arguments and hypothetical arguments.**

    Concrete arguments are supported with evidence. Hypothetical arguments are supported by an unreal situation. Unreal arguments place the reader in an imaginary situation. These statements are often made with *if*.

IDENTIFYING ORGANIZATIONAL STRUCTURES IN TEXTUAL MATERIAL

Being able to identify the mood, attitude, writer's claim, and style of argument is critical to determining the structure of the text. There are three common organizational patterns in academic reading. They are:

- Thesis structure
- Problem-solution structure
- Factual structure

If the writer makes a strong claim statement in the beginning of the text, the rest of the text is likely to follow a thesis structure. In this structure, the thesis is supported by three or four supporting ideas, evidenced with sources. A problem-solution structure is one in which the writer establishes a real or perceived problem and offers solutions to that problem. Finally, a factual structure is one in which a writer examines a topic through the use of facts.

EXERCISE 3

A. Read the passage about Hannah Arendt.

According to Hannah Arendt, a proper education is needed to create responsible, politically active citizens. Arendt also believed, however, that an attempt to actively develop citizenship as an educational goal was doomed to failure. Instead, an education should create what she called *amor mundi*, or love of the world—a sense of engagement, interest, and responsibility that would naturally lead young adults toward citizenship when they were ready for it. She arrived at her view largely due to the influence of the ancient Greek understanding of both education and the nature of public life. On the surface it seems like the ancient Greek philosophy of education would be quite similar to the modern Western practice of it; after all, the ancient Greeks have influenced Western education in one form or another almost continuously. To Arendt, however, modern Western education had kept only the most superficial attributes of the ancients and neglected both the way children experience reality and the distinction between the public and private spheres.

Moreover, Arendt did most of her writing on education during a time when many Americans were working to dramatically restructure society by ensuring the freedoms and legal rights of all citizens. After years of racial discrimination and a decade characterized by political paranoia and McCarthyist witch hunting, Arendt was supportive of the fact that her newly adopted homeland was changing for the

> **CULTURE NOTE**
> **Hannah Arendt** *Johanna "Hannah" Arendt (1906–1975) was born in Germany. Being of Jewish descent, her family escaped Europe during the Holocaust and immigrated to the United States of America like many other persecuted Jews during this time. These experiences inspired her writings and philosophies. Her works deal with the subjects of discrimination, democracy, power, politics, and totalitarianism.*

"For the things we have to learn before we can do them, we learn by doing them." – Hannah Arendt

better. She worried, however, that progressive education reforms which aimed at "liberating" students from the social hierarchy of the classroom would actually burden students with responsibilities they were not ready for. Children, she thought, needed the time spent in school to grow and develop fundamental life skills before tackling the thorny complexities of politics and power structures.

Arendt's view on politics in the classroom aligned with the manner with which she distinguished between public and private spheres. Like the ancient Greeks, Arendt saw the home life as fundamentally private and the political life as public. In contrast with her contemporaries, Arendt saw school as a private sphere that should be protected from the intrusions of the political. To her, nationally mandated educational policies aimed at social changes, including many things we take as a given today, like testing policies meant to bring students up to particular national standards, intruded upon the almost-sacred need for safety and seclusion. Children, she thought, could never develop a love of the world if they were prematurely bombarded by the concerns and demands of it. School was, above all, meant to be a protective bulwark against the concerns of the world.

How was this seemingly hands-off approach meant to create good citizens? Arendt thought that a student raised under such conditions would, as a matter of course, become a responsible and concerned individual compelled to act in the public sphere. Love of the world and qualities like responsibility were not something to be taught in a test but instead illustrated by example and developed in a location that fit the needs of the student. A love of the world was something to be carefully cultivated in private, protected spaces—but not something explicitly taught via instruction.

B. With a partner, answer the questions.

1. What is the writer's purpose?

2. What is the writer's tone? Determine mood and attitude:

   What kind of words does the writer use?

   - Are the words emotional or neutral?
   - Is the vocabulary academic or familiar and common?

   Is the writer giving specific examples, or making general statements?

   - Are the writer's examples evidenced?
   - Are the writer's examples personal, unreal, or hypothetical?

   What types of sentences exist?

   - Are there complex sentences with a third-person point of view?
   - Are there more simple sentences with a first-person point of view?

   Is the overall tone subjective or objective?

3. Does the writer make a claim?

4. Which transitional words were used? Circle any transitional words that connect ideas.

5. Were there any hypothetical statements? Underline them.

6. What organizational structure best represents this text?

C. Do you agree or disagree with Arendt's views? Prepare a one-minute emphatic argument stating your view.

Go to MyEnglishLab to complete a skill practice.

For more about IDENTIFYING MARKERS FOR ORGANIZATIONAL STRUCTURE, see HUMANITIES 1.

LANGUAGE SKILL
CREATING COHESION IN PRESENTATIONS AND DISCUSSIONS

WHY IT'S USEFUL By effectively identifying cohesive devices in academic presentations and discussions, you can better understand spoken discourse. By utilizing lexical cues in your own presentations, you can help to build cohesion and coherence for your listeners.

When participating in academic lectures, presentations, debates, and classroom discussions, you often need to highlight your ideas with **lexical cues**. These cues help your listeners understand your purpose, and they also verbally establish coherence. Whether your speaking situation is a formal rhetorical presentation or conversational, like a classroom discussion, it is important to incorporate these cues into your speech. Lexical cues generally fall under one of eight categories. These categories include: *topic markers, topic shifters, clarifiers, exemplifiers, qualifiers, relators, summarizers,* and *asides*.

Cue	Use	Example Phrases
Topic Markers	Highlight the introduction of a topic	*Let's start with …, Let's first …, Today, I'll be …*
Topic Shifters	Highlight a shift or change between topics	*Now …, Let's turn to …, This leads me to …, Another point / factor / aspect …*
Clarifiers	Clarify an idea, concept, or new item	*What I mean is …, In other words …, What that means is …*
Exemplifiers	Show an idea or concept through an example	*For example …, to illustrate …, Take X for example …*
Qualifiers	Show the importance of a topic	*The importance of this is …, The catch is …, For our purposes …*
Relators	Connect the topic to the listener(s)	*Keep in mind that …, You might think …, As you can see …*
Summarizers	Summarize the idea, topic, or concept	*To sum up …, to conclude …, All in all …*
Asides	Highlight and recognize digressions	*Where was I? …, I'm getting ahead of myself …, I'm a bit off track …*

Examples

I'd like to spend today looking at the importance that the ancient Athenian philosopher Plato placed on education.

This leads me to Plato and Socrates. For these men, acquiring knowledge and facts was only the starting point.

Plato did not simply write down what he or his mentor believed to be true; instead, Plato treated actual, living people—people he knew in real life—as characters. **What that means is** he freely crafted a conversation that demonstrated different personal beliefs.

All in all, Plato's view of education sincerely emphasized the development of character and the search for truth—in the hopes that it would allow a citizen, and by extension Athens itself, to thrive even under complex, morally challenging circumstances.

EXERCISE 4

A. Read the passage about the influence of the ancient Greeks on Western civilization. Make a note of places where you think lexical cues would help with the flow of the text.

> The ancient Greeks have influenced Western civilizations. Their influence can be seen in our governments and arts. The early Greeks believed in a government that was comprised of all citizens—regardless of social class. Citizens in early Greek culture were encouraged and expected to voice their concerns and ideas. Western civilizations adopted these ideals and established ways in which every voice could be heard. The ancient Greeks influenced Western civilizations in the arts. Western literature has clearly mirrored its early mentors. The Greeks were the first culture to widen literature. Several styles emerged from the Greeks—from poetry to history to fiction to plays. Early scholars published works on medicine, philosophy, and the arts so they could be shared and examined. The scholars of ancient Greece, like Plato, Socrates, and Aristotle, continue to influence our work today. The themes in their work remain current themes in modern Western literature. The influence of ancient Greece on Western cultures cannot be denied. Examples from government to literature reflect the huge impact the early society had on our societies today.

B. Add lexical cues as indicated. Then compare your answers with a partner.

1. Add a topic marker.

   .... The ancient Greeks have influenced Western civilizations. Their influence can be seen in our governments and arts.

2. Add an exemplifier.

   The early Greeks believed in a government that was comprised of all citizens—regardless of social class ...., citizens in early Greek culture were encouraged and expected to voice their concerns and ideas. Western civilizations adopted these ideals and established ways in which every voice could be heard.

3. Add a topic shifter.

   Western civilizations adopted these ideals and established ways in which every voice could be heard .... the ancient Greeks influenced Western civilizations in the arts.

4. Add a clarifier.

   The Greeks were the first culture to widen literature .... several styles emerged from the Greeks—from poetry to history to fiction to plays.

5. Add a summarizer.

   The themes in their work remain current themes in modern Western literature. ...., the influence of Ancient Greece on Western cultures cannot be denied. Examples from government to literature reflect the huge impact the early society had on our societies today.

C. Imagine you are preparing a presentation on this material. Add the necessary cues and present it to a partner.

Go to MyEnglishLab to complete a skill practice.

APPLY YOUR SKILLS

WHY IT'S USEFUL By applying the skills you have learned in this unit, you can better determine a speaker's style, identify his or her argument, and comprehend the organizational structure of the lecture or presentation. By utilizing lexical cues when speaking, you can develop and deliver a coherent presentation.

ASSIGNMENT

Prepare a panel discussion about the influence of educational theories from previous centuries on modern education. Use what you have learned about the views of Plato, Socrates, Goethe, and Nietzsche on past educational methods and goals. Compare their views to contemporary educational practice.

BEFORE YOU LISTEN

A. Discuss the questions with one or more students.

1. In addition to what you have learned in this unit, what are some other characteristics of ancient Greek culture?
2. What role did education play in ancient Greek life?
3. What similarities could be drawn between ancient Greek educational systems and educational systems in the Western world?

B. You will listen to a lecture about the ancient Greek system of education. As you listen, think about these questions.

1. What were some values of the ancient Greeks?
2. What was the relationship between government and education?
3. How did ancient Greeks see public and private life?
4. How did education differ for males and females in ancient Greece?

C. Review the Unit Skills Summary. As you listen to the lecture and begin preparing your panel discussion, apply the skills you learned in this unit.

UNIT SKILLS SUMMARY

Understand argumentation.
- Recognize different speaking styles.
- Identify types of argumentation.

Recognize and utilize emphatic argumentation.
- Identify and use intensifiers.
- Identify and utilize voice to make an emotional appeal.
- Identify and use repetition for effect.

Recognize and utilize succinct argumentation.
- Identify and use direct, neutral language.
- Avoid ambiguous words and rhetorical phrases.

Identify and utilize markers for organizational structure.
- Select and use markers to establish speaking purpose.
- Identify a speaker's attitude and mood.
- Identify and distinguish claim, argument, and organizational structure.

Create cohesion in discussions and presentations.
- Recognize, select, and use lexical cues to create flow in speech.

LISTEN

A. Listen to the lecture. Take notes as you listen.

B. Reread the discussion questions from Before You Listen, Part B. Is there anything you cannot answer? What listening skills can you use to help find the answers?

Go to MyEnglishLab to listen again and answer critical thinking questions.

THINKING CRITICALLY

Discuss the questions with another student.

1. How are the philosophies of the ancient Greeks similar to modern Western philosophy? How do they differ?

2. Based on the lecture, what connection can be made between civic responsibility and education?

THINKING VISUALLY

A. Review information from the lecture and your answer to the first question in "Thinking Critically." Complete the Venn diagram with characteristics of the ancient Greek philosophy of education and of the modern Western philosophy of education.

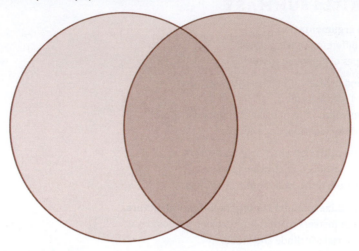

B. Compare your Venn diagram with a classmate.

THINKING ABOUT LANGUAGE

Work with a partner. Using the excerpt from the lecture below, complete the tasks.

1. Circle a topic marker.
2. Underline an exemplifier.
3. Double underline a topic shifter.

4. Highlight a relator.
5. Add a summarizer.
6. Add a qualifier.

Professor:	Now, before we begin our examination of ancient Greek culture and education, I want to remind you that we're focusing primarily on society as it would have existed in Athens around the time of Plato. The rest of the Hellenistic world was, broadly speaking, similar; don't be surprised, however, if you run into significant differences when investigating other cities and regions. Spartan culture, for example, was quite different from that of the Athenians. Having said that, let's begin.
	Greek culture at the time of Socrates and Plato has fascinated us for so long because it was a culture in transition. Literacy and the written word were just starting to become common and viable, so this was a culture that was transitioning from a focus on the spoken word to a focus on literacy. Some writers, such as Socrates, even complained about the effect that the written word may have on the mind.
Student:	Wait, Socrates thought writing was bad?
Professor:	Ah, well, you have to remember that ancient cultures valued the art of memory. The works of Homer, the poet who created *The Iliad* and *The Odyssey*, had been passed down orally for generations. Speeches, poetry, drama—all of it had been created in such a way as to aid its memorization. Men of intelligence were highly respected for their ability to memorize things. This shift toward print was gradually influencing the arts themselves; many of the dramatic works preserved from this time refer back to the ancient tales but put "new" twists on them to make a point about the society of the day.

It was not only society, but also the government that was changing rapidly. That brings us to how Athens had suffered greatly during the Peloponnesian war against Sparta, leading Sparta to force thirty of their citizens into a position of power in Athens. This "Thirty Tyrants" period was brief but oppressive and undoubtedly did irreparable damage to the Athenian democracy that had previously existed. Socrates had run afoul of the tyrants and by some accounts was in great danger; luckily for us, the tyrants were overthrown before any harm befell him. The Athenians ruled themselves once more, but the old forms of democracy would not be restored in their entirety; many would-be oligarchs now sought to take power for themselves.

PANEL DISCUSSION

A. Discuss the questions with a small group.

1. The ancient Greeks emphasized the study of literature, medicine, philosophy, and the arts. How does this compare to modern courses of study?

2. How did Goethe's and Nietzsche's views on life experience and knowledge impact current educational methods?

B. Select and research one modern educational trend. Explain how this trend is similar to or different from the educational ideals promoted by Plato, Socrates, Goethe, and Nietzsche. As you prepare, consider these questions.

1. What is the trend you will research?

2. What is the theory behind that trend?

3. How is that trend related to?

4. What speaking style can you use to best make your argument?

> **TIP**
> ....
> A panel discussion is a small group of people speaking on the same topic, each expressing their own point of view on that topic. To participate in a panel discussion, you first need to research your topic and then develop a cohesive argument.

C. Share your research with your panel members. Granting that some research might overlap, make sure that each of you has a unique point of view to present. Be sure to organize your panel's information.

D. Listen to each panel discussion.

Listen and take notes on each individual argument. Discuss how each presenter effectively made his or her argument.

Go to MyEnglishLab to listen to Professor Harrison and to complete a self-assessment.

Sound design creates a healthier world.

ENVIRONMENTAL ENGINEERING

Visuals

UNIT PROFILE

In this unit, you will learn about civil engineering and "green" building. You will also learn about systems, such as air filtration systems, which help to remove pollutants and reduce operational costs through sustainable design.

You will prepare a presentation on an existing green building and the systems, features, and technology that make this building a good model for green construction.

OUTCOMES

• Connect visuals to a lecture

• Identify different visuals and their purposes

• Read and interpret complex visuals

• Synthesize text into a visual

• Create visuals and communicate what they mean

GETTING STARTED

▶ Go to MyEnglishLab to listen to Professor Hildemann and to complete a self-assessment.

Discuss these questions with a partner or group.

1. How would you describe the building in the photo above? Does it look modern? Smart? Green?

2. What does it mean for a building to be "green"? What are some examples of green buildings?

3. In the introduction, the Professor Hildemann mentions "strategies Paris is utilizing to make an old city more environmentally friendly." What methods do you think the governments of cities or nation can implement to become more environmentally friendly?

For more about **ENVIRONMENTAL ENGINEERING**, see ② ③. See also R and W
ENVIRONMENTAL ENGINERING ① ② ③.

FUNDAMENTAL SKILL
USING VISUALS

WHY IT'S USEFUL By understanding how visuals are effectively used in academic lectures, you can better connect visual messages with verbal messages, allowing you a deeper understanding of the lecture content.

College courses involve synthesizing a wide variety of content from textbooks, handouts, lectures, and visual aids. It is vital that you be able to draw connections between and among all of these resources. College professors and your peers will frequently use **visual aids** such as charts, diagrams, graphs, maps, and tables to visually communicate a message.

To fully understand visual use in academic lectures, you first must be able to **connect the spoken word with the visual**. Why is the lecturer using a visual? What is communicated in the visual that is not conveyed in the lecture? These are important questions to consider. Visualized data can help clarify a speaker's idea by allowing the listener to "see" evidence and data.

Recognizing *why* the lecturer is using a visual aid is one step toward full comprehension. The second step involves **interpreting the information in the visual**. Interpreting complex visuals takes an understanding of the type of visual used, the data or information contained in it, and the message that it communicates. Interpreting visuals can improve your ability to recall information in a meaningful way.

NOTICING ACTIVITY

Go to MyEnglishLab to complete a vocabulary exercise.

🎧 **A.** Listen to a guest lecturer in an engineering course. As you listen, notice how and where the lecturer incorporates the visuals below and on the next page into his lecture.

This is an artist's illustration and is not meant to represent the actual Phoenix Towers.

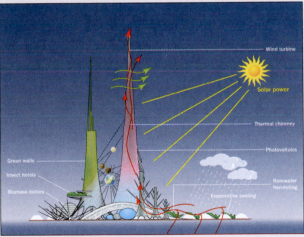

Wind turbine
Solar power
Thermal chimney
Photovoltaics
Rainwater harvesting
Evaporative cooling
Green walls
Insect hotels
Biomass boilers

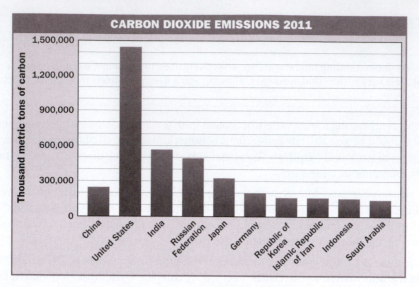

CARBON DIOXIDE EMISSIONS 2011

B. Now listen to the students' questions about the guest speaker's presentation. What does the speaker need to explain more deeply? How does he explain it?

Go to MyEnglishLab to complete a skill practice and join in collaborative activities.

SUPPORTING SKILL 1
CONNECTING VISUALS TO A LECTURE

WHY IT'S USEFUL By connecting visual content to verbal content, you can better organize and analyze new information. By making these connections when you speak, you can give a more effective presentation.

IDENTIFYING THE PURPOSE OF A VISUAL

Lecturers often use visual representations of complex information to inform, illustrate, express, and summarize. Visual content can help you recall information, which will help with your studying. When a lecturer uses a visual, identifying its purpose is the first critical step toward your understanding of the lecture.

Purposes of visuals include the presentation, illustration, or comparison of:

- data
- trends
- relationships
- processes
- proportions

Examples

1. This visual provides data and presents **proportions** of greenhouse gas-emission reductions as a result of green construction.

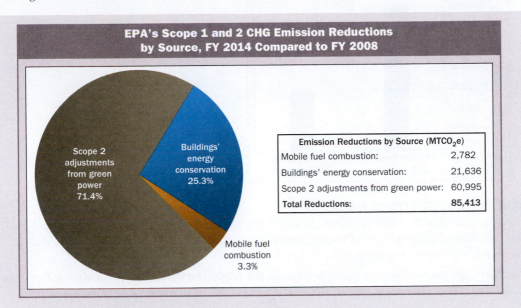

EPA's Scope 1 and 2 CHG Emission Reductions by Source, FY 2014 Compared to FY 2008

- Scope 2 adjustments from green power 71.4%
- Buildings' energy conservation 25.3%
- Mobile fuel combustion 3.3%

Emission Reductions by Source (MTCO$_2$e)	
Mobile fuel combustion:	2,782
Buildings' energy conservation:	21,636
Scope 2 adjustments from green power:	60,995
Total Reductions:	**85,413**

2. This visual provides data and illustrates **trends** in energy intensity over a twelve year period.

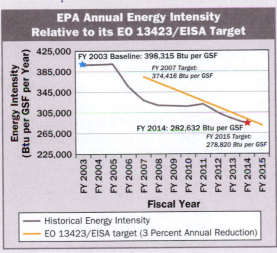

EPA Annual Energy Intensity Relative to its EO 13423/EISA Target

FY 2003 Baseline: 398,315 Btu per GSF
FY 2007 Target: 374,416 Btu per GSF
FY 2014: 282,632 Btu per GSF
FY 2015 Target: 278,820 Btu per GSF

Energy Intensity (Btu per GSF per Year) / Fiscal Year

- Historical Energy Intensity
- EO 13423/EISA target (3 Percent Annual Reduction)

3. This visual provides data and **compares** greenhouse gas emissions in 2008 and 2014.

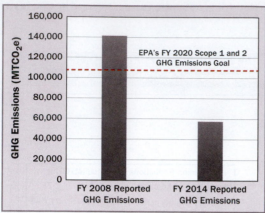

IDENTIFYING THE TYPE OF VISUAL

After you have identified the purpose of the visual, you will need to determine the type of visual used. There are several different types of visuals, and each has a specific use. Fundamental visuals include pie charts, line graphs, and bar graphs.

Pie charts, like the one shown in Example 1, are circular graphs that show a contribution toward, or division of, an overall total. The wedges, or pieces, in a pie chart illustrate proportions, often as percentages.

The pie totals 100 percent. Each division represents a piece of that 100 percent. Pie charts are easy to understand; however, they can be used accurately only when the whole of something is represented. The pie chart above, showing reductions of greenhouse gas emissions, would not be reliable if an additional reduction was not listed. All parts must be included. Pie charts are most useful when you are comparing parts of a whole.

Line graphs, like the one shown in Example 2, have a horizontal axis (x) and a vertical axis (y). Data points can be connected to form a line. Line graphs commonly show changes over time. They are useful for identifying and predicting patterns and trends.

Bar graphs, like the one shown in Example 3, also have a horizontal axis (x) and a vertical axis (y). Bars illustrate and compare two or more sets of data. Bars can be drawn either horizontally or vertically and are proportioned in length to the data. They are useful for comparing different categories or groups.

EXERCISE 1

Go to MyEnglishLab to complete a vocabulary exercise.

A. What makes a building "green"? Write down some features that make a building green.

....

....

....

B. Share your ideas with a classmate. Together, generate a list of characteristics of green buildings. Create a pie chart illustrating your predictions of these characteristics.

C. How do the characteristics on your pie chart impact a building's efficiency?

D. Listen to a student presentation on a green building. As you listen, label the visuals here, and on the next page, 1–4 in the order in which each one is used. State the purpose of each visual in the presentation.

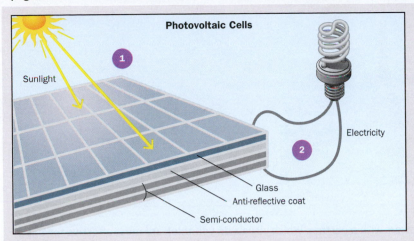

Photovoltaic Cells

Sunlight

1

2

Electricity

Glass

Anti-reflective coat

Semi-conductor

A. .... Purpose: ....

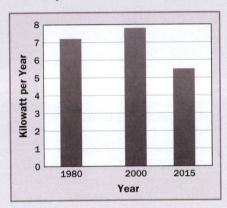

B. .... Purpose: ....

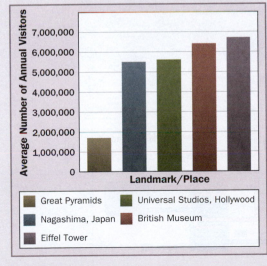

Landmark/Place

- Great Pyramids
- Nagashima, Japan
- Eiffel Tower
- Universal Studios, Hollywood
- British Museum

C. .... Purpose: ....

D. .... Purpose: ....

E. Compare your answers with a partner. Which visuals do you think are most effective for this presentation? Why?

Go to MyEnglishLab to complete a skill practice and join in collaborative activities.

SUPPORTING SKILL 2
READING AND INTERPRETING COMPLEX VISUALS

WHY IT'S USEFUL By reading and interpreting the meaning of complex visual content, you can comprehend powerful messages and information while visualizing patterns and trends.

Diagrams and tables are commonplace in academic textbooks and lectures. **Diagrams** are drawings that show how something works. The diagram below illustrates how solar panels generate energy.

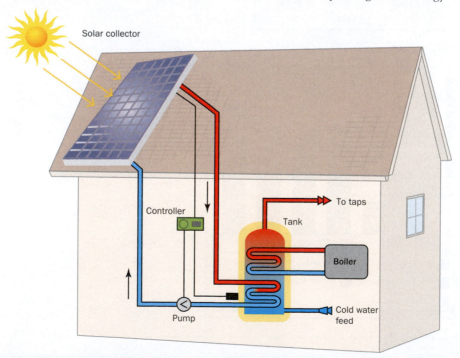

To read this diagram, it is critical to follow the arrows of the drawing. Think of a process when reading a diagram. Break each action into a step.

1. The solar collector collects energy from the sun.

2. The energy moves into the tank.

3. The tank turns energy into heat or air conditioning.

4. Cold water gets pumped back out.

Tables often collapse large amounts of data into horizontal rows and vertical columns. The data can be easily read, analyzed, and interpreted. Because they often present results, tables are especially common in scientific fields like engineering. When reading and interpreting the information, look for:

- headings
- numerical ranges
- comparisons that can be made

Example

2015 Commercial and Residential Energy End-Use Splits

Commercial	Percent	Residential	Percent
Lighting	16.7%	Space Heating	27.9%
Space Heating	14.1%	Water Heating	13.7%
Space Cooling	8.6%	Space Cooling	14.6%
Ventilation	8.9%	Lighting	7.6%
Refrigeration	5.8%	Refrigeration	6.5%
Electronics	5.2%	Electronics	4.7%
Water Heating	4.5%	Wet Cleaning	5.0%
Computers	3.1%	Cooking	2.8%
Cooking	1.4%	Computers	2.7%
Other	16.4%	Other	14.6%
Adjust to SEDS	15.2%		
	100%		100%

We can read this table by determining:

1. The headings: 2015 Commercial and Residential Energy End-Use Splits.

2. The numerical range: 1.4%–27.9%.

3. Comparisons: Commercial buildings require more lighting, ventilation, and slightly more energy for electronics and computers. Homes require more space heating, water heating, slightly more refrigeration, cooking, and wet cleaning energy than buildings.

EXERCISE 2

Go to MyEnglishLab to complete a vocabulary exercise.

A. You will hear an academic discussion on filtration systems. This diagram is used in the discussion. How would you read it? Read it to a partner.

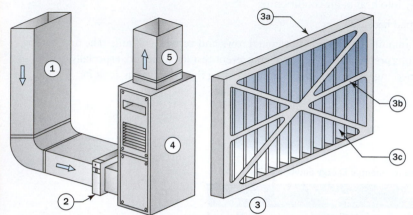

1. Return Air Duct
2. Air Filter Housing
3. Air Filter
   3a. Rigid Frame (such as a chipboard)
   3b. Filter Media Restrainer
   3c. Filter Media (installed inside the frame)
4. Air-Handling Unit that contains a recirculation fan, heating element, and cooling coil. (The unit may be in a basement, closet, or attic.)
5. Supply Air Duct

B. Listen to the academic discussion. Look at the table below and the diagram in Part A. Take notes on the information the professor gives about these visuals.

MERV Ratings*

MERV Rating	Average Particle Size Efficiency (PSE), microns – % Removal			Typical Controlled Contaminant or Material Sources (ASHRAE 52.2)
	0.3–1.0	1.0–3.0	3.0–10.0	
1–4			<20%	>10 Microns Textile Fibers Dust Mites, Dust, Pollen
5			20–35	3.0 to 10.0 Microns Cement Dust, Mold Spores, Dusting Aids
8			>70	
9		<50	>85	1.0 to 3.0 Microns Legionella, Some Auto Emissions, Humidifier Dust
12		>80	>90	
13	<75	>90	>90	0.3 to 1.0 Microns Bacteria, Droplet Nuclei (sneeze), Most Tobacco Smoke, Insecticide Dust
16	>95	>95	>90	
17**	≥ 99.97			<0.3 Microns (HEPA/ULPA filters) Viruses, Carbon Dust, Fine Combustion, Smoke
18**	≥ 99.99			
19, 20**	≥ 99.999			

C. Refer to your notes and discuss the questions with your partner.

1. The table above is entitled MERV ratings. What does MERV refer to?

2. According to the professor, what is the first thing that engineers consider when creating an air filtration system? Why?

3. What is the result of increasing air filtration efficiency?

4. For homes and offices, what are some possible drawbacks of increased air filtration efficiency?

5. Did the visuals help you to understand the discussion? How?

Go to MyEnglishLab to complete a skill practice and join in collaborative activities.

INTEGRATED SKILLS
SYNTHESIZING TEXT INTO A VISUAL

WHY IT'S USEFUL By understanding how to synthesize material from a text, you can create a focal point for your presentation and present data or information in an organized way.

When giving a presentation, it is important to use visuals. In addition to using images and organizational slides, you should also present data or other compressed information in a visual manner. This serves several purposes. By using a visual, you can:

- communicate an idea.
- support your assertions by providing a reference point.
- illustrate an example.
- provide a focal point for your presentation.
- explain a complex process.
- make your presentation more interesting.

Creating visuals involves synthesizing information, or combining ideas in a meaningful way. Synthesizing information involves:

- making specific connections between content.
- identifying key information that can support your idea or topic.
- extracting information that can be presented in the visual form.
- determining the manner in which you can best present the information.

The type of information you want to present will determine the style of visual. For example, if the information in one section of the text refers to the energy savings of a building in the year 2008, and another section refers to the energy savings of a building in 2015, you may want to create a bar graph. Bar graphs are ideal for comparisons. Being able to identify the type of information you are synthesizing is important when selecting a visual style.

This table highlights which type of visual is best for presenting different sorts of information.

Information Synthesized	Suggested Visual
Comparisons	Bar graph
Divisions or categories within one topic	Pie chart
Statistical data	Table
Textual information	Table
Relationship among different quantities or amounts	Bar graph
Relationship between two variables	Line graph
Processes	Diagram

EXERCISE 3

A. Read this excerpt from an article about air filtration systems used in the home.

At-Home Air Filtration Systems

Common Allergens in the Home

The air is filled with particulate matter: tiny specks of solids and liquids. Much of this airborne particulate matter is found inside the home and is known to be irritating to people. These allergens can stay suspended in the air for long periods of time, sometimes even for days. Even the cleanest homes can hold irritating allergens, as particulates such as pollen can be brought in from outside. Other substances like mold can grow in dark, damp corners. The corpses and feces of dust mites—tiny animals that live in the dust—represent about 36 percent of the particulate matter in a person's home. In the home of a pet owner, 42 percent of allergens come from pet dander. Pollen can represent 14 percent of particulates in the home. Molds represent about 8 percent. These figures vary greatly based on the environment, on whether or not an air filtration system is used, and on the type of system used.

Filtration Solutions Then and Now

For many years, the most common filtration system found in homes was simply built into the house's heating and air-conditioning systems. Basic, low-rated filters were added to the air intake systems on these devices to help cleanse circulating air. This was adequate for getting rid of dust, but it was insufficient to clear the air of numerous allergens. Modern, high-efficiency filters cannot be fitted to most older air conditioners, and even some modern systems cannot circulate the air sufficiently for the highest-efficiency filters to function. This has led to a rise in dedicated air filtration systems, especially portable filters designed for use in individual rooms. These devices are optimized for filtering large volumes of air, and homeowners can choose a portable filtration system that targets allergens common to their place of residence. Alternatively, modern heating and air-conditioning systems have much more advanced filtration capabilities and can be designed to fit the needs of the consumer. Concerned homeowners can always opt for adding a dedicated filtration system to the house.

True HEPA, Ionizers, and Ozone: Other Solutions

As consumers became increasingly aware of the importance of air filtration, inventors rushed to offer new solutions. One such solution was to increase the MERV (minimum efficiency reporting value) rating of air filters. In prior years, filters with a 1–6 rating were removing less than 5 percent of particulates. As technology developed, an 8-rated filter increased particulate removal up to 40 percent. This increase continues for MERV 11 at 62 percent and at 83 percent for MERV 13. However, HEPA (high-efficiency particulate arresting) filters are at nearly 100 percent, making them ideal for filtering out smaller particulates that older filters couldn't handle. Trying to run an older air-conditioning system with a HEPA filter is almost the same as running it with a clogged filter: the system cannot generate enough power to keep the air circulating. One problem that has arisen with the HEPA label is that many companies have attempted to apply this label as a marketing term, even when the filter they are promoting may not meet the standard. People who require HEPA due to allergies or asthma need to verify that the filtration system in fact conforms to HEPA standards.

Ionizers negatively charge particulates, causing them to stick to various surfaces and thus removing particulates from the air. But, particularly with cheaper models, the particulates simply land where they fall until they are stirred up again later. Moreover, the cheaper ionizer models tend to produce unhealthy quantities of ozone. For consumers, a proper filtration system—be it portable or built into the home—is a more worthwhile investment.

B. Answer the questions with a partner.

1. What specific information can be best synthesized in a visual form?

2. Which visuals would best illustrate the synthesized information?

C. Imagine you and your partner are preparing a presentation on home allergens and the reduction of these allergens with MERV rated filters. Create two visuals using the information from the article excerpt on home air filtration systems.

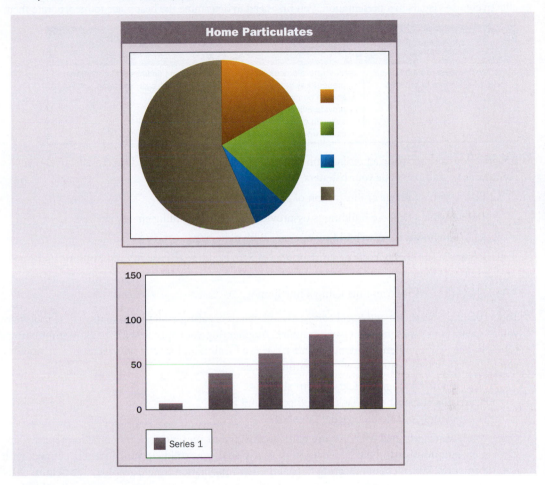

D. Present your visuals to your class.

Go to MyEnglishLab to complete a skill practice.

For more about SYNTHESIZING TEXT INTO VISUALS, see W ENVIRONMENTAL ENGINEERING 1 .

LANGUAGE SKILL
CREATING AND COMMUNICATING VISUALS

WHY IT'S USEFUL By effectively incorporating visual content in an academic presentation or discussion, you can illustrate complex information for your listeners and clearly convey your message.

Incorporating visuals in an academic presentation or discussion is a necessary skill in college courses. To effectively use visuals in a presentation, you first need to determine the best place to incorporate them.

Using Visuals in Presentations		
In the Introduction	**In the Body**	**In the Conclusion**
· show the presentation subject · define a system or process	· illustrate a process · present key data · show a comparison · provide evidence for a claim · show an example · clarify an object or process	· present findings and conclusions · summarize key systems

Imagine you are preparing a presentation on the benefits of a net-zero building. To effectively communicate and persuade your listeners, follow these steps.

1. Begin with an image or illustration of a net-zero building.
2. Define what a net-zero building is by providing a visual detailing energy savings.
3. Illustrate how a net-zero building operates with a diagram.
4. Compare the energy costs or sources of a net-zero building to a traditional building using a pie chart or table.
5. Show the savings over time using a line graph.

Tools such as PowerPoint and Excel can easily aid you in **creating effective visuals**. These tools allow you to create slides that include visual graphics. Augmenting your speech with visually stimulating slides can help keep your audience's attention and serve as a focal point for your presentation. It is important you follow a few basic strategies when creating visuals:

- Avoid putting too much text on your slides.
- Carefully consider your background colors and fonts.
- Display only one graphic visual per slide.

Once you have determined what you are going to say in your presentation, it is time to prepare your visuals. By **communicating** the information in your visual, you will help your listeners connect with the information. When communicating data and other information from a graphic, it is helpful to use cues, or signposts. Signposts let your listeners know what information is being conveyed and indicate the importance of that information to your topic. Speakers often use a signpost to introduce a visual. You can signpost your graphics in a variety of ways.

Examples

As you can see here, …
As shown in this table/graph/chart/diagram, …
As illustrated in this table/graph/chart/diagram, …
This table/graph/chart/diagram shows, …
This table/chart compares, …
Let's look at this table/graph/chart/diagram, …
On the right/left you can see, …

In addition, different visuals require different language. For example, when integrating a pie chart like the one here, the language of fractions and percentages is used.

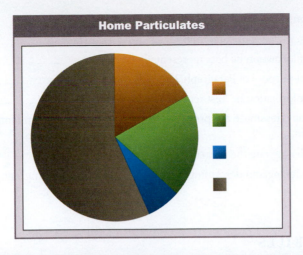

Home Particulates

Percentage of Pie	Fraction	Descriptive Language
70–51%	Over half	A large proportion; the largest proportion
49–40%	Just below half	A significant proportion
30–26%	Just above a quarter	A good proportion
25%	A quarter	A pretty good proportion
24–15%	Less than a quarter	A pretty good proportion; a small proportion
14–10%	Slightly more than a tenth	A small fraction; a small proportion
9–0%	Less than a tenth	A very small fraction

When describing information on a line graph, it is important to use the language of trends.

Line Direction	Descriptive Language
When the line is moving in an upward direction	Upward trend, increase, growth, climb
When the line is moving in a downward direction	Downward trend, decrease, decline, drop, fall
When the line remains the same or is straight	Steady, stable, constant

Similar to line graphs, bar charts may also show trends. However, they often illustrate comparisons. It is helpful to use language that compares the elements contained in the graph. Common words used when making a comparison include *more, less,* and *fewer.* To avoid repetition, consider adding adverbs like *significantly, approximately,* and *slightly.*

EXERCISE 4

A. Read this excerpt from a lecture.

Large cities all over the world have problems with air quality. Sources of particulate matter and pollutants range from vehicle emissions to dust. Take Beijing. Vehicle emissions account for 22 percent of air pollutants. Dust and industrial emissions are each 16 percent. Since coal is a source of heat and energy in Beijing, pollution generated by it represents 17 percent. Straw burning, which is also common in Beijing, accounts for 4 percent. However, the most surprising thing is that 25 percent of Beijing's pollution comes from surrounding districts.

Beijing and other large cities are investing in innovative solutions to reduce emissions. They can look to Paris as an example. The Paris city government has asked an architectural firm to develop a plan that would reduce their pollutants by 75 percent. The resulting project is called "2050 Paris Smart City" and includes eight proposals for sustainable, green structures. These structures will emphasize nature by serving as vertical gardens. Waste products and multiblade wind turbines will be used to generate electricity.

B. **Answer the questions.**

1. What is the main purpose of Paragraph 1?...
2. How could the information be best represented visually?...
3. What is the main purpose of Paragraph 2?...
4. How could the information be best represented visually?...

C. **Imagine you and your classmate are preparing a presentation on new and innovative solutions to remove air pollution.**

1. Create a visual to illustrate the sources of pollution in Beijing.
2. Take turns introducing and describing the contents of the visual using signposting.

Go to **MyEnglishLab** to complete a skill practice.

APPLY YOUR SKILLS

WHY IT'S USEFUL By applying the skills you have learned in this unit, you can make connections between information from visuals and information you hear or read, deepening your comprehension of the topic. By using visuals in your own presentations, you can convey information in an in-depth, interesting way to your audience.

> **ASSIGNMENT**
>
> Prepare a presentation on a green building. Present the key sustainable features and innovative technologies that will make it a successful green building.

BEFORE YOU LISTEN

A. **Before you listen, discuss the questions with one or more students.**

1. Why do you think there is such an emphasis on making cities green these days?
2. Are you aware of any current projects that are in progress to improve life in a city? Where?
3. What sustainable resources do you think could be used to make a building more environmentally friendly?

B. **You will listen to a lecture about urban solutions to environmental problems. Keep these questions in mind as you listen to the lecture.**

1. What factors contribute to making a city hotter?
2. How can plants and other natural matter enhance a city's environment?
3. What are innovative energy sources?
4. How do piezoelectric walkways work?

C. Review the Unit Skills Summary. As you listen to the lecture and begin preparing your presentation, apply the skills you learned in this unit.

UNIT SKILLS SUMMARY

Understand and utilize visuals.

- Make connections between visual and verbal messages.
- Identify the type and purpose of visuals.
- Recognize and interpret complex visuals.
- Synthesize text into a visual.
- Create visuals and communicate what they mean.

LISTEN

A. Listen to a lecture about one city's innovative solutions to environmental problems. Refer to the visuals here and on the next page and take notes as you listen.

Figure 1 Thermal Image Depicting a Surface Urban Heat Island (UHI).

Figure 2 "Farmscraper" with Greenery Incorporated into Walls

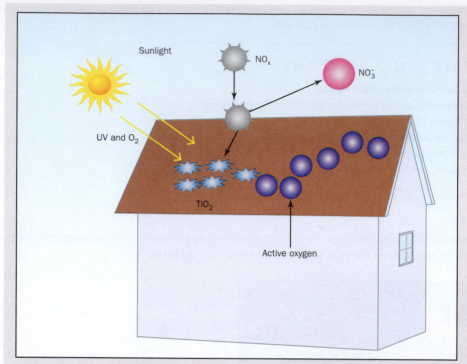

Figure 3 How Titanium Dioxide Coverings Work

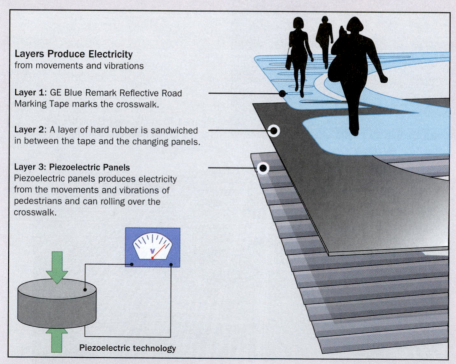

Layers Produce Electricity
from movements and vibrations

Layer 1: GE Blue Remark Reflective Road Marking Tape marks the crosswalk.

Layer 2: A layer of hard rubber is sandwiched in between the tape and the changing panels.

Layer 3: Piezoelectric Panels
Piezoelectric panels produces electricity from the movements and vibrations of pedestrians and can rolling over the crosswalk.

Piezoelectric technology

Figure 4 Walkways Powered by Piezoeletric Technology

B. Reread the discussion questions from Before You Listen, Part B. Is there anything you cannot answer? What listening skills can you use to help find the answers?

🎧 Go to MyEnglishLab to listen again and answer critical thinking questions.

THINKING CRITICALLY

Discuss the questions with another student.

1. What connection does the speaker suggest exists between air quality and quality of life?
2. Which innovative solution from the lecture would best work in your city or hometown? Why?

THINKING VISUALLY

A. Using information from the lecture, create a line graph that illustrates the cause-and-effect relationship between employing innovative strategies and emission rates.

B. Compare your line graph with a classmate.

THINKING ABOUT LANGUAGE

Study each visual. Introduce and describe each one to a partner.

1.

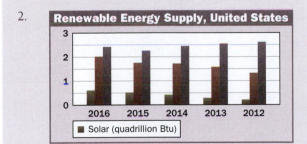

Energy Consumption by Source, United States

Natural Gas ◆ Renewable Energy ■ Electricity ▲

2.

Renewable Energy Supply, United States

■ Solar (quadrillion Btu)

3.

Innovation	Details	Purpose/Benefit
Solar panels	In various locations	Provides electricity
Window layout	Optimized for sunlight, ideal temperature	Decreases dependence on electrical light
Geothermal wells	Installed throughout the school	Helps heat or cool the school
Insulation	Top quality, carefully applied	Helps avoid wasting energy maintaining room temperature

A. **Read and discuss the question with a small group.**

Countries all over the world are moving toward sustainable design and green building. What innovative technologies do you think are most successful toward that end?

B. **You will prepare a presentation on a green building for your class. Research your building. Consider the systems, features, and innovative technologies, such as solar, wind, and organic-matter energy sources, that make this building a successful example of green construction.**

1. Which green building will you research, and what are its sustainable features?

2. What visuals will you include to best illustrate the information?

C. **Listen to each presentation.**

Listen to the presentations and take notes on each one. Discuss how effectively each presenter used visuals.

▶ Go to **MyEnglishLab** to listen to Professor Hildemann and to complete a self-assessment.

PART 2

Critical Thinking Skills

THE HUMAN EXPERIENCE
Sociology

FACTS AND OPINIONS   80

MONEY AND COMMERCE
Economics

IMPLICATIONS AND INFERENCES   96

THE SCIENCE OF NATURE
Biology

PROCESS   110

ARTS AND LETTERS
Humanities

ANALOGIES   126

STRUCTURAL SCIENCE
Environmental Engineering

SUMMARIZING AND SYNTHESIZING   140

Part 2 moves from skill building to application of the skills that require critical thinking. Practice activities tied to specific learning outcomes in each unit require a deeper level of understanding the academic content.

Struggle influences social change.

SOCIOLOGY

Facts and Opinions

UNIT PROFILE

In this unit, you will learn about social movements that have created change, such as the Black Freedom Movement. You will further investigate how activism emerges and social justice organizations are formed.

You will prepare a group presentation on what changes need to be made at your school or in your community.

OUTCOMES

- Identify facts through verbal and nonverbal signposts
- Identify opinions through verbal and nonverbal signposts
- Recognize facts and opinions in texts
- Interpret and utilize hedging devices

GETTING STARTED

▶ Go to MyEnglishLab to listen to Professor Greenberg and to complete a self-assessment.

Discuss these questions with a partner or group.

1. What does the expression "together we stand, divided we fall" mean to you? Do you think this saying is always true? Can you think of any situations in your family or in society that illustrate your beliefs about this saying?

2. Why do you think people protest? Have you or has anyone you know ever participated in a protest? What was the outcome?

3. In the introduction, the speaker says that there were "multiple grassroots campaigns that happened during the time that Dr. King was most active." What are grassroots campaigns? Can you give some examples of grassroots campaigns during Dr. King's time and today?

For more about **SOCIOLOGY**, see 1 3 . See also R and W **SOCIOLOGY** 1 2 3 .

CRITICAL THINKING SKILL
DISTINGUISHING FACTS FROM OPINIONS

WHY IT'S USEFUL By understanding how to distinguish a fact from an opinion, you can determine what can be proven through evidence and what cannot be proven. Using verbal and nonverbal signposts for facts and opinions in your own speeches or presentations will help your listeners recognize which statements are your beliefs and which statements you can support with evidence.

An important aspect of academic listening is **distinguishing a fact from an opinion**. This critical awareness can help you make the distinction between what can be proven and what may lack evidence. Many times making this distinction is very clear, while other times it is not as clear.

Facts are true statements that can be proven, or have objective evidence. Dates, percentages, and other numeric measurements are easily verified and are considered objective. Signposting factual statements with verbal cues is another indicator that the information is true and can be verified.

Opinions are statements of belief, judgment, or observation. While many people may have the same belief, that does not make it a fact. Similar to facts, opinions are easily distinguishable with signposts such as *I believe* or *I think*. However, speakers occasionally present certain information as factual, when it is not. In these cases, it is nearly impossible to distinguish it from fact without verifying the information through source-checking.

Facts and opinions are both necessary in academic discussions. Voicing opinions and using facts to support opinions are key elements for your academic success.

Go to MyEnglishLab to complete a vocabulary exercise.

NOTICING ACTIVITY

Listen to the lecture on activism and the relative deprivation theory. As you listen, notice what facts the speaker gives. How do you know they are facts? Share your ideas with a partner.

Go to MyEnglishLab to complete a skill practice and join in collaborative activities.

> **CULTURE NOTE**
>
> **Marching for a Cause** Activism has a long history in North America. Even early settlers protested against unjust laws and regulations. One common form of protest is a march. This is when citizens gather and march in the streets, blocking traffic, in an area that decision makers, such as lawmakers, would be able to see or hear them. Marches were quite popular during Dr. King's time; however, they have been used in support of a vast array of causes, such as voicing opposition to wars or to lack of rights for women.

SUPPORTING SKILL 1
IDENTIFYING FACTS THROUGH VERBAL AND NONVERBAL SIGNPOSTS

WHY IT'S USEFUL By recognizing verbal and nonverbal fact signaling, you can identify measurable, verifiable information. By using verbal fact signaling in your own presentations, you can make a stronger case to your audience, indicating which statements are verifiable.

Lecturers include both facts and opinions in their lectures. Facts are objective; they exist independently of anyone's perception or emotion. Identifying facts in spoken discourse can often be complicated. Unlike textbooks or other written material, you cannot "see" the source. There is no citation. However, speakers often use both verbal and nonverbal cues, or signposts, to indicate something is a fact.

USING VERBAL SIGNPOSTS

The language the speaker uses can help you determine whether the information is factual. When the speaker states a citation from a reliable source or mentions how the information is reliable, it is a fact. In addition, the *kind* of information given can distinguish it from an opinion. Numeric evidence is one type of information that can easily be used as evidence.

Language That Signposts a Fact	Information Given
According to Morrison, there are three keys to the relative deprivation theory.	**Sixty-four percent** of the American population felt bus segregation was unjust at the time of the Montgomery bus boycott.
Based on research conducted at Princeton, social movement organizations need charismatic leaders.	**In 1909**, the NAACP was formed in Illinois.
Well-known sociologists and historians determined that a single act of defiance brought light to the civil rights movement.	**Four in ten** African Americans report that they have been a victim of discrimination.
The government found the bus segregation unconstitutional.	Dr. King spoke out against unfair labor rights and the Vietnam War **at the Southern Christian Leadership Conference.**
As learned by past investigation, it was not Rosa Parks' intention to participate in an act of civil disobedience that day.	Dr. King visited the White House to campaign for voter rights **in the mid-1960s**.

Having a verbal signpost is not the only determiner of a fact. A fact is something that can be measured or validated. When in class, ask yourself if you can make a contrasting argument. If you can, it is most likely not a fact.

Examples

Opinion:	Social movement organizations work because they bring about change.
Contrasting argument:	Social movement organizations don't always work. Look at PETA (People for the Ethical Treatment of Animals). They are against killing animals and using their coats/skins for clothing. Yet, clothing made from animals coats/skins is still manufactured today.
Fact:	People involved in a social movement organization have a common goal.
Contrasting argument:	This is a fact. A contrasting argument cannot be formed.

USING NONVERBAL SIGNPOSTS

The language the speaker uses is one cue that the information you are hearing is a fact. The way the information is stated is a different type of cue, or signpost. It is a nonverbal signpost. Facts are generally spoken with a basic intonation pattern. Basic intonation pattern is a "step up, walk down" pattern. While your professor might use his or her voice to stress a key idea, it isn't an emphatic stress. Syllables other than the focal stress are of equal length. The vocal pattern, if diagrammed on paper, looks like this:

```
                                        -i-
                          vis-
                                              -ted
              -tor      King                              the
     Doc-                                                       White
                                                                    House.
```

Listen. When you hear this "step up, walk down" pattern, you can assume that the information stated is most likely a fact.

EXERCISE 1

Go to MyEnglishLab to complete a vocabulary exercise.

A. Are you familiar with any organizations that have been formed to make a change? What are they? List some facts about these organizations.

....

....

....

B. Share your facts with a classmate. Use signposts when stating your facts. Was the information new to your classmate?

C. One well-known organization in the United States is the National Association for the Advancement of Colored People (NAACP). Work with one or two partners and share any facts you may know about this organization.

....

....

D. Listen to this lecture about how the NAACP got its start. Which of these facts are given? For each fact identify the signpost that helped you determine it was a fact.

Fact	Verbal signpost	Nonverbal signpost
1. After the Civil War many politicians favored segregation.	....	....
2. After the war, politicians passed laws restricting the rights of African Americans.	....	....
3. African Americans who wanted to vote had to pay taxes, or take a test.	....	....
4. Organizations were formed to create more just laws.	....	....
5. Dubois led the Niagara Movement in 1905.	....	....
6. African Americans should work hard and avoid confrontation.	....	....
7. A violent race riot occurred in Springfield, Illinois.	....	....
8. NAACP is the most important advocate for African Americans.	....	....

Go to MyEnglishLab to complete a skill practice and join in collaborative activities.

SUPPORTING SKILL 2
IDENTIFYING OPINIONS THROUGH VERBAL AND NONVERBAL SIGNPOSTS

WHY IT'S USEFUL By recognizing verbal and nonverbal signposts of opinions, you can identify overgeneralizations, statements of bias, subjective statements, or statements that are observable but not measurable. By signposting your own opinions, you can make clear which statements are your beliefs, and you will be considered a more credible speaker.

Lecturers interject observations or opinions in their lectures. These are valuable and serve a purpose. Presentations often begin with an opinion and then are supported by facts. Determining which statements are opinions is not always straightforward. While some opinions may begin with "*I believe*," "*In my opinion*," or "*I think*," that is not always the case in academic settings. Like facts, speakers often use both verbal and nonverbal cues—signposts—to indicate something is an opinion.

IDENTIFYING VERBAL SIGNPOSTS
There are three main types of verbal signposts to help you identify opinions. They are

- expressions used to introduce a personal opinion
- value and judgment words
- overgeneralizations

Value words can't be measured, and when used in a statement, they can be debated easily. For example, "Social movement organizations are *useless*." While one person may believe this to be true, there are others who do not. It is debatable.

Judgment words are similar. They express what the speaker feels the outcome should be. For example, "By 2026, the government *must* ensure that all races have equal rights." The use of the modal *must* expresses a potential future outcome, rather than a proven fact.

Overgeneralizations are statements that are more general than can be proven. For example, "SMO leaders *always* are charismatic." These statements are subjective, or biased. Subjective and bias statements are influenced by personal opinions and can potentially be unfair.

Introducing a Personal Opinion	Value and Judgment Words	Overgeneralizing Words
I believe …	good	always
I bet / I'd bet …	ideal	anything
I imagine …	perfect	everything
I suspect …	bad	never
I think I'd say …	irrelevant	nothing
I think …	ordinary	
I'm sure …	outrageous	
Personally …	unnecessary	
	useless	

IDENTIFYING NONVERBAL SIGNPOSTS

Lecturers often use their voices to indicate an opinion. Strong opinions are said more emphatically, or with a stronger voice. The signposting words are generally said at a higher pitch and lengthened.

```
                              AL
                  are      WAYS
           ders              char
                              is
       lea                        ma
                                    tic.
   SMO
```

🎧 Listen. Emphatic, high-pitched statements like this one are a clue that what you are hearing is an opinion, rather than a fact.

EXERCISE 2

Go to MyEnglishLab to complete a vocabulary exercise.

🎧 **A. Listen to two students studying Dr. King's reactions to various threats and violence. What opinions do the students have? Make notes about which statements are opinions.**

B. Share your ideas with a classmate. Did you both agree on which statements were options?

🎧 **C. Listen again. Decide whether each statement is an opinion or a fact. If it is an opinion, explain how you determined that.**

1. Dr. King must have been furious that his home was bombed.

   ☐ Fact   ☐ Opinion   ....

2. Dr. King's speech after the bombing was not an easy speech to give.

   ☐ Fact   ☐ Opinion   ....

3. In his speech, Dr. King encouraged the continuation of peaceful actions.

   ☐ Fact   ☐ Opinion   ....

4. Dr. King knew that his home was wiretapped.

   ☐ Fact   ☐ Opinion   ....

5. Everyone should have a sit-down with the President.

   ☐ Fact   ☐ Opinion   ....

6. There was a backlash after the FBI authorized the wiretap on King's phone.

   ☐ Fact   ☐ Opinion   ....

> **CULTURE NOTE**
> **John F. Kennedy** sometimes called JFK, was the 35th President of the United States. He was assassinated while still in office in 1963. JFK came from a family that is often considered American royalty. His brothers were also involved in politics. His brother Robert Kennedy was the attorney general, and it was he who persuaded the president to place secret listening devices in Dr. King's home.

D. Check your answers with a classmate. Did you both find the same information?

Go to MyEnglishLab to complete a skill practice and join in collaborative activities.

INTEGRATED SKILLS
DISTINGUISHING BETWEEN FACTS AND OPINIONS IN TEXTS

WHY IT'S USEFUL By recognizing facts and opinions in written materials, you can critically analyze whether the information can be supported through evidence or whether it is the opinion of the writer.

Speakers often signal their ideas with signposts such as expressions of belief, judgment words, or terms of overgeneralizations. Like speakers, authors combine facts and opinions in writing. Reading critically allows you to better differentiate facts from opinions. The distinction is not always clear in text, as many authors avoid using the personal pronoun *I*. In addition, different types of written material lend themselves more to fact-giving, while others lend themselves more to opinion-giving. Newspaper and magazine articles tend to offer more opinion than fact. Textbook and journal articles tend to be more grounded in fact. These types of sources use citations to signal to the reader that the ideas are supported by evidence. A citation is one clear sign of a fact. Overall, textbooks tend to be more objective, while lecturers lean toward being more subjective. Although lecturers present facts, they often signal their agreement or disagreement with the information. These charts highlight the critical characteristics of fact- and opinion-giving in lectures and in printed material.

SIGNALING FACTS	
Lecturers	**Academic Printed Materials**
• use signposts such as *According to …* • use numeric or other easily proven signpost such as *In 1964 …*	• include the name of the source • offer numeric details • provide citations

SIGNALING OPINIONS	
Lecturers	**Academic Printed Materials**
• use signposts such as a personal expression of belief, a judgment term, or an overgeneralization • encourage agreement or disagreement and opinion-giving	• use an immeasurable adjective such as *good* or *interesting* or a verb of emotion, such as *worry* • use hedging devices (see Language Skill)

EXERCISE 3

A. With a partner, discuss nonviolent social movements and radical social movements. What are some characteristics of each? List your ideas.

Nonviolent Social Movements	Radical Social Movements
....	....
....	....
....	....
....	....

B. Read the textbook excerpt. As you read, pay attention to the signals used for facts and opinions.

Class Solidarity or Radical Separatism?

An Overview of Perspectives on Consciousness-Raising in the African American Civil Rights Movement

Is racial equality best achieved through hard work and quiet struggle within a socio-politic or by building a new, separate society unfettered by oppressive ideology? In the centuries-long struggle for equal rights, it seems that African American philosophers, activists, and citizens have approached the quest for equality in numerous ways, with each viewpoint offering new perspectives to the community as a whole. As far back as the early 19th century, some abolitionists and freedmen argued in favor of separatism—completely removing African Americans as a people from the direct control of the United States government (Walter 22). The nation of Liberia was formed by former North American and Caribbean slaves seeking to establish a new, sovereign nation. Decades later, faced with the violence and oppression of the Jim Crow era, figures like Marcus Garvey would try to persuade black citizens in North America to join the "back to Africa" movement, borne of the idea that true freedom from oppression could be found in their ancestral homeland.

During the civil rights era, the Black Nationalist and Black Separatist movements advocated not just for solidarity but also for a form of self-reliance that more moderate civil rights advocates found to be extreme (Kendall 21, 76). Moderate advocates, such as Dr. Martin Luther King Jr., worried that the positions of radical activists would harm the perception of the civil rights movement on the national level. For example, certain militant groups advocated in favor of armed self-defense organizations as a way to protect African Americans from violent hate groups like the Ku Klux Klan. Moderates were concerned that even raising the possibility of armed self-defense would likely inflame white racist hate groups and segregationist politicians, providing them the justification needed to enact stricter legislation.

According to meeting minutes, black radicals argued that the moderates' perspective was based in false consciousness and ended up supporting, not challenging, the ideology of an oppressive government that cared little about the safety or welfare of African Americans. Malcolm X, in his famous "The Bullet or The Ballot" speech, seemed to indicate that segregation was still in common practice by state and local governments despite being clearly and obviously illegal according to the Supreme Court. What, asked the radicals, did African Americans expect to gain from a government that could not even enforce its own laws?

In truth, despite the differing perspectives and often bitter arguments among the two sides, both groups were dedicated to raising the class consciousness of African Americans. Both groups found the ideology of American society oppressive and saw the harm done to African Americans as a serious problem. The primary difference between the two groups was simply the means by which they hoped to change society. Both were dedicated to consciousness-raising, but each group had a different understanding of what that entailed.

C. List four facts from the excerpt in one column and four opinions in the other column.

Facts	Opinions
....	....
....	....
....	....
....	....

D. Check your answers with a partner. Discuss what helped you identify opinions within the text.

CULTURE NOTE

The Black Panthers One of the more radical social and political organizations that formed in response to racial and social unrest in the 1960s was the Black Panther Party, commonly known as the Black Panthers, or BPP. The Black Panthers originated in Oakland, California in 1966. The Black Panthers were known for their practice of militant self-defense, such as carrying guns in their communities on patrols to "police the police" (monitor and challenge police brutality). Their beliefs were connected to those of Lenin and Mao Tse Dong, who believed in "armed struggle" to achieve social change rather than nonviolent resistance. They called for violent revolution. In addition to their beliefs on violence, the Black Panthers also began several social programs in African American areas to promote self-reliance. These programs included health clinics for those with little or no medical care and a free breakfast program for children. Because of leadership conflicts, membership began to decline, and after 1972, the BPP was no longer active in the United States. Their organization was very controversial; many found their beliefs and methods too extreme to be effective.

E. Work in groups of four. Two members of the group consider the benefits of nonviolent movements. Two members of the group consider the benefits of radical movements. Have an informal debate regarding which movement is more effective in creating a change.

Benefits of Nonviolent Movements	Benefits of Radical Movements
....	....
....	....
....	....
....	....

Go to MyEnglishLab to complete a skill practice.

For more about IDENTIFYING FACTS AND OPINIONS, see [R] and [W] SOCIOLOGY ②.

LANGUAGE SKILLS
INTERPRETING AND UTILIZING HEDGING DEVICES

WHY IT'S USEFUL By identifying hedging devices in presentations and lectures, you can differentiate facts from opinions more easily and determine a speaker's certainty about his or her statement. Incorporating hedging devices into your own speaking allows you to cautiously communicate your assertion.

During class lectures, presentations, and discussions, students often assert their ideas or claims. While a claim is an opinion, it is usually supported with facts. **Hedging** is a strategy used to cautiously express your assertion or opinion. Listeners are able to ascertain your level of certainty with the hedging device you use. A fact has 100 percent certainty, while an opinion has less than 100 percent certainty. The hedging device you choose shows how close to certain, or how uncertain, you are. There are several types of hedging devices. These are shown in the chart.

Device	Example	Explanation
Modal auxiliary verbs can, could, may, might, must, should	Great leaders can be a catalyst for change. The legislative changes of the 1960s **might** not have occurred it had not been for leaders like Dr. King.	Using a modal softens your opinion and expresses cautiousness to the listener. Listeners understand you are not 100% certain when you insert a modal. If the *can* is removed from the first example, it sounds like a fact. It is a very strong assertion.
Adverbs of approximation (modal adverbs) apparently, likely, perhaps, possibly, presumably, probably, arguably	The relative deprivation theory is **possibly** an explanation for the large number of SMOs during the 1960s and 1970s.	Like modal auxiliary verbs, modal adverbs communicate that you are not 100% certain.
Distancing verbs appear, indicate, look like, seem, suggest, tend	The theory **seems** to indicate that the characteristics of leaders are necessary for mobilization. Research in this area **suggests** that the organization must collectively agree on the message they wish to convey.	These statements often appear to be facts; however, the use of the distancing verb communicates that this is one's opinion. The speaker is cautiously and politely offering an informed opinion.
Compound hedges seems reasonable, seems / looks probable / likely / unlikely	It **seems reasonable** to conclude that sociologists have thoroughly examined this topic. It **looks likely** that other grassroots organizations will follow in their footsteps.	Compound hedges generally include an introductory verb and adverb of approximation. Using compound hedges communicates to your listeners why you have this opinion while at the same time remaining open to debate or argument.
Informal vagueness indicators and coordination tags Kind of, sort of And / or + everything, so, something, such, stuff, thing	Those sit-ins were **kind of** effective. The college students involved in those sit-ins spent numerous hours **or so**.	Like other hedging devices, these informal devices indicate a speaker's imprecision or approximation. These are commonly heard in small group discussions, but they are not often used in formal lectures or presentations.

EXERCISE 4

Rewrite each statement using the hedging device indicated.

1. The Southern Christian Leadership Conference made great strides in communicating the message of nonviolent protest. (distancing verb)

   ....

2. The Poor People's campaign orchestrated the massive march on the capital in Washington, D.C. (adverb of approximation)

   ....

3. The gradual rise of the African American influence mobilized the movement. (compound hedge)

   ....

4. The NAACP pushed for economic and political reforms. (informal vagueness indicator)

   ....

5. The Montgomery bus boycott signaled a change within the movement. (modal auxiliary verb)

   ....

6. Freedom rides and freedom songs promoted racial solidarity. (distancing verb)

   ....

EXERCISE 5

A. Listen to the lecture excerpt and take notes.

B. Use your notes to share what you heard with a classmate. Use hedging devices for those points that you are not certain of. Listen to your partner's ideas. How certain were you both?

Go to MyEnglishLab to complete a skill practice.

APPLY YOUR SKILLS

WHY IT'S USEFUL By applying the skills you have learned in this unit, you can successfully distinguish between facts and opinions in academic contexts. You can recognize which statements are supported by evidence and which statements show bias or reflect the speaker's perspective. By utilizing hedging language and by signposting facts and opinions in your own presentations, you can make a stronger argument in which it is clear to your listeners what your own views are.

ASSIGNMENT

Prepare a group presentation on a change that you would like to see made in your community or school. Use what you have learned on relative deprivation theory, social movement organizations, and activism to present your ideas.

BEFORE YOU LISTEN

A. Before you listen, discuss these questions with one or more students.

1. Considering historical events and cultural climates, what changes have resulted due to activism?

2. What makes a social movement organization effective in today's world?

3. What are the issues that surround social movement organizations today?

B. You will hear a lecture about a social movement called the Black Freedom Movement. This movement marked a change in how African Americans organized to fight segregation. As you listen, think about these questions.

1. What characterized the efforts of Dr. King and the NAACP to effect change?

2. How did later movements, such as the Black Freedom Movement, differ from earlier efforts?

3. What were the forces that brought about these changes?

C. Review the Unit Skills Summary. As you listen to the lecture and begin preparing your presentation, apply the skills you learned in this unit.

UNIT SKILLS SUMMARY

Identify facts.
- Listen for signposts.
- Pay close attention to voice.
- Recognize measurable evidence.

Identify opinions.
- Listen for signposts.
- Pay close attention to voice.
- Recognize judgment words and overgeneralizations.

Identify and utilize hedging devices such as:
- modal auxiliary verbs (*may, might*, etc.)
- adverbs of approximation (*apparently, probably*, etc.)
- distancing verbs (*appear, seem, tend*, etc.)
- compound hedges (*seems reasonable, looks likely*, etc.)
- indicators of vagueness and coordination tags (*kind of, and such*, etc.)

LISTEN

A. Listen to the lecture about the Black Freedom Movement. As you listen, take notes. Organize your notes according to verifiable fact versus the speaker's opinion.

B. Compare your notes with a partner. Did you both find the same facts and opinions? What listening skills from this unit can help you better identify fact versus opinion?

C. Work with a partner. Use your notes from the lecture to answer the questions from Before You Listen, Part B.

Go to MyEnglishLab to listen again and answer critical thinking questions.

THINKING CRITICALLY

Discuss the questions with another student.

1. Based on the lecture, what is the relationship between the Black Freedom Movement and Dr. King's early efforts?

2. What changes were made as a result of both movements? Based on what you heard, how did each movement play an important role toward bringing about these changes?

3. According to the speaker's conclusion, what led to further changes within these social movements? What do you think characterized the movements that followed?

THINKING VISUALLY

A. Look at this Venn diagram highlighting the similarities between social movements and collective behavior. Do you find any of these surprising? Why or why not? How does this diagram support what you heard in the lecture?

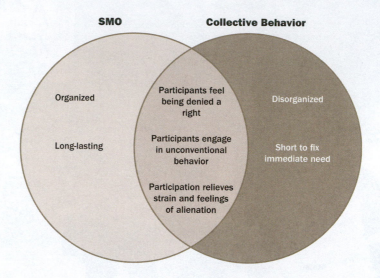

SMO   **Collective Behavior**

Organized

Long-lasting

Participants feel being denied a right

Participants engage in unconventional behavior

Participation relieves strain and feelings of alienation

Disorganized

Short to fix immediate need

B. Conduct an online search on a current social movement organization. Investigate how the group began, their message, and the way in which they get their message across. Make a Venn diagram comparing it to either the Black Freedom Movement or Dr. King's civil rights movement. Present the diagram to your classmates, and share your opinions about which group has been more effective.

THINKING ABOUT LANGUAGE

A. Listen to these excerpts from the lecture. After hearing each excerpt, rephrase the statement using a hedging device.

1. ....

2. ....

3. ....

B. Compare your answers with another student. Which hedging devices did you use? If you used different devices, how is your meaning different from your partner's?

GROUP PRESENTATION

A. Think about the lectures and other topics covered in this unit. Throughout history, people have organized themselves to make changes over a common issue, primarily over rights they felt they were being denied. Considering your current school and community, what issues need to have light shed upon them? Make a list.

B. Share your list with a small group. Prioritize your issues. Vote on which issue is most critical for the entire group.

1. With your group, create a message about this issue.

2. Develop your message, using evidence.

3. Use facts to support your group's opinions.

4. Determine the strategies you will employ to communicate your message.

5. Present your message and the strategies to your class.

C. Listen to each presentation.

As you listen, take notes. Determine what information is a fact and what information is an opinion. Consider the degree of certainty each group has in regards to the information they share.

D. Discuss these questions as a class.

Would you rally to support this group's cause? If not, what further evidence would they need to provide, or what strategies should they employ, to garner support?

▶ Go to MyEnglishLab to listen to Professor Greenberg and to complete a self-assessment.

Individual choices impact the global economy.

Implications and Inferences

UNIT PROFILE

In this unit, you will learn about market economic theory, market equilibrium, and market competition. You will also learn about different types of markets, and you will discuss how market supply and demand influence price.

You will prepare a class debate on the benefits and drawbacks of a supply-side economy and a demand-side economy.

OUTCOMES

- Identify a speaker's underlying meaning
- Determine a speaker's intent and degree of certainty
- Synthesize information from multiple sources
- Understand implied conditions

GETTING STARTED

▶ Go to MyEnglishLab to listen to Professor Clerici-Arias and to complete a self-assessment.

Discuss these questions with a partner or group.

1. Are you familiar with the expression, "What goes up must come down?" What does it mean in your life? What does it mean when applied to economics?

2. What are some advantages of having many companies who produce the same goods or services? What are some disadvantages?

3. In the introduction, Professor Clerici-Arias says "Businesses manipulate shifts in supply and demand to create demand for certain items." Do you agree with his statement? If so, how do you think they might do that?

For more about **ECONOMICS** see ❶ ❸. See also Ⓡ and Ⓦ **ECONOMICS** ❶ ❷ ❸.

CRITICAL THINKING SKILL
IMPLICATIONS AND INFERENCES

WHY IT'S USEFUL By understanding implications and by making inferences, you can determine the underlying meaning of what someone is saying, which leads to better comprehension. By making implications in your own speech, you can communicate your idea more subtly, without directly stating it.

Although speakers regularly communicate their ideas directly and explicitly, they often convey aspects of their message indirectly or through **implication**. When speakers **imply**, they give hints to their ideas, feelings, and intentions. The use of implication is not always deliberate; rather it is a natural speaking style in which the listener is simply expected to connect the dots.

As listeners, we all interpret, or **infer**, incoming messages constantly. **Inferences** are educated guesses we make based on what the speaker has implied. To accurately infer meaning, active listeners pay close attention to **rhetorical devices**. They know to listen not only for *what* is said but also for *how* it is said, as well as for what is *not stated*. For example, when a speaker tells a story, it may not be the story itself, but what the story illustrates that is the main point. Other devices include things such as a speaker's word choice and voice.

Not only are listeners responsible for decoding the language, but they must also determine the **speaker's intent**, or underlying meaning, which often includes his or her opinion on or bias toward the issue. Being able to identify implications through rhetorical cues allows you to determine the speaker's intent. This in turn allows you to **determine the speaker's degree of certainty** about the subject and to draw accurate connections and conclusions.

NOTICING ACTIVITY

Go to MyEnglishLab to complete a vocabulary exercise.

A. Listen to the lecture on the benefits of competition. As you listen, make inferences about how the lecturer feels about competition. What does the speaker say that allows you to make those inferences?

B. Continue listening as two students discuss their inferences about the lecture. Compare your own inferences with theirs.

Go to MyEnglishLab to complete a skill practice and join in collaborative activities.

SUPPORTING SKILL 1
IDENTIFYING IMPLIED MEANING

WHY IT'S USEFUL By identifying a speaker's implied meaning, you can understand unspoken messages, or the speaker's indirect ideas. This helps you to better comprehend the real meaning and gives you insight into a speaker's rhetorical style. Using rhetorical devices in your own speeches and presentations can help you convey your intent.

INTERPRETING IMPLICATIONS

To *imply* something is to convey an idea or message indirectly. Speakers use implication unintentionally all the time. They use chunks of language that are related in meaning, but they don't always connect these terms in a clear, organized manner. In the simplest form, an implication can be made through the use of similar lexical items. For example, a speaker may at first refer to his or her research as *findings*, and later as *these unexpected results*. It can be implied that the speaker *was surprised by what was learned*.

To best interpret an implication, consider the speaker's word choice. Words have meanings beyond the dictionary meaning; they have cultural meanings, or *connotations*. Connotations often communicate a positive or negative feeling. For instance, *The economic downturn has many businesses downsizing* versus *The economic downturn has many businesses firing people*. The verb *downsize* has a more neutral connotation. The implied meaning here is that businesses are doing this in an ethical and considerate manner. The verb *fire*, by contrast, gives us the idea that these businesses do not really care about their employees.

It is just as important to consider the speaker's voice. When pitch is low and words are lengthened, the speaker usually means the opposite of what is being said. For example, the phrase, "It's a wonderful day." Stretch out the word *wonderful*. Now the speaker is saying it is *not* a wonderful day.

RHETORICAL DEVICES

In addition to word choice and voice, speakers may use rhetorical devices to verbally illustrate their main idea. Lecturers often include stories, comparisons, and metaphors in their lectures in order to connect with their audience. These are useful devices to use in your own presentations. Rhetorical tools talk around the key ideas, or illustrate the main point; thus, you must infer the speaker's main ideas.

Strategy/Device	Meaning	Example
Analogy	A powerful comparison.	If the economy is a car, demand is the fuel that moves the car forward.
Anecdote	A short story which often sets the stage for a main idea.	I was at the mall the other day with my daughter. She begged me for the X tablet. No surprise, as we are bombarded on a daily basis with their advertisements, claiming we can't live without this technological tool.
Euphemism	Substituting a polite expression for something that might be unpleasant to hear, or harsh.	By using less expensive materials to produce its goods, the company is being economical. (Substituting *economical* for *cheap*.)
Metaphor and Symbolism	A nonliteral imaginative substitution for something.	When the car industry was in trouble, Detroit looked like a ghost town.
Paradox	A kind of truth that at first seems contradictory.	You have to spend money to make money.
Sarcasm	Irony. Means the opposite of what is said. Usually determined by voice.	Monopolies are clearly concerned about helping the little man.
Tone and Undertone	A way to communicate an attitude toward something. Not directly expressed, but usually can be determined by voice and facial expressions.	For many decades, the American automotive industry was protected from outside competition by highly restrictive trade barriers. They became so complacent that they actually designed cars to break down. (Said with raised eyebrows, a slower voice, and exaggerated stress to show incredulity.)

EXERCISE 1

Go to MyEnglishLab to complete a vocabulary exercise.

A. Think of a celebrity-endorsed product. Do you think the product was more successful due to the celebrity endorsement? What inferences can you make about the supply and demand of the product being endorsed? Make notes about your ideas.

B. Discuss your ideas with a classmate. Did you both infer the same thing?

C. Listen to a lecture from an economics class. Then answer the questions.

> **CULTURE NOTE**
> **Mountaineering shoes** Mountaineering is a common sport in North America and other places around the world. It involves mountain climbing, hiking through mountainous terrain, and rock climbing in a variety of weather conditions. There are special shoes or boots mountaineers usually wear. They are usually made of a very durable, waterproof fabric and have rigid soles with plates that allow a mountaineer to easily grip rough, unstable terrain.

1. When the professor says, "Be mindful of the terminology …" what can you infer from this statement?

   ....

2. When the professor says, "We just love fashion," what can you infer from how this statement is said?

   ....

3. What is the professor illustrating by using the example of the celebrity endorsement?

   ....

4. What does the professor imply when he refers to celebrities as "hotshots"?

   ....

5. What can you infer when the lecturer states, "… everyone desires a flat screen"? What does he communicate by his word choice of "desire" over "want"?

   ....

6. What connections can you draw from the examples the lecturer used?

   ....

D. Share your answers with another student. Explain how word choice, voice, and rhetorical strategies helped you infer meaning from the lecture.

Go to MyEnglishLab to complete a skill practice and join in collaborative activities.

SUPPORTING SKILL 2
DETERMINING A SPEAKER'S INTENT AND DEGREE OF CERTAINTY

WHY IT'S USEFUL By using inferences to determine a speaker's purpose or intent, you can better understand the key ideas of the lecture, or what claims the speaker is making. Identifying sources used by the speaker helps you determine the speaker's degree of certainty. This in turn helps you draw conclusions and formulate opinions about the topic.

SPEAKER'S INTENT

Speakers may not directly state their purpose. This is often something that must be inferred. While most class lectures have the purpose to educate or examine, other types of academic presentations might have a different purpose—for example, to persuade or make a claim. Determining speaker's intent involves evaluating:

- word choice
- use of sources
- tone of voice
- body language and facial expressions

DEGREE OF CERTAINTY

Inferential listening involves listening actively for subtle cues to a speaker's certainty. In academic settings, speakers often support assertions and claims with evidence when they want to establish the content as reliable and valid. Speakers do this by:

- citing sources in which the implication is that their position is grounded in research and, therefore, has credibility.
- making claims and providing evidence for that claim.

Examples

Citing Sources	Making Claims and Providing Evidence
The *Journal of Economics and Business* reported that …	It's true that …
Well-known experts say, quote …	It's certain that …
A study by The National Center for Economic Growth indicates that …	Absolutely
According to the textbook, / the experts, / Adam Smith, the famous economist, / statistics …	Certainly
	Clearly
As Dr. Sammshas pointed out …	Definitely
Evidence was given by …	As I have noted …
In an article …	For all of those reasons, you must recognize that …
In its research survey, the Federal Reserve Bank learned …	Obviously / Unquestionably / Undoubtedly / Evidently …
Many statistics prove / studies show …	
Referring to your textbook author …	
The work of Gibbs shows that …	
Based on the latest research …	

EXERCISE 2

Go to MyEnglishLab to complete a vocabulary exercise.

A. Listen to the lecture excerpt on market saturation. What is the speaker's intent? Share your idea with a classmate.

B. Listen again. Choose the words and phrases the speaker uses to make a claim.

a. It's true that

c. As recently noted

e. Referring to your textbook

b. Absolutely

d. According to

f. As I pointed out before

C. Listen again. Answer the questions.

1. What is the speaker's assertion or claim?

....

2. How does the speaker add credibility to his claim?

....

3. How does the speaker introduce the source?

....

4. What word or phrase does the speaker use to make the author of the article credible?

....

5. What sources does the speaker suggest you go back and read to understand there was a time when trade was opening up?

....

6. How does the speaker feel about *"anyone entering the market"*? How do you know?

....

D. Share your answers with a classmate. Do you agree with the speaker? Why or why not? Defend your position with examples.

Go to MyEnglishLab to complete a skill practice and join in collaborative activities.

CULTURE NOTE

"The Little Man" Businesses that are run by families or individuals rather than large corporate chains are often referred to as "the little man. These are also sometimes called mom and pop shops. Decades ago there were many more such businesses than today.

INTEGRATED SKILLS
SYNTHESIZING INFORMATION FROM MULTIPLE SOURCES

WHY IT'S USEFUL By recognizing synthesized information from multiple sources, you can determine the reliability of the information and identify where you can go for further research. Similarly, by synthesizing multiple sources in your own presentations, you can add greater credibility to your own assertion or claim.

Speakers need to support their statements with evidence in order to convince listeners that the content is valid. Using only one source, or one type of source, does not convince most listeners the information is widely accepted. Therefore, speakers often use multiple sources to assert their claim. Verbal markers are used to illustrate the relationship between sources.

Verbal Markers	Example
Similarly /Likewise	According to Hubbs, the average consumer spends nearly 15% of their income on household goods. **Similarly**, Gaston asserts that 90% of these items are unnecessary.
similar to / like	In Lenke's research, he discovered that consumers are unlikely to change brands. This was **like** the data provided by Hasten, who found only 2% of consumers make brand changes.
According to (both) X and Y . . .	**According to both Stakes and Berns**, monopolies exist in every market.
Based on the research / studies conducted by X and Y . . .	**Based on the studies conducted by Princeton University and Boston College**, trade agreements have aided larger corporations.
In addition to . . .	**In addition to** Games' research on brand selection, Cavin has also proven that a perfectly competitive market is best for consumers.
[This] is further supported by . . .	The loss of mom-and-pop shops has been heavily researched by Craggs. He found these small independent operations couldn't compete with large wholesalers. **This is further supported by** Telay and Cole, who added even mid-sized corporations were falling out of the market due to megastores and wholesalers.

Textbooks, trade magazines, and journal articles also integrate multiple sources. This is done through citations. Citation styles depend on the discipline; however, all disciplines have a system for acknowledging where the information has come from.

EXERCISE 3

A. Brainstorm markets that have regular price changes. Why do these price changes occur?

B. Listen to the lecture. Notice his references to sources.

C. Choose the ideas from the lecture that are supported by a source.

1. There has been a shift in the prices of organic strawberries.
2. Price changes are always the result of supply and demand.
3. Price changes can often be credited to fluctuations in seasonal growing patterns.
4. Consumers find a substitute good when there is a shortage of a product.
5. High fructose corn syrup is added due to shortages of cane sugar as a result of political differences.
6. Monopolies rarely move the shifts in the supply-and-demand line.
7. New or increased demand for oil creates price fluctuations.
8. There is an infrastructure for oil manufacturing.

D. Think about the lecturer's use of sources. What type of sources did he use? How did he connect multiple sources? Discuss your ideas with a partner.

Go to MyEnglishLab to complete a vocabulary exercise.

EXERCISE 4

A. Which products or services would you be willing to give up if their costs became too great? Which ones would you be unwilling to give up despite their expense? Why? Discuss your ideas with a partner.

B. Read these quotes on opportunity costs. Take notes on any similarities that you see among the quotes.

Quote One

In addition to the actual cost of an item, consumers consider the opportunity cost of a purchase. This cost refers to what a consumer has to give up in order to make the purchase. These costs are not restricted to monetary costs but are inclusive of loss of time and loss of enjoyment. Price fluctuations influence one's opportunity cost. When consumers change their purchasing based on opportunity costs, this is what is referred to as "demand elasticity." The demand is flexible, not fixed.
(*Economics Today*)

Quote Two

Elasticity, the degree to which demand and supply curves react to price changes, varies greatly among products. Goods and services that have a drastic change in the quantity demanded after a small price change is made are considered highly elastic. Economists have determined that necessities are inelastic. The opportunity costs are not considered, since these items are deemed needed for daily life.
(*Leading economist, Will Cavs*)

Quote Three

An elastic demand occurs when a slight price change creates a very large change in the quantity demanded by consumers. Thus, the opportunity cost is low for the consumer; they are willing to give up the product. Compare this with inelastic demand, where a large price increase produces only a slight change in the quantity demanded by consumers. The opportunity cost for consumers is high for inelastic goods and services. The consumers are willing to give up a lot in order to gain the needed good or service. (*Professor Ana Turner*)

C. Synthesize the information from the three quotes. Give a short presentation on the synthesized information, using verbal markers to help your listeners identify the multiple sources.

Go to MyEnglishLab to complete a skill practice.

For more about SYNTHESIZING MULTIPLE SOURCES, see W ECONOMICS 2 and R BIOLOGY 2.

LANGUAGE SKILL
UNDERSTANDING IMPLIED CONDITIONS

WHY IT'S USEFUL By understanding implied conditions, you can infer the meaning of a speaker's message more accurately and better imply your own meaning when speaking.

Rather than fully state a condition by using an if-clause, speakers sometimes imply a conditional meaning. The condition may be expressed beginning with *but for, if not, if so, otherwise, with,* and *without.* In a sentence with an implied condition, there is no grammatical change in the result clause—the conditional verb form is still used. As with other conditional sentences, the condition may precede or follow the result clause.

Examples

Conditional with *If*-clause	Implied Condition
Kara might be right. **If she is right**, demand will shift.	Kara might be right; **if so**, demand will shift.
The company would have gone bankrupt **if a celebrity had not been their spokesperson.**	The company would have gone bankrupt, **but a celebrity was their spokesperson.**
If Emma didn't have savings, she'd have no money.	**But for Emma's savings**, she'd have no money.
If he doesn't get the job, he'll go back to school.	He might get the job; **if not**, he'll go back to school.
If she weren't desperate, she wouldn't have paid that much for it.	She is desperate; **otherwise**, she wouldn't have paid that much for it.
If he hadn't guided me, I wouldn't have pursued a degree in economics.	**Without his guidance**, I wouldn't have pursued a degree in economics.

EXERCISE 5

A. Read the lecture excerpt. Underline the conditional sentences.

If there are seasonal or political changes, the supply curve can be shifted in a number of different ways. Aluminum, once an extremely rare element to find in its naturally occurring form, became commonplace after improved processing methods were developed in the 19th century. This is one of the more striking examples from history, but similar situations have occurred with all varieties of technology. Think about it … if we have a natural disaster, our food crops could be devastated. Worldwide political trends and a tendency toward free trade in an era of globalization have made products available from all over the world, increasing the supply of almost every conceivable item.

The global tendency toward free trade has increased demand dramatically as well. If raw material markets from all over the world hadn't emerged, the demand would not have been pushed to new heights. Food, rare earth elements, and fuel have become essential to dozens of nations in this age of globalization. With so many markets open and trading with each other, there are thousands of customers across the world driving up demand for every good imaginable. If there were no new markets, demand could possibly decrease. Every new market opened to trade increases the worldwide customer base, increases demand, and sometimes drives up the price. While this increased demand is often balanced out by the increase in supply that comes with globalization, the markets are volatile; small changes in seemingly insignificant sectors can have proportionately enormous impact on price.

B. Review the sentences you underlined in the excerpt. Rewrite each one as an implied conditional.

1. ....
....

2. ....
....

3. ....
....

4. ....
....

B. Work with another student to determine if the condition in each item is implied or stated explicitly. Restate it in the opposite form.

1. The supply line may shift. If it does, the price will increase.
2. We couldn't have been successful if you hadn't helped us.
3. The government had to crack down on monopolies. If it hadn't cracked down, small businesses would not exist.
4. But for a few successful products, the company had no profit.
5. They would have invested in your idea, but they were unsure of success.
6. Without supporting statistics, the agency couldn't have generated the report.

Go to **MyEnglishLab** to complete a skill practice.

APPLY YOUR SKILLS

WHY IT'S USEFUL By applying the skills you have learned in this unit, you can successfully understand implications and make inferences in academic contexts so that you have a more complete comprehension of a speaker's message and intent. You can also successfully make implications in your own presentations so that your listeners make accurate inferences about your intent.

ASSIGNMENT

Prepare a class debate on the issue of which economic theory encourages more monetary growth: supply-side economics or demand-side economics. Use what you have learned, as well as your research into both theories, to determine the advantages and disadvantages of each one. Develop your position and integrate multiple sources to support it.

BEFORE YOU LISTEN

A. Discuss the questions with one or more students.

1. Have you ever wanted to purchase something, but there was a shortage of that item? If so, what was the product? Why do you think that shortage occurred?

2. Can you think of a product that was not as successful as people thought it would be? Why do you think it wasn't a success?

3. What products have you noticed a surplus of when you shop?

B. You will listen to a lecture about how supply and demand shifts affect shortages and surpluses. As you listen, think about these questions.

1. What is demand-side economics?

2. What is supply-side economics?

3. How can demand-side economics benefit society?

4. How can supply-side economics benefit society?

C. Review the Unit Skills Summary. As you listen to the lecture and begin preparing your debate, apply the skills you learned in this unit.

UNIT SKILLS SUMMARY

Identify implications and inferences.
• Notice word choice and connotations.
• Pay close attention to voice pitch and pace.
• Recognize rhetorical devices.

Utilize inferences to determine a speaker's intent and certainty.
• Identify discourse signals for citing sources.
• Recognize cues for claims and evidence to support claims.

Use verbal markers to synthesize data from multiple sources.

Understand implied conditions.
• Identify and use implied conditional statements.

LISTEN

A. Listen to the lecture "How Supply and Demand Shifts Affect Shortages and Surpluses." As you listen, look at the diagrams below and on the next page.

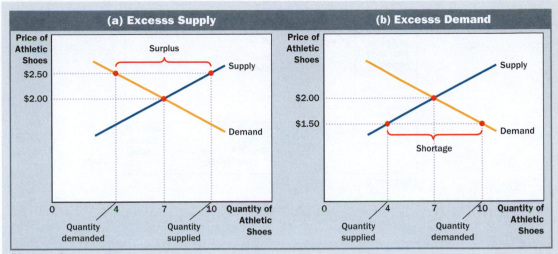

Diagram A

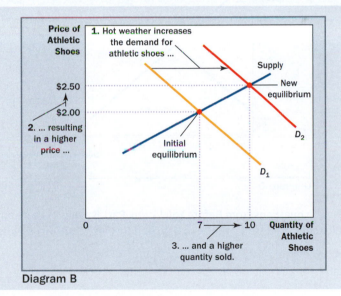

Diagram B

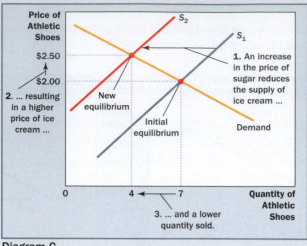

Diagram C

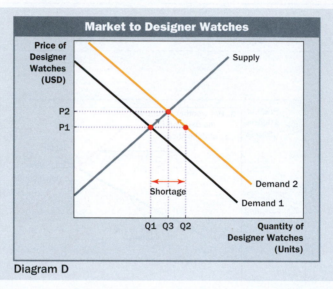

Diagram D

B. Read the discussion questions from Before You Listen, Part B again. Is there anything you cannot answer? What listening skills can you use to help find the answers? Discuss your ideas with another student.

🎧 Go to MyEnglishLab to listen again and answer critical thinking questions.

THINKING CRITICALLY

Discuss the questions with another student.

1. What connection between Nike athletic shoes and Apple® devices is the speaker making?

2. Based on the information given in the lecture, what other products do you think might create shifts in both supply and demand?

3. Considering the lecturer's tone and pitch rises, do you think the speaker sees more benefit in supply-side economics or demand-side economics?

4. How certain is the speaker that shortage of luxury brand items is artificially created? Support your idea with examples from the lecture.

THINKING VISUALLY

A. Use the diagrams from the lecture to answer the questions.

1. What information from the lecture can be seen in each diagram?

2. How does Diagram C support the information presented in the lecture?

3. What role do each of the diagrams play in understanding the content of the lecture?

B. Based on Diagram D, how has supply and demand shifted during the three quarters? According to the lecture what could be contributing causes for these shifts?

C. Conduct an online search on a product or service of your choice. Investigate how the equilibrium has shifted over a period of time, and make a graph to show the shifts. Present the graph to your classmates, and share your thoughts as to why these shifts have occurred.

THINKING ABOUT LANGUAGE

A. Listen to excerpts from the lecture. At the end of each excerpt, restate the condition using words that show the implication being made.

1. ....

2. ....

3. ....

B. Compare notes with another student. Talk about what the implied conditions mean.

CLASS DEBATE

A. Think about the lecture. There are definite consumer benefits to a shift in the supply line, and there are definite drawbacks. The same is true for the demand line. What do you think are the benefits to the consumer of each? What do you think are the drawbacks? Complete this chart with your ideas.

	Benefits	Drawbacks
Supply-Side Economics		
Demand-Side Economics		

B. Share your chart with your classmates. Divide into two teams: in favor of Supply-Side Economics and in favor of Demand-Side Economics. Follow these steps:

1. Alone, or with your team, research economic practices to support your team.

2. Develop your position, using evidence from reputable and respected sources.

3. Integrate multiple sources.

4. Prepare for your debate against the other team.

C. Debate

Establish the rules of your debate. Each team takes a turn presenting its claims. As the opposing team speaks, take notes. After the opposition has presented their argument, ask questions to ensure you understand any implications made by the other team. After the debate, take a class vote to determine which team made the strongest claim.

Go to MyEnglishLab to listen to Professor Clerici-Arias and to complete a self-assessment.

Exploring the secret lives of viruses.

BIOLOGY

Process

UNIT PROFILE

In this unit, you will learn about fast-spreading viruses. You will specifically explore how these viruses evolve over time and how they are transmitted.

You will prepare a process presentation on the transmission, symptoms, and treatment of an infectious disease.

OUTCOMES

- Understand steps of a process
- Identify purpose and structure in a process presentation
- Analyze flow in a process presentation
- Explain a complex process
- Use generalizations and specifics to introduce and define key points

GETTING STARTED

▶ Go to MyEnglishLab to listen to Professor Siegel and to complete a self-assessment.

B. Discuss these questions with a partner or group.

1. How fast do viruses, like the common cold, spread? How do they spread more easily? In what ways can we keep them from spreading?

2. What do you think are the potential dangers of a mass viral outbreak?

3. In the introduction, Professor Siegel refers to ancient viruses and how "the viruses may be extinct, but their DNA lives on in us." Are you surprised that viruses are in our DNA? Do you think these viruses cause harm to us in any way? Do you think these viruses benefit us in any way?

For more about **BIOLOGY**, see 1 3. See also R and W **BIOLOGY** 1 2 3.

CRITICAL THINKING SKILL
UNDERSTANDING AND PRESENTING PROCESSES

WHY IT'S USEFUL By understanding what a process is composed of, you can better comprehend the development of an idea or sequence of events from beginning to end, and you can develop a more cohesive, coherent presentation.

During your academic career you will most likely listen to, or be asked to outline, a process. **A process** involves steps, procedures, or a sequence of actions from beginning to end. A process presentation may be as simple as enumerating the steps in chronological order or as complex as listing the development or evolutionary changes of a virus. Whether listening to or preparing a presentation, it is important to decide on the purpose, or function, of the presentation.

Deciding on the purpose of the process presentation is critical in order to fully comprehend the information and disseminate it accurately to an audience. The purpose or function might be simply to describe the steps to inform or educate your listeners on the steps so they can be followed. Once you have decided on the function of the process, it will be easier to determine a logical flow of the information.

Flow refers to the cohesiveness of the content. Do the elements of the presentation connect together seamlessly? Planning these connections is critical and can easily be done with outlining or mapping. In addition to analyzing flow, you will need to **evaluate consistency**, both as a listener and speaker. An organized presentation contains signposts, such as headings, and the speaker often uses his or her voice effectively to help listeners determine the main points.

Another way to ensure the presentation flows and is consistent is through the inclusion of visuals. By communicating ideas, steps, events, and procedures through visual content like charts, graphs, and images, you can allow the audience to see as well as hear the information, thereby helping to elaborate and clarify complex processes.

Example

Presenter: Let's take a look at this *flow chart*. Once a patient is diagnosed with Ebola, we need to investigate, research, and disseminate information to all persons who have been in contact with the patient. *There are four courses of action* with all persons of contact. *The first* is to determine if the contact has symptoms. If they do, we must follow protocols of isolation, testing, and providing care. If that person has had other contacts, the cycle must be repeated. *The second course of action* is …

Go to MyEnglishLab to complete a vocabulary exercise.

NOTICING ACTIVITY

A. Listen to a lecture on the Ebola virus. As you listen, notice how the speaker explains the process of transmission, diagnosis, and treatment.

B. Now listen to how the students summarize the process. What are the stages they discuss?

Go to MyEnglishLab to complete a skill practice and join in collaborative activities.

SUPPORTING SKILL 1
IDENTIFYING STRUCTURE AND PURPOSE IN A PROCESS PRESENTATION

WHY IT'S USEFUL By identifying the type of structure used in a process presentation, you can better follow the logic of the presentation. By understanding the purpose of each step, event, or procedure in the process, you can better comprehend how the steps relate to one another and make sense of the complete presentation.

Academic presenters frequently lecture on events, steps, or procedures that illustrate or outline a process, method, development, or course of action. This type of presentation describes the steps in completing a task, explains how a complex procedure happens, or details why an event has produced a certain result. The first step in listening to or developing a process presentation is determining its organizational structure.

DETERMINING STRUCTURE OF A PROCESS PRESENTATION

Because process presentations often present the steps of how something functions or has evolved, they are often organized in chronological order, or topical order. With a topical organization, the presenter may choose to break the topic down into subtopics and explain how each subtopic affects a method, development, or procedure. This type of structure is often used for complex processes, like the evolution of a disease or virus. Compare the two organizational structures below.

Example

Time-Order Organization	Topical Organization
Vector Transmission	*Virus Transmission*
I. A vector develops or carries a virus	I. Droplet Transmission
II. The vector carries the virus and transmits it to a new host	II. Airborne Transmission
III. The vector transfers to the new host	III. Vector Transmission
IV. The new host transmits through air	IV. Waterborne Transmission

Once you have determined the organizational structure, be sure to differentiate between background information and actual steps, events, or procedures. A speaker provides background information to help listeners better understand the significance of the topic and set the scene for the new information. While background information helps enhance our comprehension of a topic, is not a part of the process.

DETERMINING THE PURPOSE OF STEPS IN A PROCESS

After identifying the structure of a presentation and distinguishing background information from the process itself, the next stage is to determine the purpose or function of each step, procedure, or event. To do this, ask yourself these questions:

- What is the method, development, or procedure being described?
- How is this related to the overall topic? What is the relationship?

Example

| CONTRACTION OF THE EBOLA VIRUS ||
Steps	Relationship
Step One: A victim must first have direct contact.	Shows beginning of development
Step Two: After Ebola has entered a person's body, the disease grows or incubates.	Shows progress
Step Three: Development of symptoms	Shows progress
Step Four: The Dry Phase	Shows progress
Step Five: The Wet Phase	Shows progress
Step Six: Death	Shows final result

Once you have determined each step's purpose, you can easily see relationships between the steps.

Go to MyEnglishLab to complete a vocabulary exercise.

EXERCISE 1

A. What are some ways viruses are transmitted? List your ideas.

....

....

....

B. Share your list with a classmate.

C. Listen to a lecture on virus transmission. As you listen, add the missing information to the outline.

Virus transmission

   I. Relationship between transmission and virulence
  II. Non-lethal viruses transmitted:
     a. ....
       i. Spread when someone breathes on you
     b. Droplet
       i. ....
     c. Vector
       i. Water for waterborne diseases
       ii. ....
  III. Cycle continues

D. Listen again. Check the information that is background information.

☐ Common cold not virulent

☐ Ancestors would have died out

☐ Balance between transmission and virulence

☐ Someone sneezes on you without covering their mouth

☐ Diseases can linger on an object

☐ Some diseases spread by vectors

☐ Mosquitos play a role in transmitting diseases

Go to MyEnglishLab to complete a skill practice and join in collaborative activities.

SUPPORTING SKILL 2
ANALYZING FLOW OF A PROCESS PRESENTATION

WHY IT'S USEFUL By analyzing the flow of a presentation, you can determine how cohesive and complete the information is. By creating flow and consistency in your presentations, you can elaborate and clarify complex processes for your listeners.

Just like written material, oral material should flow or move seamlessly from one idea to the next. Ensuring that the material is well organized and has an introduction, body, and conclusion helps the flow. However, in oral presentations, unlike written work, a listener cannot see where one idea ends and another begins; using cohesive strategies to tie ideas together signals movement from one idea to the next.

COHESIVE STRATEGIES
One common cohesive strategy is the use of a *transitional word or phrase and repetition*. Repetition involves repeating a key word, phrase, or idea. Using a transitional word with a repeated word or phrase not only allows the listener to understand a new topic is being introduced, but also signals the relationship between the previous idea and the new idea.

Example
Many of these diseases can linger on a fomite, which is an object like a towel or pillow, which can hold onto viruses for later. That's why you are encouraged to wash your hands during cold season!

In addition to objects, *some viruses are spread by vectors—just think of those as mediums of transmission.*

Another effective method used to establish cohesion is a *full-circle approach*. A full-circle approach is one in which the speaker directly returns to his or her starting point. If the speaker begins with a question, then the question gets restated and answered in the end. This approach allows the listener to fully understand your objective as a speaker, leaving little room for confusion or misunderstanding.

Example
Beginning: You may wonder what makes the Ebola virus different from any other viral infection. **Why is it so deadly**, especially when it is relatively difficult to transmit compared to something like the flu?

Ending: **Why so deadly?** The length of incubation, the fast attack on the body's immune system, and the way in which it attacks the immune system all make it incredibly lethal.

USING VISUALS TO CLARIFY COMPLEX IDEAS
In addition to creating flow in a presentation, it is also critical to provide details and examples and to clarify complex ideas. While clarifying or expanding on an idea is often helpful, it can also lead to more confusion for listeners, especially if the elaboration or clarification is related to a process. When presenting a process, consider using visuals such as images, charts, tables, or other visual content to provide elaboration or clarification on the topic.

Look at the image on the next page. This visual explains the chain of infection and different modes of transmission. Orally explaining each of these processes may lead to some confusion for listeners; however, presenting the information visually demonstrates the different aspects of a complex process.

Go to MyEnglishLab to complete a vocabulary exercise.

EXERCISE 2

A. How do you think ancient viruses (viruses that existed millions of years ago) could affect humans today? Brainstorm some ideas with a partner.

B. Listen to a student presentation about the ancient virus HERV-H. Choose the ways in which this virus has benefitted humans today.

The HERV-H retrovirus:

☐ helped our brains evolve into larger brains

☐ helped develop our personalities

☐ distinguished humans from other animals

☐ promotes tissue development

☐ plays a role in embryonic development

☐ helped us develop treatments for diseases

CHAIN OF INFECTION

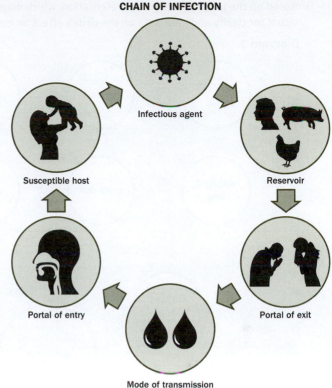

Infectious agent

Reservoir

Susceptible host

Portal of exit

Portal of entry

Mode of transmission

C. Look at the techniques the speaker used to create flow and cohesion. Write the word or phrase the speaker used for each technique.

1. Used a transitional word + repetition to signal a shift in ideas:

   ....

2. Used a full-circle approach:

   beginning: ....

   ending: ....

3. Used a visual to clarify and elaborate:

   ....

D. Based on the information in the presentation, which diagram below would serve as an effective visual for clarify and elaborate on the virus's effect on embryonic development?

Diagram 1

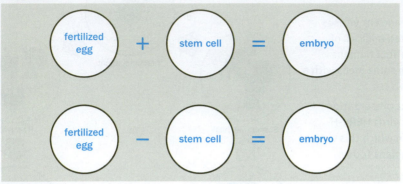

Diagram 2

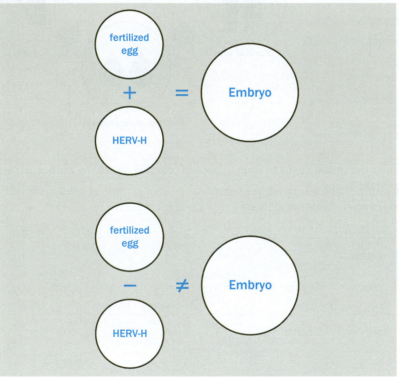

Diagram 3

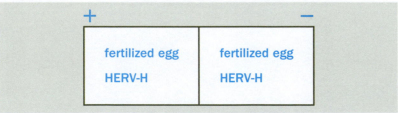

Go to MyEnglishLab to complete a skill practice and join in collaborative activities.

INTEGRATED SKILLS
EXPLAINING A COMPLEX PROCESS

WHY IT'S USEFUL By understanding how to effectively explain a complex process, you can deliver well-organized, coherent, cohesive presentations that is easier for your audience to follow.

Throughout your college career, in addition to listening to process presentations, you may be asked to give one. To prepare a process presentation, you must be able to break down a complex process into smaller, manageable steps, events, or procedures. Demonstrating your understanding of a complex process and its influences on a particular subject or topic is often the goal of a process presentation. Planning is especially critical. A well-thought-out plan will help you deliver an organized, coherent, and cohesive presentation. To create such a plan, follow these steps:

1. Identify your purpose.

Process presentations are informational, and therefore should provide new information to the listeners. Writing a specific purpose statement that conveys the information to be presented along with your objective is the first step.

2. Establish a framework.

The framework refers to the structural organization of your presentation. Will you structure it by events? Steps in a process? Types of process? Milestones?

3. Identify where background information is needed.

What information do your listeners need to fully comprehend the process? For instance, you will need to define key terms, establish the context, or identify the relative importance of the information for your process presentation to be successful.

4. Outline each step, event, or procedure.

To best outline each step, consider using a graphic organizer. A graphic organizer allows you to categorize each element and visually see the relationship between those elements. The style of graphic organizer depends on the information presented. Each step should include precise, concrete language to clearly establish each element. Use transitional words and phrases between each step to alert your listeners that the next step is coming.

5. Identify where visuals are needed.

What information is better explained through a visual? As we saw earlier in this unit, using visuals helps to clarify and elaborate on complex information.

6. Summarize key ideas.

Plan a full-circle approach by restating your objective and highlighting the key steps, events, or procedures and their effect on the overall topic, society, or the world.

Continued

Example

Identify your purpose: *To describe / explain virus origination*

Establish a framework: *Outline three working theories*

Identify needed background information for your listeners: *What is a virus; how is it transmitted*

Outline each step, event, or procedure:

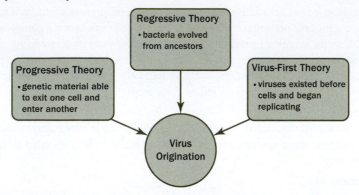

Identify where visual rhetoric may be needed: *Visual for each theory*

Summarize the key ideas: *Objective is to outline key theories of virus origination and their steps*

EXERCISE 3

A. Read the excerpt from a textbook on viral evolution.

Viruses develop genetic variation through mutation. If you compare the amount of genetic material present in a virus to even a simple form of cellular life-like bacteria, viruses seem to require very little genetic material. Because of this comparatively small amount of genetic material, a relatively small mutation can result in a relatively big change in the virus. With a high mutation rate and a large number of copies made per generation, viruses are constantly creating mutated variations of themselves. If those mutations provide any advantage, the copies possessing them can rapidly reproduce and quickly develop new strains. Once a virus is established, it mutates into several different varieties. Beneficial or harmful traits caused by a mutation will have an effect on a virus's reproductive fitness, causing favorable mutations to be passed on and unsuccessful mutations to gradually remove themselves from the population. The cycle continues when successful mutations reproduce. While evolutionary biologists would normally look at these traits in relation to biotic and abiotic factors, the specialized nature of viruses leads us to view traits a bit more narrowly: viral traits affect fitness either *within* the host, the cell being targeted, or *between*-host, everything involving the virus's survival outside of a cell until it can latch on to a target and begin reproduction. *Within-host fitness* tends to focus on how rapidly viruses can reproduce. *Between-host fitness* is tied to how many times a virus can copy itself and how many new hosts a virus is likely to infect.

Natural selection ends up favoring the viruses that can reproduce quickly, within-host, and create many copies, between-host. Reproducing too quickly and creating too many copies could ultimately be counterproductive; a virus so virulent that it kills its host organism or all available host cells before it can spread elsewhere will cease to exist. This also illustrates why the idea that viruses evolved from cellular parasites is so widely accepted. A cellular parasite that, over time, lost extraneous cell structures and developed an ability to use those of a host cell would have been able to reproduce much more efficiently than parasites that still required a complete cellular structure.

A single virus can create thousands upon thousands of copies of itself exceedingly quickly. If a new form of a virus is truly advantageous, it does not take long for it to spread. Genetic divergence can quickly lead to a new viral strain and eventually to what is thought of as a new "species" of virus. The different strains may be similar, but they require different antibodies, they have different levels of virulence, and some transfer from one person to another in different ways. Some strains can even cross species' boundaries.

B. Imagine you and a partner are presenting the process of viral evolution. Complete each of the planning steps.

1. State your purpose.

2. Establish a structure.

3. Determine needed background information.

4. Outline each step.

5. Complete the visual by adding the missing information.

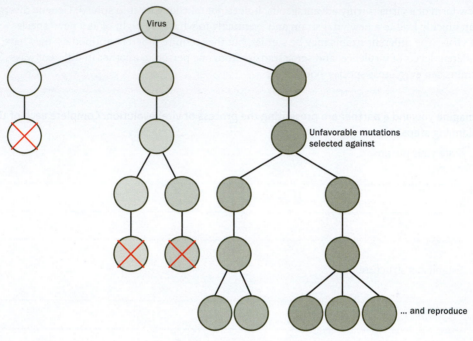

Virus

Unfavorable mutations selected against

... and reproduce

6. Summarize the key ideas.

....

....

....

....

....

D. Present the process of viral evolution. As you listen to each group, take notes about their presentation's structure, background information, and steps.

E. After each presentation, discuss how the presentations were similar and how they were different. Did each group present the same steps?

Go to MyEnglishLab to complete a skill practice.

LANGUAGE SKILL
USING GENERALIZATIONS AND SPECIFICS

WHY IT'S USEFUL By using generalizations and specifics, you can better define key ideas and communicate accurate generic or abstract meanings.

GENERALIZATIONS

A generalization is a broad statement or idea that is used to describe an entire group. Generalizations are often used to introduce, define, and summarize a topic. When introducing a process, you may make a generalization to get the audience's attention.

Example

> Viruses kill.
>
> A virus can be deadly.

In addition to using a generalization to get the audience's attention, generalizations are used to define key terms throughout a process presentation.

Example

> Vector transmission is the transmitting of a virus through a medium, like a mosquito.
>
> Viruses are small infectious organisms that replicate inside host cells.

Last, generalizations are used in a process presentation to summarize key ideas.

Example

> Overall, the Ebola virus is a deadly virus once contracted.

When making a generalization, it is common to use a generic noun or noun phrase. The use of a generic noun or noun phrase is representative of an entire class, a common marker of a definition.

Example

> A virus is a small infectious organism that replicates inside host cells.
>
> Viruses are small infectious organisms that replicate inside host cells.
>
> The mutation of a virus refers to the ability of a virus to break off and change.
>
> Vector transmission is the transmitting of a virus through a medium, like a mosquito.

To form a generic noun or noun phrase, first determine if the noun is count or noncount. There are three ways to form a generalization with count nouns:

Example

1. *a / an* + singular count noun
   A virus is a small infectious organism that replicates inside host cells.

2. no article + plural count noun
   Viruses are small infectious organisms that replicate inside host cells.

3. the + singular count noun
   The mutation of a virus refers to the ability of a virus to break off and change.

Notice the use of *the* in the third example. Abstract generics use *the*. They represent an entire class of objects, while a concrete noun, which uses *a/an* or no article, refers to one representative of the class.

Example

> Abstract: **The fear** of nuclear warfare has been replaced by the fear of viral warfare.
>
> Concrete: **A fear** of viral warfare is realistic in today's world.

There is one way to form a generalization with a noncount noun: no article + noncount noun.

> **Water** is a vector transmitter.

SPECIFICS

Unlike generalizations, specifics refer to a precise, or particular, noun by using *the* before the noun.

Examples

- When something is mentioned for a second time
  Viruses have been around longer than man. **The virus** we are going ….
- When using an indicator of a specific (*principal, one, only, time* …)
  The principal reason for the outbreak was …
- When there is known shared knowledge
  The common cold virus is a good example of airborne transmission.

EXERCISE 4

A. Complete the excerpt from a lecture on the common cold. Add *a/an*, *the*, or *X* (no article).

.... cold is a contagious viral infection. While there are dozens of viruses lumped under the name "common cold," .... term usually refers to some form of rhinovirus. This virus reproduces within the respiratory tract—making it easy to transmit through .... sneezes, a handshake, a shared pen, or a kiss with .... infected person. Since the disease is unpleasant but rarely debilitating, infected people tend to go about their business in public—making it easy for you to catch .... cold from them! Once infected, the virus may take a few days to show .... symptoms. Then, you feel that itch in your throat, develop a stuffy nose, and may even run a slight fever. It usually runs its course in 5–10 days. However, due to the virus's small size and relative durability you can spread it to .... unwary victim who comes into contact with you, or an infected item. That is the main reason the virus is so widespread. Then, ... vicious cycle continues until infecting those who haven't been mindful of handwashing. .... handwashing is the best way to protect yourself against .... rhinovirus.

B. Using the excerpt, write down one generalization that defines something.

....

C. Using the excerpt, complete the tasks.

1. Write down one sentence that contains a specific with a second mention.

....

2. Write down one sentence that contains a specific with an indicator.

....

3. Write down one sentence that contains a specific, due to shared knowledge.

....

Go to **MyEnglishLab** to complete a skill practice.

APPLY YOUR SKILLS

WHY IT'S USEFUL By applying the skills you have learned in this unit, you can effectively identify and understand complex processes, evaluate the flow of a process presentation, and organize your own process presentation.

ASSIGNMENT

You will prepare a process presentation on the transmission, symptoms, and treatment of an infectious disease.

BEFORE YOU LISTEN

A. Discuss these questions with one or more students.

1. What are some fears that people have regarding viruses?

2. How has the media portrayed mass viral infections?

3. What is a zombie? How are they depicted on TV and in movies?

4. What connections exist between zombies and mass viral infections?

CULTURE NOTE

Zombies *Zombies are a common sight in horror films, TV shows, and books. Zombies are undead beings that are created through the reanimation of a human body. It is commonly believed, by zombie fans that reanimation occurs through exposure to a virus.*

B. You will listen to a lecture on the "zombie virus," investigating its origin, infection, progress, and potential prevention measures. Keep these questions in mind as you listen to the lecture.

1. What do zombie viruses represent?

2. In theory, how can someone become infected with a zombie virus?

3. How can zombies possibly have movement and animation if they are dead?

4. What needs to happen for humanity's survival chances to increase and halt the zombie virus?

C. Review the Unit Skills Summary. As you listen to the lecture and begin preparing your presentation, apply the skills you learned in this unit.

UNIT SKILLS SUMMARY

Understand the steps of a process.
- Identify the purpose of a process presentation.
- Distinguish between different organizational structures.
- Identify the function of each step.

Analyze the flow of a process presentation.
- Use cohesive devices.
- Identify and use repetition.
- Recognize and utilize the full-circle method.
- Use visuals to elaborate on and clarify complex processes.

Explain a complex process.
- Identify your purpose.
- Establish the framework.
- Identify where background knowledge is needed.
- Outline key steps.
- Identify where visuals would be helpful.
- Summarize key ideas.

Utilize generalizations and specifics.
- Distinguish between general and specific statements.
- Use generalizations to frame an introduction, definition, or summary.

LISTEN

A. Listen to the lecture on the "zombie virus" and take notes. As you listen, determine the processes of infection and zombification.

B. Reread the questions from Before You Listen, Part B. Is there anything you cannot answer? What listening skills can you use to help find the answers?

Go to MyEnglishLab to listen again and answer critical thinking questions.

THINKING CRITICALLY

Discuss the questions with another student.

1. How does the professor describe the process of infection? Determine three steps involved in the process.

2. How does the professor describe the complex process of zombification? Determine three events or steps that occur in the process.

THINKING VISUALLY

A. Using information from the lecture and what you know about visuals, create a visual that shows the process of infection.

B. Compare your visual with a classmate's.

TIP

Presenters use different types of visual aids such as pie charts, line graphs, bar graphs, and diagrams to convey and illustrate information. For ideas on the the best type of visual to use with your information, see ENGINEERING, Part 1.

THINKING ABOUT LANGUAGE

Listen to the excerpts from the lecture. After the end of each excerpt, determine whether it is a generalization or specific statement. If it is a generalization, restate it in a different way.

1. generalization   specific statement   ....

2. generalization   specific statement   ....

3. generalization   specific statement   ....

4. generalization   specific statement   ....

INDIVIDUAL PRESENTATION

A. Read and discuss the question with a small group.

During the lecture, the professor outlined the origin, the way to become infected, the result of infection, and potential preventive measures and cures. Why do you think this lecture was organized like this? Is there another way the lecture could have been organized?

B. You will prepare a presentation on an infectious disease for your class. Research the disease you wish to present. Consider these questions as you research and prepare.

1. How will you define the disease?

2. What is its origin, if known?

3. How does a person become infected with it?

4. What are the symptoms of this disease?

5. Is this disease curable? If so, what is the cure?

6. What, if any, are preventive measures that can be taken to avoid contracting the disease?

C. Listen to each presentation.

Listen to the presentations and take notes. Discuss how effectively each presenter explained the disease and the process of infection and cure.

Go to MyEnglishLab to listen to Professor Siegel and to complete a self-assessment.

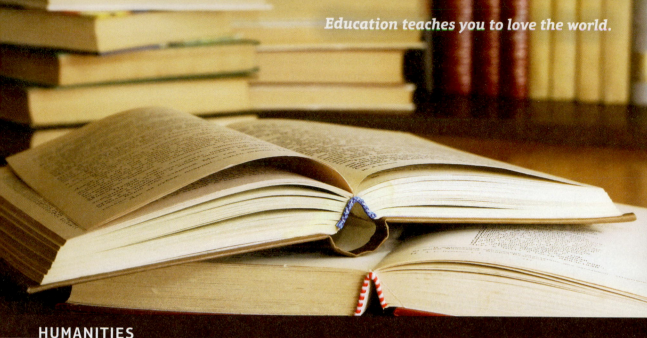

Education teaches you to love the world.

HUMANITIES

Analogies

UNIT PROFILE

In this unit you will learn how the study of literature helps us to understand the world better. You will also learn how well-known authors like Hannah Arendt and Mary Shelley use literature to reflect their ideas regarding education, morality, and shared experiences.

You will prepare a group presentation on how a classic work of literature has influenced the world today.

OUTCOMES

• Identify and use analogies

• Use metaphors and similes

• Make assumptions and identify false assumptions

• Assess the quality of a conclusion

• Recognize and use colloquial language

GETTING STARTED

▶ Go to MyEnglishLab to listen to Professor Harrison and to complete a self-assessment.

Discuss these questions with a partner or group.

1. Do you think there is a connection between the study of humanities (literature, philosophy, art, and history) and one's sense of self in the world?

2. What are some ways that literature might help in the development of responsible citizenship?

3. In his introduction, Professor Harrison refers to the value of self-education. What do you think are some ways in which one can become self-educated? What could be the benefits of a self-education?

For more about **HUMANITIES**, see ❶ ❸. See also Ⓡ and Ⓦ **HUMANITIES** ❶ ❷ ❸.

CRITICAL THINKING SKILL
IDENTIFYING AND USING ANALOGIES

WHY IT'S USEFUL By recognizing analogies in academic presentations and discussions, you can better understand dense, complex information being presented. By using analogies, you can help your listeners understand and relate to abstract information more easily.

In academic presentations and discussions, speakers use a wide variety of techniques to engage their listeners. They may tell a story, pose a hypothetical situation, or ask a question. Or, they may make an analogy. An **analogy** is a comparison between two ideas or things that appear quite dissimilar. With an analogy, the speaker makes a reference to something familiar or easily understood in order to illustrate or explain something else.

Speakers incorporate analogies into their presentations and lectures for many reasons. First, analogies often help listeners better understand theoretical ideas. By using a comparison that the listeners can relate to and understand, the speaker makes a complex idea simple. Additionally, analogies help to bridge information gaps. Presenting complex information in a way that the listener can understand helps the listener connect the information to knowledge they may already have.

Metaphors and similes are two ways in which an analogy can be made. A **metaphor** is a figure of speech that communicates a likeness between two ideas, things, or people. When you use a metaphor, you are essentially saying that something *is* something else. For example, *I love this book. It's a real gem!* In this case, the speaker feels the book is as valuable, or as precious, as a jewel. A **simile** compares two unlike things, ideas, or people in order to create a new meaning. The words *like* or *as* are used in a simile. For example, *This essay is like a diamond in the rough.* This sentence compares a piece of writing with a diamond that hasn't been cleaned yet. With both metaphors and similes, we are able to get a clearer, more definitive understanding of the speaker's meaning.

When speakers make an analogy, the listener is often required to make an assumption or draw a conclusion based on the information presented. An **assumption** is something that is believed to be true without the presence of concrete evidence. Assumptions are generally based on what we already know, coupled with the information that can be inferred.

Using analogies in spoken discourse often involves colloquial language. Colloquial language or **colloquialisms** are words and phrases that are quite informal and often used in daily life. If a friend tells you that they are "in a pickle," that means that are experiencing a conflict or some sort of trouble. Many of these colloquialisms are phrases that first appeared in works of literature and have been adapted to daily life.

NOTICING ACTIVITY

Go to MyEnglishLab to complete a vocabulary exercise.

A. Listen to a lecture about Hannah Arendt. As you listen, notice the analogies the professor uses. What assumptions are being made?

B. Now listen to two students discussing assumptions made by the lecturer. What assumptions do they mention?

Go to MyEnglishLab to complete a skill practice and join in collaborative activities.

SUPPORTING SKILL 1
USING METAPHORS AND SIMILES

WHY IT'S USEFUL By distinguishing between metaphors and similes, you can better understand comparisons made in spoken discourse. By incorporating metaphors and similes in your own speech, you can add variety to your language and help your listeners better understand complex concepts.

Metaphors and similes draw comparisons between two concepts. They are common in spoken discourse because they engage the listeners' imaginations and help them to draw connections. Metaphors and similes are often confused; however, there are distinct differences between them.

METAPHORS

Metaphors describe something by comparing it with another thing that appears unrelated. These comparisons are *implied*, rather than stated directly. The listener needs to make an inference regarding the concepts being compared. Once an inference is made, the metaphor creates a strong image in the listeners' minds.

Examples

A teacher is a coach or tour guide.
He is a monster.
Education is light.

SIMILES

Similes, like metaphors, compare two things. However, the comparison is *direct*, using the words *like* or *as*. The listener does not need to make an inference because the speaker has already done so. Using similes makes your presentations more descriptive and creative. They also emphasize key ideas by conveying vivid descriptions.

Examples

A teacher is like a coach or tour guide.
He is like a monster.
Education is like a light—it shows the way toward potential opportunities.

Strong speakers incorporate both metaphors and similes to aid in persuading their listeners. Because metaphors and similes are often memorably worded, these phrases add depth to a viewpoint, thus making an emotional appeal—enhancing both a speaker's perspective and credibility.

EXERCISE 1

Go to MyEnglishLab to complete a vocabulary exercise.

A. **What do you think of when someone says the name *Frankenstein*? Brainstorm some words or ideas.**

Frankenstein

CULTURE NOTE

Frankenstein *The full title of Mary Shelley's novel is* Frankenstein; or, The Modern Prometheus. *The title refers to the ancient Greek mythological character Prometheus, who created humans out of clay. Similarly, in Shelley's novel, the scientist Dr. Victor Frankenstein decides to create a man. He works day and night, but when he finally achieves his goal, he is filled with fear at the monstrous creation he has brought into the world. Dr. Frankenstein flees, the monster disappears, and trouble ensues throughout the city.*

Although the monster was never given a name in the novel, he is now popularly known as Frankenstein, after his creator.

B. **Share your ideas with a classmate. Together, generate a list of characteristics.**

....

....

....

....

C. **Listen to a student presentation on Mary Shelley. As you listen, complete each phrase. Which are metaphors, and which are similes? Choose the correct figure of speech.**

	Metaphor	Simile
1. Frankenstein is	☐	☐
2. Mary Shelley felt	☐	☐
3. Reading was her	☐	☐
4. Mary felt like her heart	☐	☐
5. Mary felt like a	☐	☐

D. **For each metaphor that you found in Part C, write down the inference being made.**

....

....

E. **Compare your answers with a partner. Can you turn the similes into metaphors? Can you turn the metaphors into similes?**

Go to MyEnglishLab to complete a skill practice and join in collaborative activities.

Analogies   129

SUPPORTING SKILL 2
MAKING ASSUMPTIONS

WHY IT'S USEFUL By making assumptions when listening to a discussion or presentation, you can better relate the topic to your prior knowledge and experience, creating a more complete assessment of the topic. You can also determine the validity of an argument.

Active listening involves making assumptions. **Assumptions** are things that are believed to be true, without explicit proof. It is common for professors to encourage students to make assumptions during a lecture or an academic discussion in order to anticipate possible topics. To make an effective assumption, brainstorm what you already know about a topic. When you brainstorm, you are developing assumptions between what you already know and what you anticipate hearing. Listen carefully to the lecturer, and determine the meaning of what is being said. Are the assumptions you made prior to the lecture accurate? Can you draw a connection between your assumptions and the main ideas of the lecture? **Anticipating** what might be said is an important part of listening because it allows you to assess what you already know about a topic and test the accuracy of the information.

Identifying false assumptions is also a critical part of listening. A false assumption, or a **fallacy**, is an incorrect belief that is based on an unsound argument. It may appear logical and sound convincing; however, there is no proof that it is true. Many times these statements are overgeneralizations. There are several different types of fallacious arguments. Three of the most common include bandwagon, antiquity, and authority.

A *bandwagon fallacy* is one that attempts to convince an audience that something is true because so many people believe it. An *antiquity fallacy* is one that argues that something must be true because it has been believed to be true for a long time. An *authority fallacy* is one which uses a person of authority to falsely support an idea. Remaining an active listener helps you to make and test your own assumptions and to identify any false assumptions or fallacies.

Examples

Assumption:

Professor: Our topic today is Mary Shelley's *Frankenstein*.
Student: Is it really good to try to create a living person?
Human behavior can't be learned by a machine.

Fallacies:

People believe that the more education one gets, the more money one earns later in life.
My parents say that education isn't for everyone.

EXERCISE 2

Go to MyEnglishLab to complete a vocabulary exercise.

A. How are monsters and humans different? Complete the chart with some assumptions about each.

Monsters	Humans

B. Share your ideas with a classmate. Do your lists contain similar items?

C. Listen to a presentation on the novel *Frankenstein*. Take notes as you listen, and check your assumptions.

D. Share your notes with a partner. Answer the questions.

1. Does the speaker make any assumptions? If so, what assumptions?

2. Does the speaker's presentation contain any fallacies? If so, write them under the correct heading.

Bandwagon Fallacy	Antiquity Fallacy	Authority Fallacy

Go to MyEnglishLab to complete a skill practice and join in collaborative activities.

INTEGRATED SKILLS
ASSESSING THE QUALITY OF A CONCLUSION

WHY IT'S USEFUL By assessing the quality of a conclusion, you can make a more informed decision when choosing to support or refute the ideas being presented.

Conclusions are a critical part of making an argument. Because they are the final words heard, they leave a lasting impression. Listeners and readers alike remember how something ends. Conclusions not only summarize the key points, but they also should provide closure to the listeners or readers and initiate an audience response.

An effective conclusion *summarizes key points* by explicitly restating the main ideas in concrete terms. Terms used to introduce summary statements include *to sum up, to recap, in brief, in sum*. The statements following these terms are specific to the content of the speech, lecture, or text, rather than general. General, broad statements in a conclusion are often considered weak and do not appeal to the audience.

Providing closure, or cueing the audience that the presentation is over, is a second critical function of a conclusion. One technique for providing closure is bookending. **Bookending** is when you connect the ending to the beginning. If you asked a question in the introduction, answer it in the conclusion. If you told a story in the introduction, revisit it in the conclusion.

Last, quality conclusions *initiate an audience response*. What should the audience do with the information presented? What change are you asking them to make? What new knowledge do you want them to have? What specific actions do you want the audience to take? This is often referred to as "the takeaway." The final words should challenge the audience to take concrete action.

Examples

Summarizing Key Points

To recap, Mary Shelley's *Frankenstein* illustrates how education not only provides humans with knowledge and higher-order reasoning but develops in us the desire to connect with others.

Providing Closure

Introduction: What purpose does a university serve in a journey from childhood ignorance toward a mature love of the world?

Conclusion: A university experience allows you to begin that shift toward a purposeful excellence under the guidance of wise, helpful mentors. All of the resources of the university are available to you, aiding you in this task. The bottom line here is, you get to make this shift toward a greater responsibility in the company of your peers who have chosen to do the same.

Audience Response

Today we looked at how and why education needs to play a role in civic responsibility. What changes are *you* willing to make so we can move toward a more responsible citizenry?

EXERCISE 3

Go to MyEnglishLab to complete a vocabulary exercise.

A. Read the script for a presentation on the value of the literary classics.

What can be learned from books that were published hundreds and hundreds of years ago? How can these works published hundreds of years ago be relevant in today's society? In the 20th century, a number of scholars, publishers, and businessmen began campaigning for a college curriculum built around the "Great Books" of Western literature. Some viewed this as an almost political cause, as they tried to create a clearly defined oasis of high culture in a world where radio, film, and television were overtaking the printed word as the dominant medium. Others wished to share the classics that had touched their lives and spoke to them in a meaningful way. Finally, a small but crucial portion of this movement simply looked forward to selling America a fifty-volume, hardback set of fancy-looking books—conveniently payable in monthly installments. Adherents of this philosophy spread throughout America, some finding surprising influence. Numerous colleges and universities, seeking to distinguish themselves, crafted "Great Books Curricula," creating an entire college education that looked at the world through the lens of past thinkers.

This occurred only a few decades ago, but conventional wisdom tells us that such a curriculum would be an impossibly hard sell in the present age. There seem to be more immediate, desperate concerns that rule out a college life of contemplation. Still, the Great Books curriculum remains in use at a number of small, private colleges spread throughout the United States. A dedicated group of learners from diverse backgrounds still seek out a book-centric education. Despite all the changes of society and technology witnessed in just the opening years of the 21st century, something still draws people toward these relics of another era. What, exactly, do the classics offer that you can't find anywhere else? If the books do truly offer something special, why is it so hard to get most students interested in them?

Perhaps what those book-loving students have, and what people in earlier eras also possessed, was a desire and willingness to meet the classics on their own terms. This quality was omnipresent in the years between Gutenberg and Marconi, when the printed word was the most convenient and portable method of encountering big ideas and bringing your mind into another realm. While even this era, of course, would have had students stuck reading things at times that held no

> **CULTURE NOTE**
> **Great Inventors** *Gutenberg and Marconi were both inventors whose inventions changed the world. Johannes Gutenberg is credited with printing the first book in Europe with his printing press. Guglielmo Marconi invented the radio telegraph system.*

interest for them, in general people read something because they wanted to read something. You read Cervantes because you wanted to read Cervantes. He was a respite from the world and an escape into the realm of the imagination. Now, all too often, a student reads a summary of Cervantes, merely to parrot back on a test how one is supposed to feel upon reading Cervantes. All this without ever once opening *Don Quixote*—and teachers are grateful that even *this* level of engagement can be coaxed out of a student!

If we are to argue that the classics have value, and I truly believe that they do, that value cannot be wrung out of them with all available efficiency. That value cannot be distilled from them and rapidly plunged into the ready minds of young learners in the space of a single lecture. No, such shortcuts have no place when it comes to the classics. All the more reason to embrace these classics and engage learners to delve into them. To borrow an old cliché—one that is no less true for its overuse—it is about the journey, not the destination; students and, especially, those who develop their education, would do well to remember it.

To recap, the 20th century movement of a few to enhance our educational systems through inclusion of the classics has ignited a passion in many today. The value of reading classic literature to develop thinkers and foster innovative ideas cannot be denied. In a society where print is becoming more and more obsolete, it's time to pick up the great novel and take the journey. Let's stop talking and texting so much and *think* for a change! Perhaps the problems of civilization could be neatly solved in an afternoon.

B. With a partner, answer the questions.

1. What main points of the presentation does the writer summarize in the conclusion?

2. Does the writer provide closure? If so, how?

3. Does the writer ask the audience to respond in some way? If so, how?

C. Do you agree or disagree with the writer's views? Why or why not? What other benefits come from reading books written in different time periods?

D. Read the presentation excerpt below. Use what you have learned to write a quality conclusion.

Education has a transformative power. As children grow and develop, they naturally become more aware of the world around them, more empathetic toward others, and more willing to take on responsibility. According to several researchers, education calibrates a child's sense of self. They can better understand their role in the world and become an adult who can realize his or her full potential.

Cultural norms vary from culture to culture, and these norms impact educational practices. Thus, there are variations in what it means to be an empathetic, responsible citizen in the community. One thing is known for sure: All true education draws a learner toward more responsibility and trains that learner to better interact with his or her peers, appropriately for one's culture.

....

....

....

....

Go to MyEnglishLab to complete a skill practice.

For more about QUALITY CONCLUSIONS, see W HUMANITIES 1.

LANGUAGE SKILL
COLLOQUIAL LANGUAGE

WHY IT'S USEFUL By identifying and deciphering colloquialisms in spoken discourse, you can better comprehend the message being delivered. By incorporating colloquialisms into your own speech, you can make a more vivid appeal to your listeners.

When analogies are made, colloquial language is often used. Colloquial language, or colloquialisms, are informal phrases and sentences that are common in daily life. Many colloquial expressions are not literal usages of the words but metaphorical usages. Like metaphors, they are often used to create a more vivid visual image in the listeners' minds. They are frequently used in works of literature to create a sense of authenticity and paint a clear picture. However, when you write formal papers, colloquialisms are generally unacceptable unless in dialogue form.

Colloquialisms fall under two major categories: phrasal colloquialisms and aphorisms. *Phrasal colloquialisms* are phrases while *aphorisms* are sentences. Below is a small list. Can you add others?

Colloquialism	Meaning
a can of worms	problematic
a lemon	no good, not reliable
ace it	do very well
all ears	listening / paying attention
back to the drawing board	begin again
caught in the crosshairs	stuck in the middle
doesn't cut it	isn't good enough
get a fix	get something you need
on the edge of one's seat	waiting for more; anxious
pass the buck	not take responsibility
He is larger than life.	He is very impressive.
He wasn't born yesterday.	He's not easily fooled.
It fits like a glove.	It's perfect.
Let's call it a day.	Let's stop or cease what we're doing.
She's bent out of shape.	She's annoyed or irritated with something.
That drives me up the wall.	That is something that I don't like. It really gets on my nerves.
We're behind her.	We support her.

Examples

When Mary Shelley began writing *Frankenstein*, her goal was to create a character **larger than life**.

Mary Shelley's husband felt that her writing didn't always **cut it**. Thus, he edited her original draft voraciously.

When Arendt spoke to the auditorium of university students, they were **all ears** and **on the edge of their seats**.

EXERCISE 4

A. Read the presentation excerpt below.

> Reading great literature often leaves you on the edge of your seat. When writers create characters larger than life, readers often get lost in the pages of the book. They begin to understand new worlds and slip away. In addition to the pure pleasure that we associate with reading, great stories can also make waves within a society. They can serve as a catalyst for change. When readers engage with gutsy characters who meet challenges head on, they often dig deep within themselves to find the same kind of strength.

B. Rewrite the excerpt by changing the informal colloquial language into more formal language.

_____

_____

_____

_____

_____

_____

_____

_____

C. Work with a partner. Give the modified presentation to your partner.

Go to MyEnglishLab to complete a skill practice.

APPLY YOUR SKILLS

WHY IT'S USEFUL By applying the skills you have learned in this unit, you can better understand how to form analogies and when to use them. You can also recognize the importance of making assumptions and analyzing the quality of a conclusion. By deciphering colloquial language, you can understand the formality of someone's discourse and make your own discourse more vivid.

> ### ASSIGNMENT
> Prepare a group presentation on a classic work of literature, a novel, poetry, a play, or an essay that has influence in the world today.

BEFORE YOU LISTEN

A. Discuss the questions with one or more students.

1. How do you think classic literature influences governmental infrastructures, such as education?

2. What role does literature play in advocating for changes in society?

3. Do you think other forms of art, such as visual art or theater, have the same impact on society as literature? Why or why not?

B. You will listen to a lecture on the importance of literature in developing a love of the world. As you listen, think about these questions.

1. Why do so many argue for the inclusion of the humanities in education?

2. What connection does the lecturer draw between humanity and literature?

3. How are Mary Shelley and Hannah Arendt similar?

4. According to the lecture, what is the main argument for the study of literature?

C. Review the Unit Skills Summary. As you listen to the lecture and begin preparing your group presentation, apply the skills you learned in this unit.

UNIT SKILLS SUMMARY

RECOGNIZE AND UTILIZE ANALOGIES:

Identify and understand metaphors and similes.
- Determine the meaning of metaphors and similes.
- Analyze the structural differences.
- Interpret the reasons a speaker is using a metaphor or simile.

Identify assumptions.
- Determine credible assumptions.
- Identify and assess fallacies by recognizing false generalizations.

Determine the quality of a conclusion.
- Identify restated main ideas.
- Recognize the closure of an idea.
- Predict audience response.

Identify and interpret colloquial language.
- Recognize colloquial language in speech and text.
- Deduce the meaning of colloquial expressions.
- Conclude why a speaker is using a colloquial expression.

LISTEN

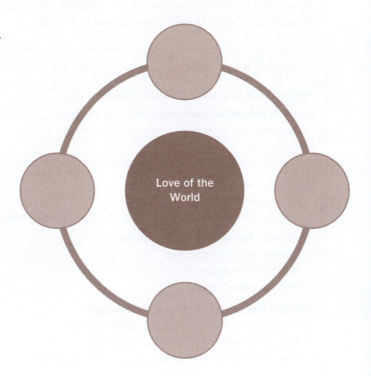 A. Listen to the lecture about the value of studying literature. Take notes as you listen.

B. Reread the discussion questions from Before You Listen, Part B. Is there anything you cannot answer? What listening skills can you use to help find the answers?

Go to MyEnglishLab to listen again and answer critical thinking questions.

THINKING CRITICALLY

Discuss the questions with another student.

1. How does the accumulation of facts differ from real learning?

2. What connection does Hannah Arendt make between human brutality and education? Do you agree? Why or why not?

3. Do you think there are other fields of study that instill the same sense of "love for the world" into people? Why or why not?

THINKING VISUALLY

A. Using information from the lecture, determine the elements of a humanities education that help to form a "love of the world."

B. Compare your chart with a classmate's.

Love of the World

THINKING ABOUT LANGUAGE

Read an excerpt from the lecture.

For Mary Shelley, then, literature is a bridge—something that builds a connection between our lived experiences and the shared experience of humanity. Hannah Arendt hit upon a similar insight when she developed *amor mundi*, love of the world, in her own writings. Mary Shelley distinguished knowledge, which Victor Frankenstein possessed in great quantity, from meaningful experience and human connection, which the Monster sought; the implication of the book is that, had Victor been more connected to the world and the human experience, he would not have made so many terrible mistakes.

Arendt made a similar distinction—knowledge, representing the accumulation of facts and skills, differed greatly from education, which was the process in which a young learner grows into the world while becoming aware of its complexity and taking up the responsibility of improving it. Arendt had experienced the monstrous brutality of industrialized society in World War II; she knew all too well from her analysis of war criminals that knowledge without humanity or empathy could lead to terrible things.

B. Give a summary of the excerpt to a partner, using colloquialisms.

SMALL GROUP PRESENTATION

A. Read and discuss the following questions with a small group.

Western philosophy and literature have created social change by developing a greater awareness of our world and by igniting innovation and action. Thinking of your own culture, has it been influenced by the humanities? How has it been influenced?

B. With a small group, research a classic work of literature that has influenced society. Be prepared to illustrate how the theme of the work you selected has influenced our world today. Remember to plan an effective conclusion for your presentation.

1. What is the work you will research?

2. What are the characteristics of the theme that are relevant to modern society?

3. How can you best conclude your presentation?

C. Listen to each small group presentation.

Listen carefully to each presentation. Take notes on each presentation and discuss how each presenter presented his or her ideas and concluded effectively.

▶ Go to MyEnglishLab to listen to Professor Harrison and to complete a self-assessment.

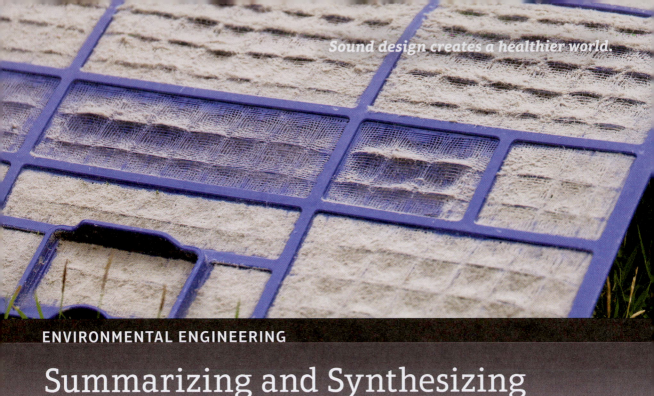
Sound design creates a healthier world.

ENVIRONMENTAL ENGINEERING

Summarizing and Synthesizing

UNIT PROFILE

In this unit, you will learn about civil engineering and "green" building. You will specifically explore the dangers of indoor air pollution and the systems that can improve indoor air quality.

You will prepare a group presentation on building systems and government regulations.

OUTCOMES

• Summarize and synthesize research
• Select suitable research to support your ideas
• Present integrated research
• Understand and present a research report
• Cite sources of academic references in presentations, speeches, or discussions

GETTING STARTED

▶ Go to MyEnglishLab to listen to Professor Hildemann and to complete a self-assessment.

Discuss these questions with a partner or group.

1. What do you see in the photo above? What is its purpose, and what is the current problem with it?

2. What is indoor air pollution? What are the dangers of indoor air pollution?

3. In the introduction, Professor Hildemann states that "As families the world over begin living in 'energy efficient' homes, people are encountering new problems caused by a lack of air circulation." What do you think are the reasons this might happen?

For more about **ENVIRONMENTAL ENGINEERING**, see 1 3. See also R and W **ENVIRONMENTAL ENGINEERING** 1 2 3.

CRITICAL THINKING SKILL
SUMMARIZING AND SYNTHESIZING RESEARCH

WHY IT'S USEFUL By understanding how to summarize and synthesize academic research, you will better support your ideas in discussions and presentations. Supporting your ideas with expert evidence gives you more credibility as a speaker.

Professors typically require students to summarize information from both written and oral sources. **Summarizing research** is an essential skill for college success. It involves distinguishing important ideas from unimportant ones and combining these main ideas in an organized and meaningful way. Summarizing shows your understanding of a topic. In academic prose, however, not all main ideas are explicitly stated; sometimes they are implied. It is necessary to fully understand the text in order to accurately determine the main ideas.

Once you have determined the main ideas of your sources, it is necessary to synthesize the research. **Synthesizing research** involves comparing and contrasting information from multiple sources and looking for similarities and differences in both the data and perspective in order to arrive at newer and more fully formed versions of your own ideas.

Summarizing and synthesizing research not only shows your understanding of the information, but it also plays an essential role in supporting your ideas. **Using research to support your own** ideas gives you more credibility as a speaker. Credibility creates trust in your audience which makes it easier for them to accept your ideas and assertions.

Summarizing and synthesizing research and using it to support your ideas are the initial steps of developing a strong academic presentation. The final step is **presenting your research** in a well-organized manner and integrating it into your own ideas with appropriate language. By explicitly linking your ideas to the research, you will create a more interesting and convincing presentation. By using visuals such as charts, graphs, and diagrams to illustrate data, you will not only keep your audience engaged, but you will also make the content easier for your audience to comprehend. Better comprehension often leads to audience support, or agreement.

NOTICING ACTIVITY

Go to MyEnglishLab to complete a vocabulary exercise.

A. Listen to an academic discussion on indoor air quality. As you listen, notice where and how each speaker references the reading they are summarizing.

B. Now listen to the students discuss how they summarize. What two suggestions are given about summarizing?

Go to MyEnglishLab to complete a skill practice and join in collaborative activities.

SUPPORTING SKILL 1
SELECTING SUITABLE RESEARCH TO SUPPORT YOUR IDEAS

WHY IT'S USEFUL By using suitable research to support your own ideas, you establish credibility with your audience and demonstrate your ability to identify and utilize sources that reinforce and broaden your ideas.

Using research to support your ideas in presentations, debates, or academic discussions is critical for establishing the **credibility**, or trustworthiness, of your claims with your listeners. Ways in which you can establish credibility include:

- using related research to support your ideas
- using relevant academic sources to demonstrate your reasoning
- using multiple sources to draw conclusions

SELECTING APPROPRIATE SOURCES

When researching, it is important to use reliable sources. Searching on the internet is often helpful and can allow you to get information quickly; however, it does not always return the most valid or accurate information. Professors expect their students to use valid, reliable sources. Researching through your school's library or another library database ensures a return of valid sources. Other ways to establish the reliability of your sources include:

- checking the author's qualifications and affiliations
- confirming the sources of the author's supporting evidence
- determining which organization is sponsoring the content
- establishing the date of publication to ensure that the information is current

Example

> **Your search:** "Indoor air pollution"
>
> **Your returns:** *Today's Problem with Indoor Air Pollution* by Emma Lin. You found this on http://airfiltersforsale.com
>
> Particulate Air Pollution: A Public Health Issue by Dr. Will Kane, Lane University You found this in a journal entitled "American Journal of Public Health"

USING SOURCES TO EFFECTIVELY SUPPORT YOUR IDEAS

Once you have identified which sources are reliable, you need to connect the information you research to the ideas you want to present. You can use research to support your ideas in a number of ways. It can support a statement you want to make, help demonstrate your reasoning, or show how you came to a particular conclusion.

Examples

> **Your idea / statement:** Indoor air pollution is a serious problem in today's world, and it can greatly affect your family's health.
>
> **Source to support:** According to the Occupational Safety and Health Administration, symptoms like headaches, fatigue, trouble concentrating, and even cancer can be linked to poor indoor air quality.

Your reasoning:	Because we spend a large number of our day inside, air ventilation is critical for our nation's health.
Source to support:	Based on current government research, 90% of our time is spent indoors, and our buildings are making us sick.
Your conclusion:	Thus, one possible solution to indoor air pollution is to develop cleaner air filtration systems.
Source to support:	Scientific evidence shows that high-efficiency filtration systems enhance air quality.

EXERCISE 1

Go to MyEnglishLab to complete a vocabulary exercise.

A. What are some causes of indoor air pollution? List your ideas.

B. Share your list with a classmate. Discuss the reasons why you believe the items on your list cause indoor air pollution. How do they impact our health?

C. Listen to a student presentation on indoor air pollution. As you listen, complete the tasks.

1. Choose the reasons the student used sources.
   a. to support speaker's ideas
   b. to show speaker's reasoning
   c. to draw a conclusion

2. Match each source with the reason you chose above.

   .... According to Dr. Scale from the Environmental Protection Agency, while many people assume an energy efficient home is safer because it is better for the environment, it can actually be quite dangerous to the occupants due to indoor air pollution.

   .... Take for instance, research from studies conducted in the United Kingdom. Due to changing energy regulations, many older houses have been retrofitted with modern insulation to be more energy efficient. Problems occurred because many of these houses did not have their ventilation systems upgraded to a similarly high standard.

   .... The EPA supports this by offering numerous guidelines available online to help you estimate your home's hourly air change rate.

D. Compare your answers with those of another student. Did you agree?

Go to MyEnglishLab to complete a skill practice and join in collaborative activities.

SUPPORTING SKILL 2
PRESENTING WELL-INTEGRATED RESEARCH

WHY IT'S USEFUL By understanding how to effectively integrate and present research, you will be able to construct a well-organized presentation that demonstrates your working knowledge of the topic and better communicates your key points to your audience.

The research you present depends on the evidence you need to support your idea. Evidence takes many forms. Determining the best evidence to use helps you deliver the information in an organized manner. Common types of evidence to present include:

- statistics or other numerical data
- quotes from experts or expert sources
- research study summary (*further detailed in Integrated Skills section*)
- survey results summary
- visuals (table, chart, diagram, graph) summary

When presenting research, you must effectively **integrate** it into your presentation to make sure that your listeners can properly absorb it. Placing most of your research in the beginning or at the end of a presentation is often referred to as "dumping" because it shows a lack of cohesion, which and can overwhelm the audience. Proper integration involves balancing ideas with research. One such technique for integration is known as "sandwiching." Sandwiching involves beginning and ending with your idea. Look at these steps.

1. Begin with your idea.
2. Explain your idea.
3. Use a source to support your idea.
4. Restate or explain the source or conclude your idea.

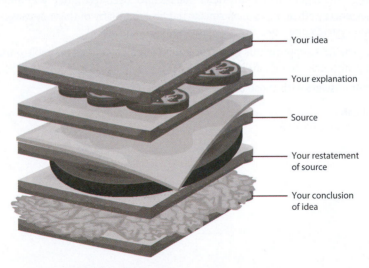

Your idea
Your explanation
Source
Your restatement of source
Your conclusion of idea

Example

> **Your idea:** We see the phrase "energy-efficient home," and we assume the home is green.
>
> **Your explanation:** Well, that is not the case. Energy-efficient homes can actually be more harmful than helpful.

Your research: According to Dr. Scale from the Environmental Protection Agency, while many people assume an energy-efficient home is safer because it is better for the environment, it can actually be quite dangerous to the occupants due to indoor air pollution.

Your restatement / conclusion: That's right. Your energy-efficient home is hurting you.

EXERCISE 2

Go to MyEnglishLab to complete a vocabulary exercise.

A. Imagine you are giving a persuasive presentation on the need for government regulations regarding air ventilation systems in homes. What types of research evidence would you look for? Why? Discuss your ideas with a partner.

B. Listen to a student presentation. Choose the types of evidence used.

    a. statistic or other numerical data

    b. quotation

    c. research summary

    d. survey

    e. visual

C. How was the research in the presentation sandwiched? First, number the sentences in the order in which they were stated in the presentation. Then label each sentence with its purpose: SI = speaker's idea, E = evidence, RS = restatement, EX / C = explain and / or conclude.

.... In other words, we are constantly exposed to these contaminants.

.... There are dozens of common contaminants that, in sufficient quantity, can turn your home or office into a dangerous place.

.... If we take actions to enact policies regarding improved ventilation, homeowners can move towards reducing pollutants and improving air quality.

.... Between 70–90% of our time is spent indoors, according to a research study from a university in the United Kingdom.

D. Listen to the excerpt and check your organization. Were you able to identify the order? Were you able to identify the organizational purposes?

Go to MyEnglishLab to complete a skill practice and join in collaborative activities.

INTEGRATED SKILLS
UNDERSTANDING AND PRESENTING A RESEARCH REPORT

WHY IT'S USEFUL By understanding how to extract key information from a research report, you can better summarize information in a presentation. By using a presentation aid, you can better organize your speeches and keep your audience engaged.

When researching a topic, you will probably come across a research article. A research article is a study that was conducted on a specific topic. There are often several graphs, charts, and tables included. In addition, there are five main sections in a research article. They are:

- abstract
- introduction
- methods
- results / findings
- discussion / recommendations

These reports are often difficult to read. They are dense and include many discipline-specific vocabulary terms. The first step to understanding a research report is to identify the type of information you can find in each section.

Abstract	This section gives a summary of the research and its findings.
Introduction	This section provides background. It states why the research is necessary and presents the goal of the research.
Methods	This section explains the process the author(s) followed. It often includes who, what, where, when, and how.
Results / Findings	This section summarizes the findings. This is where many visuals are found.
Discussion / Recommendations	This section describes what the findings mean, why they are important and what action is recommended as result.

After you have a clear idea of what you can find in each section, read the research study. Begin with the introduction. Save the abstract for last, since it is very concise, and many key ideas may be left out. However, do not disregard it all together. Reading the abstract last may help you check your understanding of the most important concepts in the article.

Once you have identified sources and extracted key information, it is time to put your presentation together. When giving a presentation, there are some general tips to ensure your success:

- prepare and practice
- vary the pitch of your voice
- make eye contact with the audience
- do not read your presentation
- provide signposts
- cite your sources, orally and in written form
- provide a visually stimulating presentation

To prepare a visually stimulating presentation, consider using a presentation aid. Presentation aids can help you communicate your ideas in an appealing visual manner. Presentation software like PowerPoint® and Prezi not only help you better organize your ideas, but also enhance your audience's experience, increase their understanding, maintain their attention, and illustrate your process. When creating visual aids, it is important to consider:

- amount of text on each screen
- use of images
- choice of font
- choice of color
- inclusion of citations

Examples

This first example has too much text and the images are distracting.

Necessity of Air Filtration Systems

- Current issues
- Common ailments
- Solutions

This second example is a simple, well-organized slide.

EXERCISE 3

A. Read the short research study. Notice the information presented in the different sections of the report.

Abstract:

This study investigated 124 homes in four climate zones to evaluate the effectiveness and variation in air ventilation systems through measuring the air change rate (ACR) in communal living spaces. Little variation in ACRs exist when updated mechanical balanced air ventilation systems are installed.

Introduction:

In today's world, homes need to be both energy efficient and well ventilated. Energy efficiency and ventilation can be achieved by using updated mechanical ventilation systems. By installing this type of system, homes can decrease their air change rate, creating less variation in temperatures (Homes, Tent 2008 and McArt 2012). However, new technologies do not always produce the same result in different homes. Variables such as a home's location greatly affect the air change rate (Tent, et. al). By analyzing the communal living space in four different climates, ventilation requirements are determined, and efficient and appropriate ventilation systems can be selected.

Methods:

During September 2015–November 2015, 124 homes were evaluated. The homes were located in four climate zones in the United States. These climate temperatures are provided in the table.

Zone	Climate	Median Temperatures During Period of Study
One	Hot–humid	93°F / 110% relative humidity
Two	Mixed–humid	72°F / 70% relative humidity
Three	Cold	64°F / 30% relative humidity
Four	Mixed–dry	91°F / 10% relative humidity

The homes ranged between 1800 square feet and 2100 square feet. All homes had four occupants and one pet. The median age of the homes studied was 1.25 years old. A communal living space, such as a family room, was studied. For each home, the median room was 800 cubic feet. All homes had balanced mechanical ventilation systems. The two most common balanced systems, as diagrammed here, bring equal quantities of air in and out of the home.

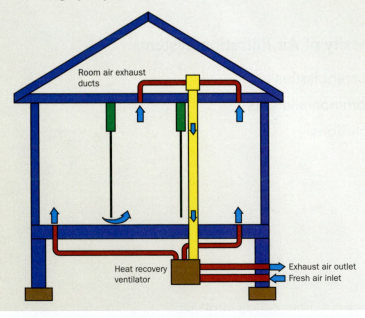

Room air exhaust ducts

Heat recovery ventilator

Exhaust air outlet
Fresh air inlet

These systems are referred to as energy recovery ventilation (known as ERV) and heat recovery ventilation (known as HRV). ERVs dehumidify air by reducing moisture in warmer months and adding moisture in cooler months. HRVs transfer heat from either incoming or exhaust air, depending on residents' desire.

The air change rate (ACR) of the communal living spaces was measured six times per day. The ACR was measured at:

ACR = 60 X CFM/V (1)

CFM = air flow through the room (cubic feet per minute)

V = volume of the room (cubic feet)

Results:

In living spaces, ACRs averaged .73 ± .76 h.

Zone	Air Change Rate Average
One	.73
Two	.74
Three	.745
Four	.76

Outdoor temperatures varied smoothly from about 65°F to about 94°F.

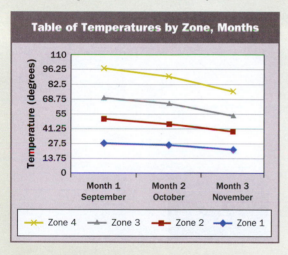

Recommendations:

The results of this study indicate that very little fluctuation occurred based on climate when a new energy-efficient balance system was used. When planning the ventilation system for a room, architects and engineers must consider the natural airflow of the room and the placement of mechanical ventilation systems to the location of the room relative to the rest of the structure. The concept of hourly air change rate (ACR) can be used to help provide a quantifiable way to measure ventilation benchmarks. According to James and Cingello (2014), the average air change rate of a new home is .6 per hour. This is considerably less than the required industry code, but it ensures the residents greater comfort and less exchange of air. Utilizing newer air ventilation systems with balanced exchanges produces a lower air change rate and is not directly affected by climate. Previous studies indicate that older systems are affected by climate and produce great variations in air change rates (Jones 2008, Tempelton 2009, and Yan 2012).

B. **Work with a partner to answer the questions.**

1. Look at the abstract section of the report. What is the purpose of the study? What were the findings?
2. Look at the introduction of the report. Why is the research necessary?
3. Look at the methods section. What was studied? Where were they studied? When were they studied? How were they studied?
4. Look at the results of the report. What was learned?
5. Look at the discussion section. What do these findings mean?

C. **Review the slides that the speaker used to present this material. Are the slides effective? Why or why not?**

Climate and Air Ventilation Systems

Emma Linger

SCI 104

Slide 1

Climate and Air Ventilation Systems

- Introduction:
  - Today's homes need to be energy efficient and well ventilated.
  - Need to install updated mechanical systems can decrease air change rate, creating less variation in temperatures.
  - Variables affect ACR.
  - Four climates
  - Is the demand the same?

Slide 2

Climate and Air Ventilation Systems

- Methods:
    - September 2015 November 2015
    - 124 homes
    - 4 Climate Zones
    - Communal living space (i.e., living room)
    - ACR measured 6 times a day

Slide 3

Climate and Air Ventilation Systems

- Results:
    - ACR averaged .73–.76

Zone	Air Change Rate Average
One	.73
Two	.74
Three	.745
Four	.76

Slide 4

Climate and Air Ventilation Systems

- Recommendation:
  - New balanced systems
  - New industry standards

Slide 5

Climate and Air Ventilation Systems

- Questions?

Slide 6

D. Slide 2 is not effective. Based on the information in the report, create a new, effective slide.

Go to MyEnglishLab to complete a skill practice.

LANGUAGE SKILL
SOURCING ACADEMIC REFERENCES

WHY IT'S USEFUL By using appropriate language to refer to academic sources and research in presentations, speeches, and discussions, you can create verbal signposts for your listener and establish credibility as a speaker.

When summarizing academic sources and research, it is important to *signpost* your sources. Signposting lets your listeners know that you are supporting your ideas with evidence, establishes your credibility, and helps you avoid plagiarizing. To summarize other's ideas, we often use the **source + a reporting verb**. Reporting verbs reflect your purpose as well as your attitude toward the source. Consider these two sentences:

> Brassan <u>says</u> that upgrading home air filters can greatly reduce ailments caused by indoor air pollution.

> Brassan <u>asserts</u> that upgrading home air filters can greatly reduce ailments caused by indoor air pollution.

The second sentence is much stronger and conveys the speaker's attitude towards the source. In the first sentence, by contrast, the reporting verb *say* only indicates that words were spoken, without conveying a purpose or feeling.

Examples

If your purpose is to use the source ...	Strong Verbs	Neutral Verbs
To add something to your idea		*adds*
To give advice		*advises*
To show evidence in agreement with your idea	*applauds, praises, supports*	*acknowledges, concurs, recognizes*
To argue and persuade	*argues, contends, insists, justifies, promises, persuades*	*assures, reasons*
To draw a conclusion		*concludes, discovers, finds*
To show a disagreement to an idea	*contradicts, dismisses, disputes, refutes*	*challenges, debates, disagrees*
To emphasize your idea	*emphasizes, highlights, stresses*	*discusses, explores*
To further explain or illustrate your idea	*evaluates, investigates*	*articulates, illustrates, examines, shows*

EXERCISE 4

A. Reread the introduction from the research study from Integrated Skills.

> In today's world, homes need to be both energy efficient and well ventilated. Energy efficiency and ventilation can be achieved by using updated mechanical ventilation systems. By installing this type of system, homes can decrease their air change rate, creating less variation in temperatures (Homes, Tent 2008, and McArt 2012). However, new technologies do not always produce the same result in different homes. Variables such as the home's location greatly affect the air change rate (Tent, et. al). By analyzing the communal living space in four different climates, ventilation requirements are determined, and efficient and appropriate ventilation systems can be selected.

B. Answer the questions.

   1. Your idea is that there is a need for updated mechanical ventilation systems. What evidence in the introduction can be used to support your idea?

   2. Your idea is that it is not climate that affects the air change rates, but the system used in a home. What evidence in the introduction can be used to emphasize your idea?

C. Imagine you are preparing a presentation. Work with a partner and restate the evidence in the Part B questions using strong reporting verbs.

Go to MyEnglishLab to complete a skill practice.

APPLY YOUR SKILLS

WHY IT'S USEFUL By applying the skills you have learned in this unit, you can effectively summarize research, use it to support your ideas, and prepare a persuasive presentation.

ASSIGNMENT

Prepare a small group presentation on government regulations and building systems. Use what you have learned about common indoor pollutants and contaminants, their effect on health, and the role that government energy regulations have played in increasing health problems.

BEFORE YOU LISTEN

A. Discuss the questions with one or more students.

   1. What are the concerns surrounding indoor air quality?

   2. Are you concerned with indoor air quality? Why or why not?

   3. Why do you think some people are not concerned with indoor air quality?

   4. What are some solutions to improve indoor air quality?

B. You will listen to a lecture on air distribution and how it is the key to maintaining clean indoor air. As you listen, think about these questions.

   1. What evidence exists that illustrates how air diffusers do not remove all pollutants?

   2. What is the process of how displacement flow purifies the air in a room?

   3. Why is mixed flow more common if displacement flow does a better job of purifying the air?

   4. What conclusion can be drawn from the professor's prediction?

C. Review the Unit Skills Summary. As you listen to the lecture and begin preparing your presentation, apply the skills you learned in this unit.

UNIT SKILLS SUMMARY

Select suitable research to support your ideas.
- Choose appropriate sources.
- Identify, summarize, and synthesize key ideas.

Integrate and present research.
- Determine the best evidence to support your idea.
- Integrate research into your presentation through "sandwiching."

Understand and present a research report.
- Identify the sections of a research report (abstract, introduction, methods, results / findings, discussion / recommendations).
- Prepare your presentation.
- Use visual tools effectively.

Cite sources of academic references.
- Determine your purpose in using those references.
- Choose strong or neutral reporting verbs to signpost your sources.

LISTEN

A. Listen to the lecture about mixed and displacement airflow. Take notes as you listen. Determine what evidence the professor uses, and the purpose of the evidence presented.

B. Reread the discussion questions from Before You Listen, Part B. Is there anything you cannot answer? What listening skills can you use to help find the answers?

Go to MyEnglishLab to listen again and answer critical thinking questions.

THINKING CRITICALLY

Discuss the questions with another student.

1. How does the professor incorporate evidence into his lecture? Point out at least four places where evidence is used. What is the purpose of the use of evidence? How is it integrated with the professor's own ideas?

2. Based on the lecture, what technologies need to be furthered developed to ensure buildings and residential spaces are green? Why?

THINKING VISUALLY

A. Using information from the lecture, label the diagram.

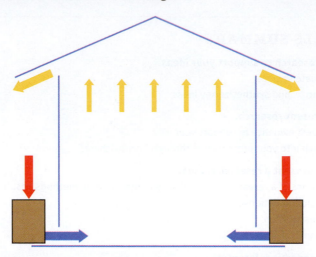

B. Compare your diagram with a classmate.

THINKING ABOUT LANGUAGE

Work with a partner. Listen to the excerpts from the lecture. After the end of each excerpt, take turns summarizing the text using your own words. Use the professor's comments as evidence, and introduce the evidence with a strong reporting verb.

GROUP PRESENTATION

A. Read and discuss these questions with a small group.

During the lecture, the professor outlined the benefits of displacement flow systems over mixed-flow systems. He highlighted how mixed flow is more common—even though displacement flow has greater benefits. Why do you think certain systems are used over others? Do you think governments should have stricter regulations for which systems are used?

B. You will work with a group to frame an argument regarding government regulations and building systems, like air ventilation systems. Research a building system and its current regulations. Based on your research, make an assertion regarding a change in regulations.

1. What building system is your group researching?

2. What are the current regulations for this system?

3. What assertions can your group make?

4. What evidence exists to support your idea(s)?

C. Listen to each presentation.

Listen carefully and take notes on each presentation. Discuss how each group effectively used evidence.

Go to MyEnglishLab to listen to Professor Hildemann and to complete a self-assessment.

Extended Lectures

THE HUMAN EXPERIENCE

Sociology

FIVE REVOLUTIONS   **158**

MONEY AND COMMERCE

Economics

SUPPLY AND DEMAND   **164**

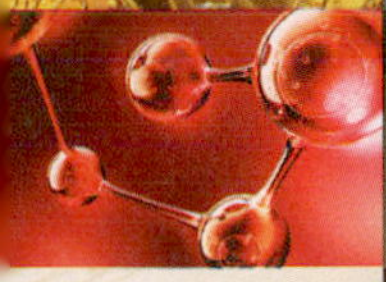

THE SCIENCE OF NATURE

Biology

ARE VIRUSES ALIVE?   **170**

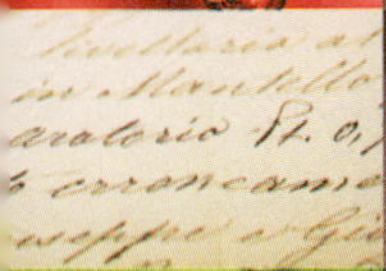

ARTS AND LETTERS

Humanities

LOVE AND EDUCATION   **176**

STRUCTURAL SCIENCE

Environmental Engineering

AIR FILTRATION SYSTEMS FOR THE HOME   **182**

Part 3 presents authentic content written and delivered by university professors. Academically rigorous application and assessment activities allow for a synthesis of the skills developed in Parts 1 and 2.

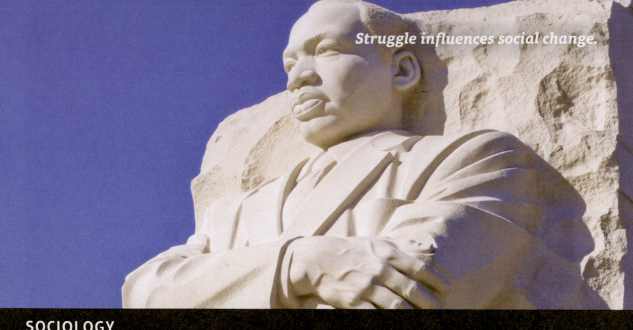

Struggle influences social change.

SOCIOLOGY

Five Revolutions

UNIT PROFILE

In this unit you will watch a lecture entitled "Five Revolutions." This lecture examines the peaceful revolutionary work of Dr. Martin Luther King, Jr. and evaluates events that have influenced social change movements throughout North American history.

You will research a grassroots movement that has impacted people's lives in a positive way and prepare a short presentation on the movement.

EXTENDED LECTURE

BEFORE YOU VIEW

Think about these questions before watching the lecture "Five Revolutions." Discuss them with another student.

1. What is a revolution?

2. Why do you think people revolt? What are some of the reasons people organize together to revolt?

3. Are you familiar with any 20th century revolutions? How have they impacted people's lives today?

4. Are there any revolutions happening now? What are they fighting for?

LECTURE

Go to MyEnglishLab to watch a lecture by Professor Jonathan Greenberg. Take notes while you listen. Then answer the questions in Check What You've Learned.

> **TIP**
> ....
> ***Taking notes*** *Three common methods for taking notes are outlining, the Cornell method, and charting or mapping. To learn more or to review these methods, refer to SOCIOLOGY Part 1.*

CHECK WHAT YOU'VE LEARNED

Think about the lecture you have just watched and refer to your notes. Answer each question.

1. In his introduction, Professor Greenberg refers to two revolutions. What are these revolutions and what connection do they have to one another?

   ....

   ....

2. What was Dr. King's purpose in referring to the story of Rip Van Winkle? Why does Professor Greenberg continue to refer to Rip Van Winkle?

   ....

   ....

3. Professor Greenberg mentions Dr. King's reference to a triple revolution. What are the other three revolutions the professor refers to? What are the similarities between those three revolutions and the two revolutions he mentions earlier?

   ....

   ....

   ....

4. What were the implications of the two questions Dr. King posed during his last sermon? What did he want people to understand?

   ....

   ....

5. What is Professor Greenberg referring to when he mentions the "moral force" of the Declaration of Independence? How does that force relate to the work of Dr. Martin Luther King, Jr.?

   ....

   ....

6. What is meant by the term "rotten compromise and radical evil"? What rotten compromise does refer to?

   ....

   ....

7. Can you identify Professor Greenberg's opinion regarding the Reconstruction period in relation to Civil Rights? What is it?

   > **TIP**
   >
   > ***Identifying opinions*** *When listening to a lecture, you can identify the speaker's opinion through verbal and nonverbal signposts. For more on identifying opinions and on distinguishing opinions from facts, refer to SOCIOLOGY Part 2.*

   ....

   ....

8. What are two things people in the 1950s and 1960s did to bring on the second revolution?

....

....

> **TIP**
> ....
> **Paraphrasing** To clarify complex ideas, it can be helpful for speakers to paraphrase. This means that the speaker restates what was just said—a word, phrase, or idea—using different words. For more on paraphrasing, refer to SOCIOLOGY Part 1.

9. Based on the lecture, what are Professor Greenberg's ideas regarding the *Brown vs. Board of Education* decision and its impact on segregation? Paraphrase them.

....

....

10. According to the lecture, how can you summarize our responsibilities as citizens?

....

....

THINKING CRITICALLY

Consider each situation in light of what you heard in the lecture. By yourself or with a partner, apply what you know about nonviolent protest movements to address each situation.

Situation 1 In his lecture, Professor Greenberg describes how nonviolent actions were pivotal acts of revolution. In the 1960s, nonviolence had an impact on problems of racism, poverty, and militarism. Choose one of these problems and describe how nonviolent protest can bring attention to the situation and create long long-lasting change.

Situation 2 Science and technology have had an extraordinary impact on the course of human history over the last fifty 50 years. These advances, however, have not come without consequences. Improvements in science and technology have been linked to overpopulation, global food shortages, and radical climate change. The same technology that provides solutions is fraught with challenges. Using strategies from nonviolent protest movements, how could you design a campaign that would effectively address one of these challenges?

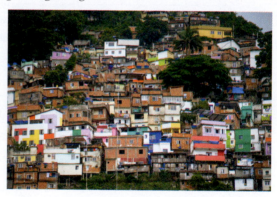

Go to MyEnglishLab to complete a critical thinking activity.

THINKING VISUALLY

A. Review the lecture, paying particular attention to important events and the years during which they occurred. Then create a timeline of 10 events mentioned by Professor Greenberg.

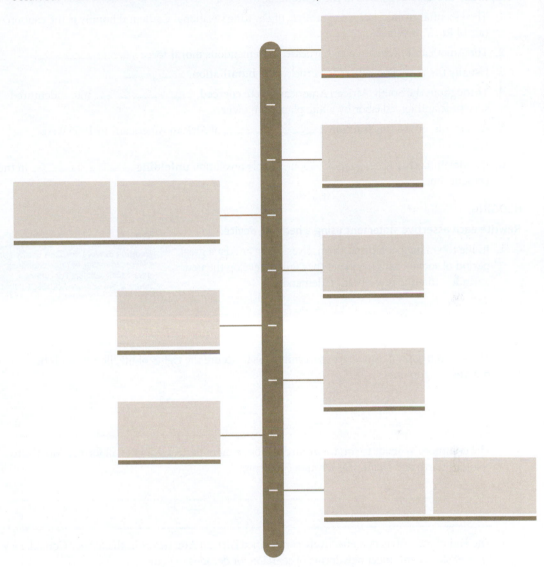

B. Compare your timeline with a partner. Follow these steps.

1. Take turns stating key events in your timeline.

2. When possible, explain how each event grew out of the previous event(s).

3. Work together and extend your timelines. Add key events from more recent years from international struggles for freedom and human rights.

THINKING ABOUT LANGUAGE

PARAPHRASING

Paraphrase the boldface words in the sentences.

1. The essential **trope**, ... of Dr. King's National Cathedral homily is the cautionary tale of Rip Van Winkle.

2. The American Revolution also harnessed a tremendous **moral force**. ....

3. Usually the party that suffers the cruelty and **humiliation**. ....

4. Throughout the South, African Americans were **coerced**, ..., into indentured servitude and forced labor by white plantation owners.

5. As a result, only a tiny **fraction**, ..., of African Americans in 1955 were registered to vote.

6. Dr. Martin Luther King, Jr. spoke about a triple revolution **unfolding**, ..., in the present time.

HEDGING

Rewrite each assertive statement using a hedging device.

> **TIP**
>
> **Hedging devices** Speakers use hedging devices to soften, or more cautiously assert their opinion. For common hedging devices, see SOCIOLOGY Part 2.

1. In life too many people find themselves living amidst a great period of social change, and yet they fail to develop the new attitudes, that the new situation demands.

....

....

2. The sole purpose of democratic government is to secure the rights of life, liberty, and the pursuit of happiness.

....

....

3. The compromise made to forge a unified nation, a more perfect union of all former American colonies north and south, was a rotten compromise.

....

....

4. The end of reconstruction effectively condemned African Americans in the former Confederacy to re-enslavement under new forms of coercion for decades to come.

....

....

5. Time after time Dr. Martin Luther King, Jr. brought community and municipal struggles to the national media, thus triggering the pressure required to end local injustices.

....

....

6. Our responsibility as human beings is to join the powerful nonviolent struggle against racism, poverty, and militarism in the United States and throughout the world.

....

....

INDIVIDUAL PRESENTATION

The second revolution highlighted in the lecture began as a grassroots movement that spread across the country and the world to ignite a change. What are some other grassroots movements that have impacted people's lives? When and where did they begin? How did the message spread? How have people's lives been changed as a result?

Topic: Grassroots movement that has impacted people's lives in a positive way.

RESEARCH

A. **Investigate other grassroots movements. Select a movement that interests you.**

   Grassroots movement..

B. **Research your grassroots movement by seeking out primary sources. Check that the materials you use and cite are from reputable and respected publication.**

C. **Prepare your presentation. Be sure to present your main ideas clearly and to support your ideas with evidence.**

D. **Practice presenting to a partner.**

E. **While listening to your partner, ask him or her to elaborate on ideas where you would like more information.**

> **TIP**
> *Elaborating on ideas* To explore a topic in greater depth, it is important to ask the speaker for more details about a particular point in order to receive a deeper explanation. For more information on elaboration, refer to SOCIOLOGY Part 1.

PRESENT

A. **Listen to each class member's presentation. As you listen, complete the chart.**

Movement	Time Period	Place	Key Leaders	Changes

B. **After the presentations, have a class discussion on each movement. Be sure to utilize turn-taking techniques. Discuss how each movement has impacted people's lives. Which movements have impacted the greatest number of lives? Which movements have brought about the most critical changes?**

Go to MyEnglishLab to complete a collaborative activity.

For more about **SOCIOLOGY**, see **1** **2**. See also [R] and [W] **ECONOMICS** **1** **2** **3**.

Individual choices impact the global economy.

ECONOMICS

Supply and Demand

UNIT PROFILE

In this unit you will watch a lecture entitled "Supply and Demand." This lecture focuses on the fundamentals of how buyers and sellers behave and how their interactions affect society.

You will research and present your ideas on how a life-saving product or service might potentially affect consumer and seller behavior.

EXTENDED LECTURE

BEFORE YOU VIEW

Think about these questions before watching the lecture "Supply and Demand." Discuss them with another student.

1. What do you know about the concept of supply and demand? What is supply? What is demand?

2. What are some factors that could affect the pricing of a product?

3. What are some factors that influence consumers' purchasing decisions? Is price always the most important issue or does it depend on the circumstances? Explain.

4. Do you think competition in a market is helpful or harmful for society? Why?

LECTURE

▶ Go to **MyEnglishLab** to watch a lecture by Professor Marcelo Clerici-Arias. Take notes while you listen. Then answer the questions in Check What You've Learned.

CHECK WHAT YOU'VE LEARNED

Think about the lecture you have just watched and refer to your notes. Answer each question.

1. Which of the statements best summarizes the main idea of the lecture?

    TIP

    Main ideas and supporting details
    Speakers often use verbal cues to signpost which of their statements are main ideas and which are supporting details. For some examples of these verbal cues, refer to ECONOMICS Part 1.

    a. Consumers and producers drive market trends.
    b. Markets provide benefits for both sellers and buyers.
    c. Economists analyze how consumers and producers drive markets.
    d. Trade is critical for meeting production goals.

2. Consumer behavior and seller behavior are supporting ideas in the lecture. Which statement best summarizes these supporting ideas?

    a. Consumer behavior is driven by seller behavior.
    b. Seller behavior is driven by consumer behavior.
    c. Consumers impact demand; sellers impact supply.
    d. Sellers impact demand; consumers impact supply.

3. What example does Professor Clerici-Arias use to illustrate consumer behavior? Explain the example in your own words.

    ....

    ....

4. How does Professor Clerici-Arias define the phenomenon of diminishing marginal utility (DMU)?

    ....

    ....

5. Based on what you heard, how would the demand curve look if there were many consumers in the market, and many products being bought and sold?

    ....

    ....

6. How does the professor define increasing opportunity cost and how does this phenomenon affect the supply curve?

    ....

    ....

7. What does Professor Clerici-Arias imply about the reason why there is an excess supply of eyeglasses?

....

....

TIP
....
Inferences and implications *Speakers often imply meaning rather than stating it directly. Meaning can be inferred by listening for key rhetorical devices. For examples of these rhetorical devices, refer to ECONOMICS Part 2.*

8. According to the lecture, at what point do neither sellers nor buyers have an incentive to change their behavior?

....

....

9. How certain is the professor regarding these economic models of how people behave? Why do you think so?

....

....

....

TIP
....
Degree of certainty *In order to establish their credibility, academic speakers support their claims with evidence . This evidence is signposted by verbal cues, word choice, tone of voice, and facial expressions. For some examples of these signposts, refer to ECONOMICS Part 2.*

10. What does Professor Clerici-Arias use to support his claim that supply and demand has benefitted all those who participate in it?

....

....

THINKING CRITICALLY

Consider each situation in light of what you heard in the lecture. By yourself or with a partner, apply what you know about supply and demand to address each situation.

Situation 1 In the lecture, the professor explains supply and demand and buyer-seller interaction by using the examples of two highly sought after products: water bottles and eyeglasses. Consider highly sought after products taken from natural resources, such as oil, gas, and water. These resources are being depleted at a rapid rate. As you see it, in what ways does this depletion affect the market for high-demand, low-supply products and services?

Situation 2 Professor Clerici-Arias asserts that societies are better off when consumers and sellers interact. He states that this interaction is a key reason for humanity's great advances in the last millennia. However, these advances have not come without consequences. Market fluctuations have been responsible for economic recessions, the loss of jobs and homes, and other tragic events. Using what you know about trade and economic models, how might these negative events have been prevented?

Go to **MyEnglishLab** to complete a critical thinking activity.

THINKING VISUALLY

A. Look at these graphs from the lecture. With a partner, take turns explaining a graph to each other. Replace eyeglasses with a different product, such as athletic shoes or a fitness tracker.

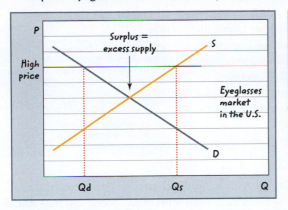

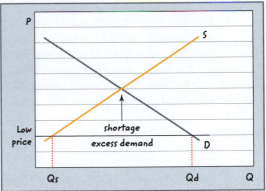

B. Read this excerpt from Professor Clerici-Arias' lecture. Create a graph to illustrate the information he describes.

So, imagine you and I are the only people in the room and that we are locked in here for the next two hours of class, … And you are thirsty and you would love to have some water, but you forgot to bring some.

Fortunately, I did bring with me three bottles of water and perhaps, for the right price, you might be able to convince me to part with one or more of them. …

So imagine that, you'd be willing to pay (WTP1) $1.00 for this one bottle of water. Fast forward a few minutes. You've drunk this water bottle, but you're still somewhat thirsty, you're feeling better, and now you want to purchase the second bottle from me. How much would you be willing to pay for this second bottle?

I would be willing to bet is that …the willingness to pay (WTP2) for the second water bottle was lower than for the first. … Once you have drunk that first water bottle, then probably your willingness to pay (WTP2) for the second bottle might be $ .50. At that point you might say, "Well, I've drunk enough, I have to be locked in here until the end of class," and all that water you have drunk is accumulating, so your willingness to pay (WTP3) for the third bottle might even be as low as $0.00.

Now that we have our demand, let's turn our attention to the behavior of the sellers. Now, if you wanted to buy the second bottle from me, it's causing me [to have] second thoughts because I, many times, do end up drinking this second water bottle, and if I don't get to finish the first one, my dry mouth would cause me trouble with teaching. So, I'm sacrificing more by selling you a second bottle of water. And perhaps I would want at least $10.00 to part with this second [bottle], so the willingness to sell (WTS2) the second increases to $10.00.

And, if you really wanted to push it and buy the third water bottle, then that would mean I wouldn't be able to teach the class. I might even hurt my throat, so that sacrifice would be so high for me that if I'm still willing to sell (WTS3) it to you, it might require $1,000.00 in payment.

CLARIFYING

Check your understanding of each paraphrased excerpt by clarifying the ideas with a confirmation question.

1. The place where buyers and sellers meet (whether physically or virtually) is called a *market*. We have seen markets evolve from simple locations where people bartered their goods and services to very complex markets, such as stock markets, with millions of participants connected through an intricate network of communication, transportation, and regulations.

   ....

   ....

> **TIP**
> ....
> ***Clarifying or Confirming Meaning*** *To make sure that you have understood a speaker correctly, it is important to ask clarifying or confirming questions. This not only checks your understanding, but it also lets the speaker know that you have been listening carefully. For examples of clarification and confirmation language and their use, refer to ECONOMICS, Part 1.*

2. Economists call this phenomenon *diminishing marginal utility*, which in their jargon means that a person would get less satisfaction out of consuming additional units of any goods and thus would be willing to pay less.

   ....

   ....

3. Competitive markets result in a win-win situation for both buyers and sellers—everyone is better off!

   ....

4. Look around you at your clothes, food, house, computer, and phone. Think about how you and your family were able to obtain these products. Now imagine what would happen if you tried to create all these products from scratch yourself, without trading anything with anyone—it's absolutely impossible!

   ....

   ....

USING IMPLIED CONDITIONS

Rewrite each implied condition with a conditional *if* clause.

1. There may be more buyers in the market; if so, demand will shift.

   ....

2. Without trade, buyers and sellers would suffer.

   ....

3. The company might have a surplus; if not, the demand may increase.

   ....

4. Without interaction between buyers and sellers, economic models would appear very different.

   ....

GROUP PRESENTATION

As outlined in the lecture, the supply and demand of products and services can greatly benefit our personal lives and our societies. Trading not only breaks down social barriers, but also advances humanity so both benefit equally. Should the same be true for life-saving drugs and products as well? Take the case of a life-saving prescription drug, for example. Should a company be able to set any price it likes on that drug because they know it is in great demand? Should consumers be willing to pay anything for a drug that could save their lives?

Topic: How a life-saving product or service might affect consumer and seller behavior.

RESEARCH

A. Investigate the economic history of a life-saving drug. Select a fatal disorder that interests you and a drug that is used to treat it.

Life-saving product / service ....

B. Research your drug by seeking out primary sources. Check that the materials you use and cite are from reputable and respected publications.

C. Prepare your presentation with your group. Decide which group members will present each section. Be sure to use verbal cues to signpost main ideas and supporting details, clarifying any new ideas.

D. Practice presenting your part of the presentation to the group. Review your section with your group members to ensure the entire presentation is cohesive.

E. While listening to other group members, comment on any rhetorical devices, such as stories and comparisons, that they use to illustrate their points.

PRESENT

A. Listen to each group's presentation and take notes. Be sure to ask questions about any points that need clarification.

B. After the presentations, discuss how supply and demand would be affected if companies chose not to set prices based on demand. Explore how the demand curve and the supply curve can be adapted to cover ethical considerations.

Go to MyEnglishLab to complete a collaborative activity.

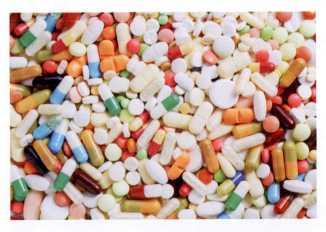

For more about **ECONOMICS**, see **1** **2**. See also **R** and **W** **ECONOMICS** **1** **2** **3**.

Exploring the secret lives of viruses.

Are Viruses Alive?

UNIT PROFILE

In this unit you will watch a lecture entitled "Are Viruses Alive?" This lecture focuses on defining what viruses are, describing their components, and exploring whether or not they are alive.

You will research and prepare a panel discussion on the controversial issue of requiring genetic testing for fatal diseases.

EXTENDED LECTURE

BEFORE YOU VIEW

Think about these questions before watching the lecture "Are Viruses Alive?" Discuss them with another student.

1. What does it mean to be alive?

2. What is a virus? Can you name some common diseases that are caused by viruses?

3. Do you think viruses are alive? Why or why not?

4. What is DNA? What do you know the relationship between DNA and viruses?

LECTURE

▶ Go to MyEnglishLab to watch a lecture by Professor Robert Siegel. Take notes while you listen. Then answer the questions in Check What You've Learned.

CHECK WHAT YOU'VE LEARNED

Think about the lecture you have just watched and refer to your notes. Answer each question.

1. Which of these phrases best summarizes Professor Siegel's goal for the lecture?
   a. to examine the structure of a virus
   b. to examine virus evolution
   c. to examine whether or not viruses are living beings
   d. to examine common characteristics of viruses

2. Based on the complexity of the introduction, what can be inferred about the answer to the topic question, "Are viruses alive?"

   ....

   ....

3. Professor Siegel makes several digressions during the lecture. He mentions Samuel Clemens, gets his pointer out, and refers to Horton, the elephant in a Dr. Seuss book. Which phrase best describes the purpose of his digressions?
   a. to exemplify a point or idea
   b. to utilize a story that relates indirectly to the topic
   c. to get the audience to relax and take a short break
   d. to connect the content of the lecture to the audience

4. What are the three definitions of life Professor Siegel uses to answer the question of whether or not viruses are alive?

   ....

   ....

   ....

5. What conclusion does Professor Siegel make about viruses regarding the *first* definition of life?

   ....

   ....

6. What conclusion does he make about viruses regarding the *second* definition of life?

   ....

   ....

7. In his third definition, the professor refers to The Central Dogma of Biology that involves possessing and processing of biological information into protein. *Dogma* is usually defined as "a set of firm beliefs by a group who expects unquestioning acceptance of these beliefs." How does Professor Siegel define the word *dogma* for the purposes of this lecture?

   ....

   ....

8. The professor shows an illustration of the process involved in the Central Dogma of Biology. Which statement best outlines this process?

   a. DNA, which possesses biological material, sends biological information to messenger RNA, which provides the structure. Once this biological information is structured, it forms a protein.
   b. RNA, which possesses biological material, sends biological information to messenger DNA, which provides the structure. Once this biological information is structured, it forms a protein.
   c. DNA, which possesses biological material, develops into a structure. Once this biological information is structured, it becomes protein with the help of RNA.
   d. RNA, which possesses biological material, develops into a structure. Once this biological information is structured, it becomes to protein with the help of DNA.

9. The professor outlines the flow of biological information in a virus. Can you explain the process of *RNA replicase*? How does that differ from the process described in the Central Dogma of Biology?

   ....

   ....

10. At the end of the lecture, Professor Siegel summarizes the key ideas and returns to his starting point. How does he ultimately answer the question posed in the lecture, "Are Viruses Alive"?

   ....

   ....

THINKING CRITICALLY

Consider each situation in light of what you heard in the lecture. By yourself or with a partner, apply what you know about biological processes to address each situation.

Situation 1 Professor Siegel refers to the Central Dogma of Biology as "something that is true until it isn't." There are numerous examples of this sort of dogma throughout history, such as the belief that the sun rotated around the earth. Technological and scientific advances have helped disprove many such beliefs. Outline a process in which another scientific belief was widely accepted until a new understanding was reached through technology or other advances.

Situation 2 The question "What is life?" is raised by Professor Siegel. While he noted this might be simple to answer on the surface, he also states that this could be a very complicated question if life were found on another planet. Imagine life is found on another planet; however, this life is not cellular based. Following the process Professor Siegel used in his lecture, construct a similar argument for defining life.

Go to MyEnglishLab to complete a critical thinking activity.

THINKING VISUALLY

Work with a partner on a visual aid documenting causes of disease other than viruses. Follow the steps below.

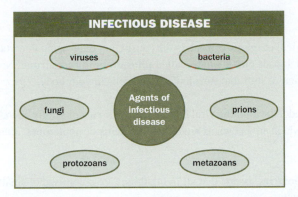

1. Partner A looks at the visual map; Partner B does not.
2. A describes the information in the visual map. B listens and draws the visual.
3. When B's map is complete, B describes the information on his or her map to A.
4. Once finished, compare visual maps. How are they similar? How are they different?

Go to MyEnglishLab to complete a critical thinking activity.

THINKING ABOUT LANGUAGE

USING INTERROGATIVES AND DECLARATIVES

Read each situation. Then, write one interrogative and one declarative for each situation.

> **TIP**
> ....
> **Using Interrogatives and Declaratives** *To gain support and authority with an audience, use interrogatives and declaratives. For more on the grammar and usage of interrogatives and declaratives, refer to BIOLOGY, Part 1.*

Situation 1 A remote island in the South Pacific with a population of under a thousand people has had an outbreak of a virus that causes people to become paralyzed. While many healthy adults and children have recovered after a few weeks, the very young and the elderly are not recovering. The island has no airport, and it takes days to get resources by boat to the island.

.... (interrogative)

.... (declarative)

Situation 2 Researchers at a major university have discovered a new strain of influenza. During their research, they also pinpointed its causes. Armed with this information, researchers are ready to start developing a vaccine. However, due to limited funding, their research is on hold.

.... (interrogative)

.... (declarative)

Situation 3 The government would like to add a tax to cover research on a new virus that poses a biological threat. Citizens have expressed strong opposition to the tax, citing that taxes are already too high. However, without money for this research, citizens' health could be at stake.

.... (interrogative)

.... (declarative)

Read the excerpts from the lecture. Look at the boldfaced words and / phrases. Put each word or / phrase under the correct heading in the chart below.

1. Now, **the viral envelope** surrounds the capsid. It's only found in certain **viral families**. It's made out of what's called **phospholipid membrane**. Now that's the same kind of stuff that surrounds all the cells in your body.

2. Now, embedded within the viral envelope are **a series** of virally encoded **proteins**, which are known as **enveloped proteins** or **peplomers**, after the **peplos**

3. **The Cell Doctrine** asserts that all living things are comprised of small units known as **cells**.

General	Specific

PANEL DISCUSSION

In the lecture, a seemingly simple question was raised: are viruses alive? However, the answer to this question is not simple. Answering it requires defining what a virus is and what it means to be alive. Biology is a field in which simple questions can have very complex answers. In addition, many of these questions are controversial and challenge traditional ethical standards. For instance, should we always vaccinate our children? Does taking a large amount of medication cause complications later in life? Should stem cells be used to further scientific research? One such question concerns genetic testing. Should people be tested to find out if they carry genes that could lead to cancer and other deadly diseases in order to seek treatment before developing the disease? One such example is women who discovered they had the gene for breast cancer opting for surgeries to remove their breasts before developing cancer.

Topic: Should people be required to undergo genetic testing to determine risk factors for deadly diseases?

RESEARCH

A. Investigate the advantages and disadvantages of genetic testing. Consider factors such as cost, availability, and the reliability of test results. Think about any diseases such as cancer or diabetes that you could inherit from your family members. What is your point of view on required genetic testing?

Your point of view: ....

B. Research genetic testing by seeking out primary sources. Check that the materials you use and cite are from reputable and respected publication.

C. Prepare your discussion points. Be sure to present your point of view clearly and to support your opinions with evidence. Review your discussion points with your panel members to ensure there is a cohesive presentation.

D. Choose one panel member to lead the discussion and ensure equal participation by all on the panel.

E. Practice presenting your discussion points to the other panel members. Where possible, include interrogative and declarative sentences to establish authority.

F. While listening to other panel members, evaluate and critique the arguments they use to justify their positions.

DISCUSS

A. Establish the rules and time limits for the panel discussion before beginning.

B. As you listen, write down questions you have for panelists. Consider asking questions for clarification or to gain more insight.

....

....

....

Go to MyEnglishLab to complete a collaborative activity.

For more about **BIOLOGY**, see ❶❷. See also ⟦R⟧ and ⟦W⟧ **BIOLOGY** ❶❷❸.

Education teaches you to love the world.

HUMANITIES

Love and Education

UNIT PROFILE

In this unit you will watch a lecture entitled "Love and Education." This lecture focuses on the relationship between love and education. Additionally, you will learn about the Ancient Greek philosopher, Plato and hear diverging views on Plato's philosophy.

You will research and prepare a presentation on ways a love of the world can be developed and fostered through volunteer organizations and private foundations.

EXTENDED LECTURE

BEFORE YOU VIEW

Think about these questions before watching the lecture "Love and Education." Discuss them with another student.

1. Do you think there is a relationship between love and education? If so, what is it?
2. How does education help to develop people's awareness of their world?
3. Is it necessary to be passionate about a subject to excel in it? Why do you think so?
4. What role does history play in developing students' understanding and appreciation of their world?

LECTURE

▶ Go to MyEnglishLab to watch a lecture by Professor Robert Pogue Harrison. Take notes while you listen. Then answer the questions in Check What You've Learned.

CHECK WHAT YOU'VE LEARNED

Think about the lecture you have just watched and refer to your notes. Answer each question.

1. Which of the following statements best summarizes the main idea of the lecture?

   a. The connection between love and education has existed for centuries. Greek philosopher Plato believed deeply that if a passion for one's world could be developed, more learning would occur.

   b. The connection between love and education has existed for centuries. Like Plato, Professor Harrison believes that a love of learning can only be developed in conversations between teachers and their students.

   c. The connection between love and education has existed for centuries. Plato believed that if a passion for learning could be ignited, more responsible citizenship could be developed. Like Plato, Professor Harrison asserts that compassion for one's world must be taught.

   d. The connection between love and education has existed for centuries. Professor Harrison believes that a love for the world comes naturally in youth, unlike Plato, who asserted that it must be developed.

2. What claim does the professor make regarding the relationship between love and education? In his opinion, how is that relationship regarded today?

   ....

   ....

3. Professor Harrison defines *educe* in the lecture. What analogy does he use to illustrate the meaning of *educe*?

   ....

   ....

4. According to the lecture, what is the most intense kind of learning? What evidence does he provide for the idea?

   ....

   ....

5. Professor Harrison makes an emphatic claim regarding Plato and the role of love in education. What is that claim?

   ....

   ....

6. Which of these statements best summarizes Plato's philosophy on the soundest method of gaining knowledge?

   a. Learning comes alive after a long period of eager study under another individual's guidance.

   b. Learning occurs after a long period of devoted study when the mind and soul are awakened.

   c. Learning occurs when the soul is fertile enough for knowledge.

   d. Learning flourishes when a student develops love for both the subject and himself.

7. How are Professor Harrison's views about education similar to the beliefs of Plato?

....

....

8. The professor states that his views on love and education diverge from Plato's in two important ways. How do they differ?

....

....

....

9. What is Professor Harrison referring to when he states, "For world love to take root in a student, he or she must acquire a basic knowledge of how it [the world] came to be"?

....

....

10. In his conclusion, what does he ask his listeners to do with the information?

....

....

THINKING CRITICALLY

Consider each situation in light of what you heard in the lecture. By yourself or with a partner, apply what you know about the relationship between love and education to address each situation.

Situation 1 In the lecture, Professor Harrison asserts that education does not fulfill its worldly mandate by putting an electronic device in every student's hands, or by promoting a purblind vision of the present. However, in today's world, students are often encouraged, and even required, to engage deeply with digital content that allows for little interaction or collaboration. While digital literacy is critical, it often takes away from interpersonal skills. How could these two be better balanced? Design an assignment that would balance these instructional forms.

Situation 2 Through science and technology, life has evolved greatly over the last 50 years. However, not all of these advancements have impacted the world in a positive way. Professor Harrison shared his belief that love and learning involve fully understanding world history, so we can make a better future. However, many students today focus only on current events and pay little or no attention to the cultural and historical events that have shaped current affairs. So many past events have shaped our current lives and will continue to shape future generations. Create a public service announcement that would raise awareness about a key historical event that has shaped our current world and will continue to shape our future world.

Go to MyEnglishLab to complete a critical thinking activity.

THINKING VISUALLY

A. Review the lecture, paying attention to Professor Harrison's statements about European, British, and American college campuses. These campuses are often organized around a central meeting place, such as a quad or courtyard. Use the example map and consider how your campus is organized. Is there a central meeting place and places for students to gather, collaborate, and exchange ideas? Create a map showing these areas of your campus.

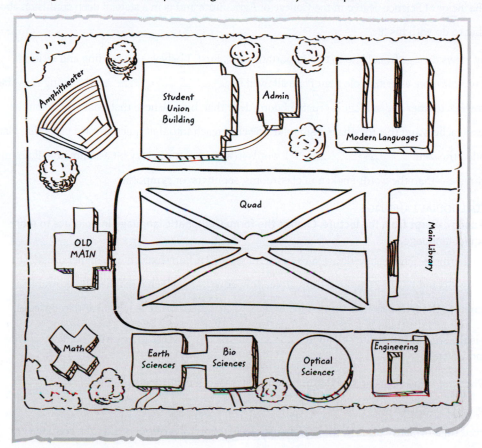

B. Compare your map with a classmate's. Discuss why some buildings were included on the map and others were not.

THINKING ABOUT LANGUAGE

CREATING COHESION IN PRESENTATIONS AND DISCUSSIONS

Read the paraphrased excerpts from the lecture and add lexical cues (transitions) to help create cohesion.

> **TIP**
>
> **Using Lexical Cues to Build Cohesion** To help listeners better understand the relationship between complex ideas, it is helpful for speakers to use key words and phrases to link those ideas. For more information on building cohesion, refer to HUMANITIES Part 1.

1. .... explore love and education. My lecture has three parts. .... I will offer some general reflections on the theme. .... I'll discuss the ancient Greek philosopher Plato. .... I will offer you my own views on the topic.

Continued

2. The connection forms part of the everyday experience of the students who frequently feel not only respect but also affection for the teachers they learn from, or the teachers who manage to "educe" or draw out from them their passion for a given subject matter. .... in John Williams' novel *Stoner*, an undergraduate at a university in Missouri is about to graduate with a Bachelor of Science degree in the College of Agriculture and is in a state of deep confusion about what to do with his life.

3. My views diverge from Plato in two important ways. First, I believe that reading and writing play a far more essential role than Plato allowed for. .... the living converse between teacher and student is crucial, I don't deny that, but I believe that books are often the best teachers and that they have a singular power to reach into that quiet, inward place that Plato called the soul. .... words in a book can be every bit as animate—if not more animate—than the words spoken in classrooms, seminars, or symposia.

USING COLLOQUIAL LANGUAGE

A. Read each excerpt from the lecture. Change the formal, emphatic language in boldface to more colloquial language.

1. Furthermore, Plato believed that such knowledge—call it knowledge of the higher order of being—could NOT be acquired through reading or writing, which don't have the power to **generate the living sparks that ignite** .... true insight and knowledge.

2. It is the student's **animate selfhood** .... that receives the seeds of knowledge.

3. What was unusual about Socrates in the context of Greek education, where professional sophists taught for wages, is that he loved each one of his students personally. Or better, he loved that formative place in the student's soul where love of wisdom could **take root and germinate** ....

4. That is why it is important for education to resist the **siren calls** .... of the contemporary and keep open the dimension of the untimely.

B. Compare the original excerpts with those using more colloquial language. Which versions do you think are more powerful? Why? Discuss your ideas with another student.

INDIVIDUAL PRESENTATION

As highlighted in the lecture, education helps us to better understand our world, enabling us to take more responsibility for it and the footprint we leave behind. In today's society, there are numerous unaffiliated volunteer organizations and foundations, which aim at making the world a better place and developing people to become better citizens. Many of these organizations are calling on volunteers who have a love for the world, whether it is for helping the hungry, the poor, the oceans, or the animals. What is the primary purpose of these organizations? What initiated their beginnings? What are they doing to further develop citizens and promote a greater love for the world?

Topic: Volunteer organizations and foundations promote a greater love for the world.

RESEARCH

A. Investigate volunteer organizations or private foundations that you associate with having a love of the world. Select an organization that interests you.

Organization/ Foundation ....

B. Research your organization by seeking out primary sources. Check that the materials you use and cite are from reputable and respected publications.

C. Prepare your presentation. Be sure to present your main ideas clearly and emphatically and to support your ideas with evidence.

D. Practice presenting to a partner.

E. While listening to your partner, suggest places where the use of intensifiers, voice stress, and repetition of key words or phrases could make the ideas more compelling.

> **TIP**
>
> **Emphatic argumentation** To better understand a speaker's feelings toward a topic and the reasoning at the heart of these feelings, focus on the language, voice stress, and repetition used by the speaker. For more on the use emphatic argumentation, refer to HUMANITIES Part 1.

PRESENT

A. Listen to each class member's presentation. As you listen, complete the chart below.

Organization or Foundation	Primary Purpose	Circumstances of Its Origins	Key Projects

B. After the presentations, have a class discussion about each organization or foundation presented. Which ones have impacted the greatest number of lives? Which are demonstrating a true love for the world?

Go to MyEnglishLab to complete a collaborative activity.

For more about **HUMANITIES**, see ❶ ❷. See also Ⓡand Ⓦ **HUMANITIES** ❶ ❷ ❸.

Sound design creates a healthier world.

Air Filtration Systems for the Home

UNIT PROFILE

In this unit you will watch a lecture entitled "Air Filtration Systems for the Home." This lecture focuses on air filtration used in homes to reduce the particulates and allergens that cause indoor air pollution. Additionally, you will learn about the characteristics of air filters and how they affect their efficiency.

You will research and debate whether or not further government intervention is needed to ensure the clarity and veracity of claims made to consumers about the effectiveness of health-related products.

EXTENDED LECTURE

BEFORE YOU VIEW

Think about these questions before watching the lecture "Air Filtration Systems for the Home." Discuss them with another student.

1. What are some air particulates commonly found in homes?

2. Is anyone in your family allergic to particulates, or unwanted matter, in the air of your home? Why do you think so?

3. What are some methods you use to remove these particulates from your home?

4. Have you ever used a portable air filter in your home? If so, was it beneficial? Why or why not?

LECTURE

▶ Go to MyEnglishLab watch a lecture by Professor Lynn Hildemann. Take notes while you listen. Then answer the questions in Check What You've Learned.

CHECK WHAT YOU'VE LEARNED

Think about the lecture you have just watched, and refer to your notes. Answer each question.

1. How would you summarize the main idea of the lecture?

   ....

   ....

2. Based on your understanding of the lecture, what can be inferred about manufacturers' claims regarding HEPA-like or micron filtration filters?

   ....

   ....

3. What can be learned from this bar graph that Professor Hildemann used in the lecture?

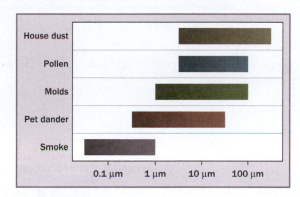

   ....

   ....

4. Identify and describe the three mechanisms a filter can use to collect particulate matter.

   ....

   ....

   ....

5. Paraphrase the lecturer's information on a "true HEPA" filter.

   ....

   ....

6. What information is presented in this line graph?

....

....

....

7. What can be learned from calculating the CADR value?

....

....

....

....

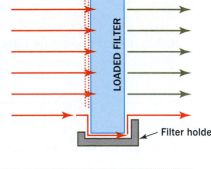

8. Professor Hildemann presents evidence to highlight the positive side and negative side of using an existing filter. Which evidence is stronger? Why?

....

....

9. How would you describe what this diagram shows?

....

....

....

....

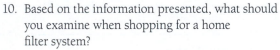

10. Based on the information presented, what should you examine when shopping for a home filter system?

....

....

THINKING CRITICALLY

Consider each situation in light of what you heard in the lecture. By yourself or with a partner, apply what you know about the effects of unwanted particulate matter to address each situation.

> **Situation 1** In the lecture, Professor Hildemann outlines the issues regarding advertising on portable home filtration systems. This advertising does not include the depth of information needed in order to make informed purchasing decisions. Consider other such systems in our homes, like water filtration systems and air conditioning units. What are some potential dangers of these systems? What could a potential homeowner do to be well-informed in order to make the best choices?
>
> **Situation 2** Professor Hildemann raises the issue of how important it is to be an informed consumer. While this is particularly important for you and your family's health in the home, it is also true in other areas of our lives. A good number of our daily decisions could directly or indirectly affect our health, or the health of our family members. While there are a number of government regulations in place to help protect consumers, they do not cover all situations. Are there areas that you feel need more government oversight? What are they? What should the government do to better protect consumers?

Go to MyEnglishLab to complete a critical thinking activity.

THINKING VISUALLY

A. Look at the line graph shown in the lecture. Then follow the steps below the graph.

1. Work with a partner. One partner will compare Filter (a) with Filter (b) on the graph; the other will compare Filter (b) with Filter (c).

2. Together, draw conclusions regarding which is the best, and which is the worst to use. Be sure to give your reasons, using the information in the graph.

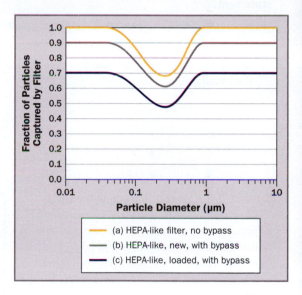

B. Look at the table presented in Professor Hildemann's lecture. Create a bar graph illustrating the flow rate and the dust spot efficiency for each filter.

TIP

Creating visuals To help listeners absorb new and complex data effectively, it is important to use the best type of visual aid for your purpose. For a list of different graph types, refer to ENVIRONMENTAL ENGINEERING Part 1.

	Flow Rate (ft³/min)	Dust spot Efficiency
Filter #1	40	40%
Filter #2	20	80%

THINKING ABOUT LANGUAGE

CREATING VISUALS AND COMMUNICATING WHAT THEY MEAN

Using the visual aids as a reference, complete each statement.

1. .... on this diagram, A, wards off larger particulates. .... wards off medium sized particulates. .... C wards off the smallest of particulates.

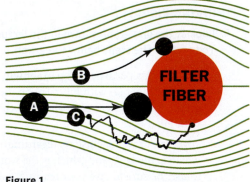

Figure 1

2. .... on this line graph, the cheap filter captures approximately .... of particles that are about .5 in diameter, whereas the HEPA-like filter captures nearly .... of that size particles. However, both show a much greater .... trend than the True HEPA filter.

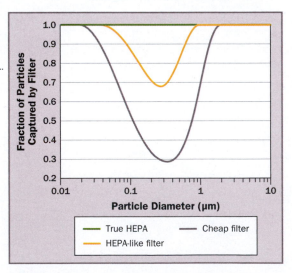

Figure 2

SOURCING ACADEMIC REFERENCES IN PRESENTATIONS, SPEECHES, OR DISCUSSIONS

Rewrite each statement replacing the verb in boldface with a stronger reporting verb.

1. Professor Hildemann **discusses** that advertisers make false claims regarding the actual removal of particulates when using a home filter system.

   ....

   ....

TIP

Using reporting verbs When presenting your sources of information, it is helpful to create verbal signposts by using strong reporting verbs with your data. To review strong reporting verbs, see ENVIRONMENTAL ENGINEERING, Part 2.

2. She **shows** how to accurately calculate the clean air delivery rate.

   ....

   ....

3. She **challenges** the use of older home filtration systems.

   ....

4. Professor Hildemann **states** the reasons consumers should be cautious when purchasing a portable home filter.

   ....

CLASS DEBATE

As outlined in the lecture, manufacturers often present consumers with claims in advertising or on packaging that contain half-truths. Half-truths are statements that are only partly true and are intended to deceive people in some way. These deceptive statements misrepresent the product. When considering products that are related to health, do you think it is the government's responsibility to ensure complete truth in packaging and advertisement, or do you think the consumer needs to take more responsibility by researching if the claims are completely true or not?

You will participate in a debate in which the class is divided into two teams. Team A will argue in favor of the proposition; Team B will argue against the proposition.

Proposition: The federal government should regulate marketing claims of health products to protect consumers.

RESEARCH

A. **Investigate issues of federal regulations and consumer safety. Discuss your central argument with your team, and make a list of points that support your side of the debate (your argument) and of points that support the opposing team's argument (the counter argument).**

   Our Central Argument (Claim): ....

B. **Choose team members (individuals or pairs) to give the introductory and closing statements. Then divide the supporting arguments and counterarguments among the other team members.**

C. **Research alone or with a classmate by seeking out primary sources. Check that the materials you use are from reputable and respected publications. Generate evidence supporting your argument and the opposition's counterargument.**

D. **Prepare your statements. Be sure to present your main ideas clearly and to support your argument with evidence and details. Consider what you already know about the counterarguments so you can anticipate what your opponent will say. If applicable, prepare visual presentation aids.**

E. **Practice presenting your arguments to your team members.**

F. **While listening to your team members, ask them for specifics when you want more information.**

Continued

DEBATE

A. Establish the rules and time limits of the debate before beginning. Begin the debate and follow these steps:

1. Team A delivers its introductory statement.

2. Team B delivers its introductory statement.

3. Teams A and B alternate presenting specific arguments, counterarguments, and responses.

5. Team A delivers its closing statement.

6. Team B delivers its closing statement.

B. After the debate, have a class discussion. Discuss your experience with the points raised. Which team's argument was the most compelling? Why? Are there any issues that you would like to know more about?

Go to MyEnglishLab to complete a collaborative activity.

For more about **Environmental Engineering**, see ❶ ❷. See also ⟦R⟧ and ⟦W⟧
Environmental Engineering ❶ ❷ ❸.

Credits

Front Cover: Roman Babakin/Shutterstock; Part and unit openers (multi use): Budai Romeo Gabor/Fotolia (gold coins), Nik_Merkulov/Fotolia (leaf with water droplets), Scisetti Alfio/Fotolia (old letter), Vichly4thai/Fotolia (red molecule dna cell), Tobkatrina/123RF (children's hands holding earth). Page 2: Bettmann/Corbis/Getty Images; 3: Ian Dagnall/Alamy Stock Photo; 5: Joe Gough/Shutterstock; 15 (TR): Everett Historical/Shutterstock; 15 (BR): Everett Historical/Shutterstock; 15 (TL): Todd Bannor/Alamy Stock Photo; 15 (BL): Rashid Lombard/AFP/Getty Images; 16: Ajgul/Shutterstock; 22 (CL): Mike Booth/Alamy Stock Photo; 22 (CR): Elena11/Shutterstock; 30: Dreamerb/Shutterstock; 31: Alexander Raths/Shutterstock; 33: Digital Vision/Photodisc/Getty Images; 35: Ellepigrafica/Shutterstock; 37: Cla78/Shutterstock; 41: Solarseven/Shutterstock; 46: Agence73Bis/Fotolia; 47 (BL): Anastasios71/Shutterstock; 47 (BR): Stefanel/Shutterstock; 49: Georgios Kollidas/Shutterstock; 52: Dpa picture alliance/Alamy Stock Photo; 56: Photo stella/Shutterstock; 60: Alice-photo/Shutterstock; 66: Looper/Shutterstock; 75 (CL): B.A.E. Inc./Alamy Stock Photo; 75 (BT): Moosician/Shutterstock; 80: Everett Historical/Shutterstock; 81: Pixel Embargo/Shutterstock; 84: Photos 12/Alamy Stock Photo; 91: Bettmann/Getty Images; 93: Everett Collection/Newscom; 96: Solarseven/Shutterstock; 97: Suphakit73/Shutterstock; 98: Bratovanov/Shutterstock; 99: iQoncept/Shutterstock; 101: keith morris/Alamy Stock Photo; 110: Sebastian Gauert/Shutterstock; 111: Centers for Disease Control and Prevention (CDC); 123: Welburnstuart/Shutterstock; 126: Tatiana Morozova/Shutterstock; 128: Sergey Nivens/Shutterstock; 131: Derrick Neill/Fotolia; 134: stockphoto mania/Fotolia; 140: Anupong Thiprot/Shutterstock; 145: Dotshock/Shutterstock; 150(TC): Luciano Mortula/Shutterstock; 150 (BC): Ryan McVay/Photodisc/Getty Images; 158: Brandon Bourdages/123RF; 160: Skreidzeleu/Shutterstock; 161: Boris15/Shutterstock; 164: Photofriday/Shutterstock; 169: Robert Kneschke/Shutterstock; 170: nobeastsofierce/Shutterstock; 176: Nivens/Shutterstock; 182: Lightspring/Shutterstock.

Index

Page numbers in bold refer to visuals (tables and figures). Page numbers in italics refer to terms found in audio referenced on those pages.

academic reading
  purposes of, **51**, 51
  read with writer's purpose in mind, 51
active participation, 2–15
  encouraging, 7, *8*
  encouraging participation, 6–7
  requests for elaboration, 3–4
  turn-taking, 6–7
activism, *81*. *see also* civil rights movement
  marching for a cause, 81
  in North America, 81
adjectives of urgency/suggestion, **40**
adverbs of approximation (modal adverbs), **90**
African Americans, 3, 88
  civil rights issues, *3*
  "Class Solidarity or Radical Separatism: An Overview of Perspectives on Consciousness-Raising in the African American Civil Rights Movement" (Sociology reading), 88
  Martin Luther King Jr., *10*
  War on Poverty, *3*
AIDS, *43*
air change rate (ACR), *143*, 148, **149**, 149, 150
air distribution, *155*
air-filtration systems
  "Air Filtration Systems for the Home" (environmental engineering lecture on video), 182
  allergens and, 70
  asthma and, 70
  necessity of, 147
air terminal devices (ATDs), *155*
air ventilation systems, climate and, 150
airflow, *155*
  mixed and displacement, *155*
allergens, 70
  air-filtration systems and, 70
analogies, 126–139, *127*
  assumptions, 130
  using metaphors and similes, 128–129
anticipating, 130
antiquity fallacy, **131**
antivirals, *31*
Apple, *97*, *107*, *109*
Apple Watch, *107*
"Are Viruses Alive?" (biology lecture on video), 170
Arendt, Hannah, 52, *127*, *138*
  Adolf Eichmann research and, *127*
  amor mundi (love of the world), 52, *127*, *139*
  education and, 52–53, *127*, *139*
  Holocaust, 52
  politics in the classroom and, 52
  Third Reich, *127*

war criminals and, *138*
World War II, *127*, *138*
argumentation, emphatic, 48, 50, 53
  language used with, **48**
  repetition, 48
  use of intensifier, 48
  use of voice, 48
argumentation, succinct, 50
  clear, 50
  neutral, 50
arguments
  concrete, 51
  hypothetical, 51
  supporting ideas and, *50*
Aristotle, 55
aside, 31
assumptions, *127*, 127, 130
asthma, air-filtration systems and, 70
"At-home Air Filtration Systems" (Enviromental Engineering reading), 70
Athens, 59
  democracy in, *57*
attitude, recognizing in a text, 51, 53
  assess word choice and sentence structure, 51
  concrete arguments vs hypothetical arguments, 51
  look for a writer's claim, 51
  look for transitional words and phrases, 51
audience response, 132
authority, asserting, 39
authority fallacy, **131**

"back to Africa" movement, 88
background information, 113
bacteriophages, **35**, *35*
Baltimore Classification System, *35*
Baltimore, David, *35*
Bamboo Nesting Towers, *75*
bandwagon fallacy, **131**
bar graphs, 64, **183**
biomass boilers, *61*
bird flu, *43*
Black Freedom Movement, 93, *93*
Black Nationalist Movement, 88
Black Panther Party (BPP), 89, *93*
Black Panthers, *10*
Black Separatist movements, 88
blocked expectation, *81*
bookending, 132
Boston University, *10*
Browder, Aurelia, *13*
Browder v. Gayle, *13*
Brown v. Board of Education, *93*

Calvin Study, *155*
Camp, Garrett, *17*
Carbon Dioxide Emissions 2011, **62**

Caudovirales, 35
caveat emptor, 185
celebrity endorsements, *99*
Center for Health, *102*
Cervantes, 133
challenging ideas of others, 31, 40
charting, 10
chicken pox, *31*
China
    air pollution in, *61*
    particulate matter in Beijing, 73
    Wuhan, *61*
civil disobedience, 10, *13*
Civil Rights Act of 1964, 3, 93
civil rights issues, **14**
    access to clean water, **14**
    access to education, **14**
    access to health care, **14**
    gender equality, **14**
    racial equality, **14**
Civil Rights Movement, *10*
    African Americans and, 88
    "Class Solidarity or Radical Separatism: An Overview
        of Perspectives on Consciousness-Raising in
        the African American Civil Rights Movement"
        (Sociology reading), 88
Civil War, *84*
claims, making, **100**
clarification. *see also* confirmation
    asking for, 36
    clarifying questions, **32**
    clarifying statement, 38
    paraphrasing, 36, *38*
    tag questions, 36, *38*
    using a confirmation expression, 36
class debate, 45, 188
    supply side and demand side economics, 109
"Class Solidarity or Radical Separatism: An Overview
    of Perspectives on Consciousness-Raising in the
    African American Civil Rights Movement"
    (Sociology reading), 88
classics, value of reading, 132–133
clean water, access to as a civil rights
    issues, **14**
climate, 150
    air ventilation systems and, 150
    table of temperatures by zone, months, **149**
    zones in the US, **148**
closure, providing, 132
Coca-Cola, *28*
cohesion, 115
    in discussions and presentations,
        54-56, 179
    full-circle approach, 114
    repetition, 114
    strategies for, 114
    transitional word or phrase, 114

collective behavior, 94
college campus, modern
    Plato and, 47
colloquial language, 180
colloquialisms, 127, **135**, 139
Colvin, Claudette, *13*
Commercial and Residential Energy End-Use Splits,
    2015, **67**
competition, 97
    benefits of, 97
competitive market, 23, 29
complex process, explaining, 117
    establish a framework, 117
    identify purpose, 117
    identify where background information
        is needed, 117
    identify where visuals are needed, 117
    outline each step, event, or procedure, 117
    summarize key ideas, 117
complexity, 47, 48
conclusion, effective
    providing closure, 132
    summarize key ideas, 132
conditional meaning
    if-clause, **104**
    implied condition, **104**
confirmation. *see also* clarification
    asking for, 36
    of meaning, 168
    paraphrasing, 36, 38
    tag questions, 36, 38
    using a confirmation expression, 36
controversial topics, discussing and responding to,
    31–33
conversation, entering, 6
    expressions used for, **6**
    signals of, 8
conversation, exiting, 7
coordination tags, **90**
Cornell Method, 9
cost elasticity, 103
credibility, 142
critical thinking
    analogies, 124
    apply what you know, 160, 166, 172, 178, 185
    cause and effect, 76
    comparisons, 43, 57, 138
    evidence and, *155*
    facts and opinions, 79–95
    implications, 13
    listening skills, 28
Crozer Theological Seminary, *10*
cultural norms, 134

debate, 42, 106, 188
declaratives, 39, 44, 174
Defense Threat Reduction Agency (DTRA), *33*

degree of certainty, 100, 166
  citing sources and, 100
  determine for speaker, 97
demand. *see also* supply and demand
  curve, *28*
  elasticity, 103
  excess, **107**
  shifts, *99*
demand side economics, 109
Dexter Avenue Baptist Church, *5, 10*
diagrams, 66, **183**
digressions, 31
  recognizing, 34–35
  signals for a return to topic, **34**
  signposts for, **34**
  using, 34–35
discussions
  asking for clarification or confirmation, 36
  cohesion in, 56
  controversial topics and, 31–33
  encouraging participation, 36
  leading, 36–37
  researching information, 37
distancing with introductory verbs, **90**
DNA, *35, 37, 115*
  viruses and, *38*
Don Quixote (Cervantes), 133
DuBois, W. E. B., *84*

Ebola virus, *31, 43,* **43**, *44, 112, 124*
  cycle of infection, *111*
  dry stage, *111*
  epidemics and, *33*
  immune system and, *111*
  incubation phase, *111*
  single-stranded RNA-based, *35*
  (steps in) contraction of, **113**
  wet stage, *111*
economic disruption, *17*
economic theory, monetary growth and, 106
economics. *see also* markets; supply and demand
  demand side, 109
  external economies, *17*
  supply side, 109
education
  access to as a civil rights issues, **14**
  ancient Greek philosophy of, **58**
  ancient Greek system of, 57
  elementary, 57
  of girls and women, 57
  Hannah Arendt and, 52–53, *127, 139*
  importance of, *131*
  modern theories about, 56
  modern Western philosophy of, **58**
  in North America and Europe, 57
  transformative power of, 134
Eichmann, Adolf, *127*

Eiffel Tower, *65*
  green engineering, *65*
  wind power, *65*
elaboration
  asking for, 3, **4**
  responding to requests for, 3
  signaling, **4**
emphatic argumentation, 48, 181
Ems, Will, *101*
energy. *see also* wind power
  consumption by source in US, **77**
  efficiency and decreased airflow, *145*
  solar, *61*
energy recovery ventilation (ERV), 149
environmental problems
  innovative solutions to, 75–76
  urban solutions, 74
Environmental Protection Agency, *143*
EPA Annual Energy Intensity Relative to its
  EO 13423/EISA target, **63**
EPA's Scope 1 and 2 CHG Emission Reductions by
  Source, FY 2014 compared to FY 2008, **63**
epidemics
  AIDS, *43*
  Ebola, *33*
  European diseases in 15th and 16th century
    America, *124*
  procedures, *33*
  smallpox, *31*
  Spanish Influenza, *43*
  swine flu 2009, *43*
equilibrium, 23
European diseases, in 15th and 16th century
  Americas, *124*
evidence, providing, **100**, *145, 155*
evolutionary fitness, theory of, 38
extended discourse, 30–45, *31*
  discussing and responding to controversial topics,
    32–33
  recognizing and using digressions, 34–35
extended lectures
  "Air Filtration Systems for the Home" (environmental
    engineering lecture on video), 182
  "Are Viruses Alive?" (biology lecture on video), 170
  "The Five Revolutions" (sociology lecture
    on video), 157
  "Love and Education" (humanities lecture
    on video), 176
  "Supply and Demand" (economics lecture
    on video), 164

Facebook, *17, 18, 19,* 19
facts, 81
  identifying, 82–83
  intonation pattern for, 83
  non-verbal signposts for identifying, 83
  vs. opinions, 80, 81–82, *81–82,* 86

signaling in lectures vs. texts, **87**
signposts of, **82**
verbal signposts for identifying, 82
Fair Housing Act 1968, *93*
fallacies, 130
    antiquity fallacy, **131**
    authority fallacy, **131**
    bandwagon fallacy, **131**
'farmscrapers', 75
Faust (Goethe), 49, *49*
FBI, *86*
filtration systems, 68, 70. *see also* air filtration
  systems
    "Air Filtration Systems for the Home"
      (environmental engineering lecture
      on video), 182
    then and now, 70
"The Five Revolutions" (extended lecture
  in sociology), 159
flow, 115
flow chart, 111
flu, 44. *see also* influenza
flu vaccine, 41
    mutations of, 44
Ford, Henry, *21*
Frankenstein, 129
Frankenstein; or, The Modern Prometheus (Shelley),
  129, *129, 131, 138, 139*
Frankenstein, Victor (character), *131, 138*
free trade, 104

Galloway, Darrell, *33*
Gandhi, Mahatma, *10*
Garvey, Marcus, *88*
gender equality, as a civil rights issues, **14**
generalizations, 121, 174
    grammar and, 121
    specifics and, 121–122
germ warfare, *33*
    government funding of, *33*
globalization, *104*
Goethe, Johann Wolfgang, 49, 56, *138*
    education and, *49*
    Nietzsche and, *50, 50*
government
    flu vaccine and, 41
    funding of germ warfare, *33*
    regulations of air ventilation systems
      and, 156
    regulations of building systems, 156
grammar
    declaratives and, 39–40
    generalizations and, 121
    specifics and, 122
    subjunctive, 40
grass-roots movement, 159
"Great Books" curriculum, 132–133

Greece, ancient
    culture and, *57*
    education and, 56, 57, *58*
    influence on Western civilization, 55
Greek tragedy, 47
green buildings, 64–65, 78
green engineering, *61, 65*
    Eiffel Tower, 65
    urban areas and, 75
greenhouse gas emissions, **63**
Greensboro Four, *93*
group presentation, 92, **94**
Gutenberg, Johannes, 133
gymnasium, 57

health care, access to as a civil rights issues, **14**
heat recovery ventilation (HRV), 149
hedging devices, 94, 162
    adverbs of approximation (modal adverbs), **90**
    compound hedges, **90**
    distancing with introductory verbs, **90**
    informal vagueness indicators and coordination
      tags, **90**
    modal auxiliary verbs, **90**
HEPA (high-efficiency particulate arresting) filters,
  68, 70
HERV-H retrovirus, *115*
    evolution of brain and, *115*
    stem cells as pluripotent and, *115*
HIV (human immunodeficiency virus), **43**, *43*
    modern antiviral drugs and, 44
home particulates, **71**, 73
Homer, *57*
    Iliad, 57, 58
    Odyssey, 57, 58
"How Supply and Demand Shifts Affect Shortages and
  Surpluses", *107*

"I Have a Dream" speech (King), *3, 10*
ideas
    development of, 16–29
    elaborating on, 163
    main ideas and supporting details, 20
    prior knowledge about a topic and, 18
Iliad (Homer), 57
immunization, *31. see also* vaccinations
    arguments for and against, 45
implications, 97
    degree of certainty, 100
    determining speaker's intent, 100
    identifying implied meaning, 98
    inferences and, 96–109
implied conditions, understanding, 104–105
implied meaning
    identifying, 98
    interpreting implications, 98
    rhetorical devices and, 98

indoor air pollution, *143*, **155**
    government regulations and, *143*
    health problems and, *145*, *146*
indoor air quality, *141*, 155
infectious diseases, 125, **173**. *see also* epidemics
infer, 97
inferences, 99, 165
    determining speaker's intent and degree of
        certainty, 100
    identifying implied meaning, 98
    implications and, 96–109
influenza, **43**, *43*
informal vagueness indicators, **90**
Instagram, 19
integrated skills
    assessing the quality of a conclusion, **132**
    comparing textbooks to lectures, **22**, *22–23*, **24**
    explaining a complex process, 117
    facts versus opinions in texts, 87
    leading discussions, 36
    markers for organizational structure, 51
    synthesizing information from multiple sources, 102
    synthesizing text into a visual, 69
    taking notes, 9–10
    understanding and presenting a research report, 146
intensifier, use of, *48*
International Committee on Taxonomy of Virus
    (ICTV), *35*
interrogatives, 39, 44, 174
intonation pattern, *84*
    for facts, *83*
    for opinions, *86*
inventors, 133

Jim Crow era, 88
Johnson, Lyndon, *3*
Journal of Environmental and Civil Engineering, *145*

Kalanick, Travis, *17*
Kennedy, John F., 86, *86*
Kennedy, Robert, 86, *86*
King, Coretta Scott, *5*, *10*
King, Martin Luther Jr., *8*, 81, *81*, *83*, 92, 159
    African Americans and, *10*
    in Alabama, *10*
    arrests of, *10*, *13*
    assassination of, *3*, *10*
    in Atlanta, *5*
    bombing of his house, *3*, *10*, *86*
    in Boston, *5*, *10*
    civil disobedience, *10*
    death threats, *3*
    early years of, *5*
    education of, *5*, *10*
    march on Washington, *10*
    in Memphis, *5*
    in Montgomery, Alabama, *13*
    Montgomery bus boycott, *10*
    Nobel Peace Prize, *10*
    non-violence and, *10*, 86, *86*
    wiretapping of, 86, *86*
Ku Klux Klan, *84*, 88

landmarks, average number of annual visitors, **66**
language skill
    clarifying, 25, **25**
    colloquial language, 135
    creating and communicating with visuals, 72–73
    creating cohesion in presentation and
        discussion, 54
    interpreting and using hedging devices, 90
    paraphrasing, 11–12
    sourcing academic references, 153–154
    understanding implied conditions, 104–105
    using generalizations and specifics, 121
    using interrogatives and declaratives, 39
language, thinking about, 179
    clarifying, 168
    creating visuals and communicating what they
        mean, 186
    generalizations and specifics, 125
    hedging devices, **94**
    interrogatives and declaratives, 44
    lexical cues, 57
    paraphrasing, 160
    reporting verbs, *156*
    summarizing, *156*
    using colloquialisms, 139
    using generalizations and specifics, 174
    using interrogatives and declaratives, 174
    visuals, 77
lectures, compared to textbooks, **22**, *22–23*, **24**
legitimate expectation, *81*
"Letter from Birmingham Jail" (King), *10*
lexical cues, **54**, *54–55*
    asides, 54, **54**
    clarifiers, **54**, *54*
    exemplifiers, **54**, *54*
    qualifiers, 54, **54**
    relators, 54, **54**
    summarizers, **54**, *54*
    topic markers, 54, **54**
    topic shifters, **54**, *54*
    using to build cohesion, 179
Liberia, 88
Lincoln, Abraham, *84*
line graphs, 64, 73, **184**
LinkedIn, 19
literacy, 58
    in Ancient Greece, 57
literature, *138*
    human experience, *138*
    love of the world and, *138*
    value of studying, *138*

"the little man" businesses (AKA mom and pop businesses), *101*, 101

Locke, *131*

"Love and Education" (humanities lecture on video), 176

lynching, *84*

main ideas, *21*
  identifying, *17*
  signals of, **20**, 20
  supporting details and, 17, 165
  verbal cues, *21*

Mao Tse Dong, 89

mapping, 10

Marconi, Guglielmo, 133

markets, *23*, 23, *24*
  competitive, 23, *24*, 28, 29
  perfectly competitive, 23
  saturation of, *101*

Mays, Benjamin, *5*

meaning
  clarifying, 168
  confirming meaning, 168

MERV (minimum efficiency reporting value), *68*, 70
  filter, *68*
  ratings, **68**
  table, *68*

metaphors, 127–128, *129*

Milton, John, *138*

mind map, **18**, **19**
  theories of supply and demand, **27**

modal adverbs, **90**

modal auxiliary verbs, **90**

molds, 70

monetary growth, economic theory and, 106

Mononegavirales, 35

monopoly, 97

Montgomery bus boycott, *3*, *5*, *10*, *13*, *81*, 93

Montgomery Improvement Association, *13*

Montgomery, march from Selma to (1965), 93

Morehouse College, *5*, *10*

mountaineering shoes, 99

multiple sclerosis, *115*

NAACP (National Association for the Advancement of Colored People), *13*, *84*, 84, 92, 93

National Association for the Advancement of Colored People. *see* NAACP (National Association for the Advancement of Colored People)

Niagara Movement, *84*

Nietzsche, Friedrich, 50, *50*, 56
  Goethe and, *50*, 50

Nike, *107*

non-violence
  Martin Luther King Jr. and, *10*, *86*
  protest and, *10*

note-taking, 9–10, 159, 164
  charting or mapping, 9, 159
  Cornell Method, 9, 159
  methods, 9
  outlining, 9, 159

noticing activity, 141
  extended discourse, 31
  identify main ideas, 17
  incorporation of visuals into lecture, *61*
  speaking styles, 47–48

Odyssey (Homer), 57

opinions, 81
  distinguishing from facts, 81–82
  giving, **32**
  identifying, 159
  responding to or challenging, **32**
  signaling, in lectures vs texts, **87**
  using markers for organizational structure, 159

opinions, nonverbal signposts, 85
  high-pitched statements, *86*
  pitch and emphasis, 86

opinions, verbal signposts of, 85
  expressions used to introduce, 85
  overgeneralizations, 85
  value and judgment words, 85

oral communication skills
  active participation, 2–15
  analogies, 126–139
  extended discourse, 30–45
  idea development, 16–29
  implications and inferences, 96–109
  process, understanding and presenting, 110–125
  speaking styles, 46–59
  summarizing research, 141–142
  synthesis and summarizing, 140–156
  using visuals, 60–78

oral presentation, tips for, 146

organization, *145*

organizational structure, 52–53
  factual structure, 52
  identifying and using markers for, 51
  problem-solution structure, 52
  recognizing attitude in a text, 51
  in textual material, 52–53
  thesis structure, 52

Our Common Future, (United Nations Commission on the Environment), 64

outlining, 9, **118**

panel discussion, 59, 175

paraphrasing, **11**, 11–12, 36, 160

Paris
  greenhouse emission reductions, 75
  pollution and, 73

Paris Smart City, 2050, 73, 75

Parkinson's, *115*

Parks, Rosa, *10*, *13*, *81. see also* Montgomery bus boycott
   arrest of, *13*
participation. *see* active participation
Peloponnesian War, 57, 59
Pentagon, 33
   Defense Threat Reduction Agency, *33*
Pepsi, *28*
Phoenix Towers, *61*
'Photosynthesis Tower", *75*
photovoltaic cells, *61*, **66**, *75*
pie charts, 63–64
piezoelectric capacitor walkways, *75*, *76*
plague, *33*
Plato, 47, 55–56, 57, 58, *138*, 176
   dialogues of, *47*, *48*
   education and, *47*
poll tax, *84*
pollution. *see also* indoor air pollution
   dangers of exposure to, *141*
prelistening, 56, 92, 106, 123, 137, 154
presentations
   cohesion in, 54
   individual, 78
   listening to, *29*
   using visuals in, 72
previewing, 159, 170, 182
price changes, *102*
price takers, *28*
prior knowledge, activating, 18
process presentation
   analyzing flow of, 114–115
   cohesive strategies, 114
   determining structure of a process presentation, 112
   determining the purpose of steps in a process, 112
   structure and purpose in, 112–113
   time-order organization, 112
   topical organization, 112
   using visuals to clarify complex ideas, 114
processes, 110–125
   analyzing flow of a process presentation, 114–115
   deciding on the purpose of, 111
   evaluate consistency, 111
   flow, 111
   identifying structure and purpose in a process
     presentation, 112–113
   summary of, 112
   understanding and presenting, 110–125
propositions, 44

rabies, *35*
   single-stranded RNA-based, *35*
race riot, Springfield, IL 1908, *84*
racial equality, 88
   as a civil rights issues, **14**
Ray, James Earl, *3*
Reconstruction, *84*
relative deprivation theory, *81*

Renewable Energy Supply, US, **77**
repetition, *48*
reporting verbs, using, 187
research, 169, 180
   federal regulations and consumer safety, 188
   genetic testing, 175
   grassroots movement, 163
   presenting, 141
   using to support your own ideas, 141–143
research article
   abstract, 146, 148
   discussion/recommendations, 146
   introduction, 146, 148, 150
   main sections of, 146
   methods, 146, 148, 151
   recommendations, 149, 152
   results/findings, 146, 149, 151
research, presenting, 144–145
   sandwiching, **144**, 144
rhetorical devices, 97, **98**
RNA, *35*
Romantic poets, *138*
Rousseau, Jean-Jacques, *131*

segregation, *13*
   on buses, *81*
self-driving cars, *17*
sentence structure, attitude and, 51
separate but equal, *93*
separatism, 88
   "Class Solidarity or Radical Separatism: An Overview
     of Perspectives on Consciousness-Raising in
     the African American Civil Rights Movement"
     (Sociology reading), 88
Shelley, Mary, 129, *129*, *131*, *138*
Shelley, Percy, *129*
shortages, *102*
signal words, 17
Silicon Valley, *17*, *17*
similes, 127–128, *129*
skills, applying, 12, 27, 74, 92, 106, 136
   debate, 42
   group presentation, 154
   lexical cues, 56
   process presentation, 123
smallpox, *31*
smartphone technology, *17*
SMEs (small and medium-sized enterprises), *19*
SMO (social movement organization), *8*, *81*, 94
smoke, second-hand, *155*
social change, struggle and, 2–15
social movements, 15
Socrates, 48, *48*, 55–56, 57, 58–59, 127
   education and, *47*
solar chimneys, *61*
solar collector, **66**
solar energy, *61*

solar panels, *65*
sources
    academic references in presentations, speeches, or discussions, 187
    citing, **100**
    references to, 102
    reporting verb and, **153**, 153
    selecting appropriate, 142
    signposts for, 153
    using research to support your own ideas, 142–144
    verbal markers and, **102**
Spain, *43*
Spanish Influenza, *43*
    epidemic, *43*
Sparta, *57, 59*
speaker's intent, *97, 100, 101*
speaking styles, *46–59, 47, 47–48*
    create cohesion in discussions and presentations, 56
    emphatic argumentation, 48
    succinct argumentation, 50
specifics, *122, 174*
    generalizations and, 121
    grammar and, 122
spoken word, connecting with the visual, 61
Standard Oil, *102*
Stanford University, *115*
start-up companies, *17, 19, 19*
summarizing, *141*
    key ideas, **120**, 132
    research, 141–142
    synthesis and, 140–156
supply. *see also* supply and demand
    curve, 104
    excess, **107**
supply and demand, *28*
    "How Supply and Demand Shifts Affect Shortages and Surpluses", *107*
    mind map, **27**
    shifts affecting shortages and surpluses, 107
    "Supply and Demand" (economics lecture on video), 164
    theories of, *27, 28, 102, 107*
"Supply and Demand" (economics lecture on video), 164
supply side economics, 109
support, confirming, 39
supporting details
    main ideas and, 17, 165
    signals of, **20**, 20
Supreme Court
    decision on bus segregation, *13*
    segregation and, 88
sustainable design, 78
swine flu epidemic 2009, *33, 43*
synthesis
    of information from multiple sources, 102
    summarizing and, 140–156

tables, 67
tag questions, 36
technology, *17, 19*
textbooks, compared to lectures, **22**, 22–23, **24**
"The Bullet or The Ballot" speech (Malcolm X), 88
"Thirty Tyrants period", *59*
titanium dioxide coverings, 76
topic, prior knowledge about, 17–18
totalitarianism, *138*
Transformational Medical Technologies Initiative (TMTI), *33*
transitional words and phrases, attitude and, 51
"tulip bubble", *21*
turn-taking, *3, 6*
    signals of, *8*

Uber, *17, 19, 28*
urban heat island (UHI), 75
US Department of Defense, 33
US, energy consumption by source in, **77**
US Military, disease research and, 33
USDA Economic Research division, *102*

vaccines, 42
    vs antivirals, *31*
Venn diagram, **43**, **58**
    SMO (social movement organization) and Collective behavior, **94**
ventilation system, *143. see also* indoor air pollution; indoor air quality
    balanced, **148**
    health problems and, *145*
verbs of urgency/suggestion, **40**
Vietnam War, *3, 10*
Vincent Callebaut Architectures, *75*
viral evolution, *37, 118*
    between-host fitness, 118
    process of, 118–119
    within-host fitness, 118
viruses, 42
    21st century, *43*
    airborne, *31, 113*
    alien, *124*
    ancient, *115*
    cellular parasites and, 118
    classification of, *35*, **35**
    dangerous, *43*
    evolution of, *37, 38*
    HIV and, *43, 43*, 44
    mutations of, *31*
    reproduction and transmission, *31*
    single-stranded RNA-based, *35*
    theory of evolutionary fitness and, 38
    transmission of, *113*
    virulence, *31, 113*
    warfare and, *33*

viruses, ancient, *115*
visual aids, **23**, 60-78, 125
visual map, 18, **173**
visual thinking, 77, 173
    bar graphs, 13–14
    campus map, **179**
    chart, **138**
    diagrams, 108, 156
    graphs, 167
    line graphs, **185**
    supply and demand graph, *29f*
    timeline, 161
    Venn diagram, **43**, **58**, 94
visuals
    communication of information in, 72
    connecting to a lecture, 62
    creating, 72, 186
    data and comparison, 63
    interpreting information in, 61
    line graphs, 64
    pie charts, 64
    proportions, 63
    purpose of, 62
    reading and interpreting complex, 66

trends, 63
types of, 64, 125
types of information presented in, **69**
using, 60–78
voice, use of, *48*
voting, restrictions of, *84*
Voting Rights Act 1965, 3, *10*, 93

War on Poverty, *3*
watches, designer, **108**
wind power, *61*, *65*
Wollstonecraft, Mary, *129*
word choice, attitude and, 51
World Health Organization, *43*
World War I, *43*
World War II, *138*, 139
writer's claim, attitude and, 51

X, Malcolm, 88

zombie viruses, *124*
zombies, 123
    virus analogy and, *124*
Zuckerberg, Mark, 18